F

Thomas Merton's Betrayers

THE CASE AGAINST ABBOT JAMES FOX AND
AUTHOR JOHN HOWARD GRIFFIN

Hugh Turley
David Martin

McCabe Publishing
Hyattsville, Maryland

Authors Hugh Turley and David Martin/McCabe Publishing
http://themartyrdomofthomasmerton.com

Book Layout ©2017 BookDesignTemplates.com

Thomas Merton's Betrayers: The Case against Abbot James Fox and Author John Howard Griffin/ Hugh Turley and David Martin. —1st ed.
ISBN 978-0-9673521-6-9

Acknowledgements

We could not have written this book without the help of friends, university libraries, and professional archivists.

We are especially appreciative of the warm welcome afforded to David Martin by Father Bernard Sawicki, O.S.B., and his assistant, Claudia Burger, at the Thomas Merton symposium that they organized at the Pontificio Ateneo Sant' Anselmo, the headquarters of the Benedictine Order in Rome, in June of 2018 in the wake of the publication of *The Martyrdom of Thomas Merton: An Investigation*.

We offer our gratitude to Dr. Paul M. Pearson, director of the Thomas Merton Center of Bellarmine University for his assistance. In addition many helpful experts at various institutions contributed to this project, including Tara C. Craig, Head of Public Services, Rare Book & Manuscript Library, Columbia University; Nick Munigan, library assistant, Charles Deering McCormick Library Special Collections Library at Northwestern University; Anne Causey and Penny White at the Albert and Shirley Small Special Collections Library at the University of Virginia; Dennis Frank, Friedsam Memorial Library, St. Bonaventure University; and Cate Brennan, Textual Reference Branch, National Archives at College Park, Maryland.

Our appreciation goes as well to Father Patrick Henry Reardon for permission to quote and Brother Paul Quenon, O.C.S.O., for his advice.

The photograph of Thomas Merton by John Howard Griffin was used with permission of the Thomas Merton Center at Bellarmine University. The photograph of Thomas Merton, Patrick Hart, and Maurice Flood was used with permission of the Thomas Merton Center at Bellarmine University. The photograph of John T. Wheeler was used with permission of The Oklahoman-USA TODAY NETWORK.

We thank Patricia Lefevere for permission to reprint her article, "The Strange Case of the Monk in the Shower – Questions Surrounding the Death of Thomas Merton." We thank Fons Vitae Books for permission to quote. We thank F. Dean Lucas for permission to quote. We thank John OLoughlin for permission to quote from *McDuff Lives! The Life and Untimely Death of Thomas F. O'Loughlin, Jr*. We also thank Phillip F. Nelson for permission to quote from his review, "The Mysterious Death of Thomas Merton." We thank Fr. Emmanuel Charles McCarthy for his support. His work can be accessed at emmanuelcharlesmccarthy.org.

Contents

In memory of
Makiko Turley

Foreword

Rationalized Reason

When he told me he didn't believe it,
I didn't know how to receive it.
But now I can see
That his message for me
Was he couldn't afford to believe it.

When we published *The Martyrdom of Thomas Merton: An Investigation* in March of 2018, Merton, the famous Trappist monk, had been dead for almost a half century, and all that time the prevailing view had been that he had died in a freak accident, killed by a faulty electric fan while attending a monastic conference in Thailand. No one had attempted any sort of independent examination of what actually transpired there at the Red Cross retreat center outside Bangkok on the afternoon of December 10, 1968.

Such a total lack of curiosity became even more remarkable after the long-awaited publication of Michael Mott's critically acclaimed "authorized biography" in 1984, *The Seven Mountains of Thomas Merton.* Mott had access to evidence that had not been made public—much of which is still not public—and he also arrived at the conclusion that Merton had died from accidental electrocution. Anyone reading Mott with anything resembling a critical mind must see, though, that he makes a very weak case for such a conclusion. (See appendix 1.) His conclusion, he tells us in so many words, is based upon his own guesswork, because the Thai police only conducted a sham investigation—a cover-up, if you will—and they didn't conclude that Merton had been killed by a faulty fan. That would have reflected too badly upon the local Thai hosts, Mott speculates. Rather, the Thai police concluded that Merton had died naturally of "sudden heart failure" and had fallen into the fan, already dead at the time, but the fan did happen to be mis-wired and faulty, producing burns on his body. In case you might not believe such a fantastic story, Mott quotes from the previously secret police report, which states exactly that. He also reveals something that would have been new to most people at that time, that there was no autopsy. Furthermore, Mott tells us something that was missing from the police report completely, that there was a wound in the back of Merton's head that he informs us had "bled considerably."

Though our book has been generally well received by the public, even getting several excellent reviews, none of them were published in what might be called a large-circulation, mainstream organ.[1] The closest it has come is with the article by the journalist Patricia Lefevere, "The Strange Case of the Monk in the Shower – Questions Surrounding the Death of Thomas Merton." The article, which was written for the 50th anniversary of Merton's death, appeared only on the web site of Paul Pearson, the head of the Thomas Merton Center at Bellarmine University, although Lefevere writes for the *National Catholic Reporter*. We have reproduced it here as appendix 2.

That article has the following passage: "Commemorations of the 50th anniversary of whatever death Merton experienced have been going on for months across the nation and the world. From Argentina to Britain, Canada to Poland and across 12 American states exhibitions, Masses and services of remembrances have been held or are planned." A list of such services was published by the Thomas Merton Center of Bellarmine

---

[1] See http://www.themartyrdomofthomasmerton.com/reviews.html.

University.[2] As one reads this book, he should bear in mind that no such commemoration from Merton's home abbey of Our Lady of Gethsemani is to be found on the Merton Center's list, and we may conclude that they did not have one.

The largest concentration of scholars and experts on Thomas Merton are at the International Thomas Merton Society (ITMS). Since they had been among those repeating the poorly founded story that Merton had died from accidental electrocution for so long, we should perhaps have not been surprised that, rather than being receptive to our revelations as we had hoped they would be, the ITMS has been very nearly the most hostile of any organization. As explained in David Martin's "An Enemy of the Thomas Merton Society," with reference to Henrik Ibsen's play, *An Enemy of the People,* they have rejected all our submissions for publication, including a proposal to present a paper to their 2019 biennial conference.[3] As this book was going to press the Program Committee rejected our proposal to discuss this book at the 2023 ITMS conference. It is hardly an exaggeration to say that they have acted less like truth seekers than as gatekeepers. The gate that they are keeping is what their designated first reviewer called the "standard account" of Merton's death, that being the oft-repeated proven-to-be-false story that Merton was electrocuted by a faulty fan when he touched it while emerging wet from a shower. The reviewer can't call it the "official account," because the only official ruling is that Merton died of "heart failure" that was not caused by the fan, and there is no trace of a shower in that account.

That review, published in the ITMS's quarterly *The Merton Seasonal,* Winter 2018 edition, is the only purely negative review that we have had in any formal publication. Our response to it entitled "Befuddled Juror in

---

[2] See, http://merton.org/50th/events.aspx#A and
http://merton.org/50th/default.aspx.

[3] https://www.dcdave.com/article5/191031.html.

3

Merton Book Verdict," also written by David Martin, was published in January of 2019.[4]

Another stalwart member of the ITMS wrote a review of sorts, which he has since taken down, on his very active Twitter site. Martin's response to that review, "Professor Secretly Trashes Merton Book," reveals the review to be little more than a collection of nos. 2, 5, 6, 7, and 11 of the "Seventeen Techniques of Truth Suppression," based upon a fundamental mischaracterization of the book.[5] In response to Martin's review, the Twitter site has blocked him from reading it.

Amazing as it may seem, right up to the spring of 2022, the ITMS has hardly wavered from this standard account. As you will see in the article, the professor in question is Greg Hillis of Bellarmine University. He recently published a book entitled, ironically enough, considering his own behavior with respect to the question of Merton's death, *Man of Dialog: Thomas Merton's Catholic Vision.* The vice president of the ITMS, journalist Judith Valente, wrote demonstrably falsely in a review of that book, "Merton died...of what was determined to be an accidental electrocution, caused when he apparently touched a faulty fan wire as he was coming out of the shower in the cottage where he was staying outside of Bangkok."[6] In response to our email to her about this assertion, Valente informed us that what she had written had been reviewed and approved by a "prominent Merton scholar," whom she did not name. Our guess is that, if the scholar exists, he or she is also prominent in the ITMS.

We can be sure, unless he is extremely two-faced, that the scholar to whom she is referring is not the man who might well be the ITMS's most prestigious scholar, the Canadian, Michael W. Higgins.[7] While, for its last quarterly of 2018, the ITMS had used a member of what we call in our

---

[4] https://www.dcdave.com/article5/190108.htm.

[5] "Professor Secretly Trashes Merton Book," February 27, 2019, https://dcdave.com/article5/190227.html; The "Seventeen Techniques for Truth Suppression" are this book's appendix 9.

[6] *America, the Jesuit Review*, May 19, 2022.

[7] https://en.wikipedia.org/wiki/Michael_W._Higgins.

response a member of the junior varsity to review our book, for *The Merton Annual* of 2019 they used Higgins, whom one might characterize as the captain of the varsity. And while we are characterizing, the review that he produced, it might be said, is a truly masterful job of tightrope walking. He says so many good things about our book that, with our own selective quotations, we have used parts of four paragraphs of his review on our book's web site as a sort of promotional blurb.[8] His tone is such, though, that he manages to leave the reader with an overall negative impression. The whole thing must be seen to be believed, and one can freely access it online for that purpose.[9] For one not wanting to take the time, the concluding paragraph gives some appreciation of the man's tightrope skills:

> In the end, Turley and Martin have written a not negligible contribution to the literature around Merton's death—and by highlighting many of the mistakes and discrepancies around the official Thai, U.S. embassy and abbatial records, as well as conflicting witness testimony by those in attendance at the conference, they have assured that "controversial" and" contentious" are appropriate adjectives in defining the circumstances around Merton's death. But by ascribing motives behind the actions, foibles and fumbles of many of the principal players, motives that are insidious if not pernicious, the Turley/Martin team profoundly weaken their argument. In the end, they have written a polemic—inelegant in much of its phrasing and ploddingly repetitive— that is yet another symptom of the Steve Bannon, Alex Jones, Donald Trump era.

One gathers that he thinks we would have done better had we not told readers that the Merton biographer Michael Mott consciously lied when he told readers that the photographs that Fr. Celestine Say took of Merton's body were taken after the scene had been disturbed or that when Brother Patrick Hart left out the words "in his pajamas" from the initial written description of how the body was found that it was just a slip up and had not been done so in order to leave open the possibility that Merton, as Br. Patrick stated from whole cloth five years after the fact in that same volume, had just emerged from a shower.

---

[8] http://www.themartyrdomofthomasmerton.com/book.html.

[9] http://www.merton.org/ITMS/Annual/32/HigginsRevTurley279-282.pdf.

We are forced to conclude that, taken all in all, Professor Higgins has produced a work of truth suppression that relies heavily upon nos. 2, 5, 6, 7, and 14 of David Martin's "Seventeen Techniques for Truth Suppression." (See appendix 9.)

The ITMS may be contrasted with some other important organizations. The Catholic Worker was founded in New York City in 1933 by social activists Dorothy Day and Peter Maurin. It publishes a newspaper, also called *The Catholic Worker*, seven times a year. Day was the editor of the newspaper until her death in 1980. Merton's views on civil rights and matters of war and peace were very similar to those of Day, and *The Catholic Worker* published many of Merton's writings. *The Catholic Worker* had a very favorable review of *The Martyrdom of Thomas Merton* in its August-September 2019 edition, written by Anthony Donovan. Hugh Turley has given presentations sponsored by The Catholic Worker in December of 2018 in Washington, DC and at the organization's headquarters in New York City in September of 2019.

Island Catholic News, a quarterly in Victoria, British Columbia, Canada, edited by Patrick Jamieson, has perhaps been our book's biggest booster, with editorials, articles, some by us and some by others, and reviews that consistently support the book's thesis that Merton was assassinated.

Culture Wars, a monthly in South Bend, Indiana, like *Island Catholic News*, is closely identified with one man, in this case, its founder, the conservative E. Michael Jones. Its December 2018 edition had an article by James G. Bruen, Jr., entitled "The Shocking Death of Thomas Merton." Consistent with the magazine's political orientation, which is pretty much at the opposite end of the political spectrum from that of *Island Catholic News*, Bruen lets the readers know that he is no fan of Merton, taking what we believe are gratuitous, unwarranted shots at the man and his writings, but he comes down foursquare on the side of our book when it comes to how Merton most likely met his end.[10]

---

[10] Perhaps Bruen should be excused that, in his effort to put Merton in the worst possible light, he should state that in his wild youth as a first-year student at

The largest and most influential organization we believe we can count as among the book's supporters are the Benedictine monastic order. We should remind readers that we dedicated *The Martyrdom of Thomas Merton* to four members of the order who were eyewitnesses on the scene in Thailand who had the presence of mind to record events in a clear and truthful fashion, unlike the Thai investigating authorities. Father Rembert Weakland was the abbot primate of the Benedictines, based in Rome, when he presided over the conference in Thailand, and his sharing of official documents that he had retained has been very helpful to our inquiry. And, unlike the ITMS, the Benedictines invited us to present a paper at their conference entitled "Thomas Merton: Prophecy and Renewal," which took place at their headquarters, the *Pontificio Ateneo Sant'Anselmo,* in Rome in June of 2018. The paper that David Martin presented in person is the previously referenced appendix 1. The venue, on the first floor of the abbey, was almost directly under the office of the Benedictine Abbot Primate Weakland at the time of the Thai conference.

In 2021, Hugh Turley was invited to speak about Merton's death to students at the Benedictine St. Anselm's Abbey School in Washington, D.C. Later he was invited to return and discuss our book with the Benedictine monks at St. Anselm's. After reading our book, a former Trappist, now a Benedictine at St. Anselm's, Brother Matthew Nyland, told Turley that he found it "unassailable."

Cambridge University in England, Merton had fathered an illegitimate child. After all, the story has been repeated as accepted truth by many people who have written about the man, most of whom are professed Merton admirers. It is far from an established fact, however. In the "Declaration of Intention" to the U.S. Immigration and Naturalization Service in February 1938, "subscribed and sworn to" by Merton, he stated that he had no children and there is no legal record in England of his fathering a child. In the oft-told tale, both mother and child were killed in the blitz during the war, but the Germans never bombed Cambridge where they were presumed to have been living.

When Martin began his presentation in Rome, he paid tribute to the Benedictines to whom the book is dedicated, Father Celestine Say, Sister Edeltrud Weist, Father Egbert Donovan, and Father Odo Haas, but he was forced to acknowledge that a very likely collaborator in the murder plot, as explained in the book, was the mysterious Belgian Benedictine monk, Father François de Grunne, who was the last man seen with Merton alive and was also the discoverer of Merton's body.

There has turned out to be one other exception to the Benedictine heroes list. That is the recipient of the 2019 Thomas Merton Award, presented "to an individual who has written and published in the period between the [biennial] General Meetings a work on Merton and his concerns that has brought provocative insight and fresh direction to Merton studies."   Perhaps the young Korean monk, Father Jaechan Anselm Park, realized that he would never get the coveted award from the ITMS if he did not repeat in his book, *Thomas Merton's Encounter with Buddhism and Beyond: His Interreligious Dialogue, Inter-Monastic Exchanges, and Their Legacy,* the "standard account" that Merton had been "accidentally electrocuted by an electric fan."[11]

As it happens, Fr. Park is not the only one to break ranks from the larger group when it comes to public positions in the wake of our book on what caused Merton's death. Professor Joseph Quinn Raab, as editor of *The Merton Annual,* is a far more important figure in the accident-story-promoting ITMS than the young Fr. Park is among the Benedictines. Yet, in 2021 he wrote, "It is no longer plausible to conclude that Merton's death was the result of accidental electrocution."[12]

Finally, in the realm of popular culture, we had some hope that at least one influential person who shared Merton's sentiments with respect to the Vietnam War and racial justice would learn of our discoveries about his death and would speak up on behalf of his memory.

---

[11] Liturgical Press, 2019, p. 26.

[12] *Opening New Horizons: Seeds of a Theology of Religious Pluralism in Thomas Merton's Dialogue with D.T. Suzuki,* Pickwick Publications, 2021, p. 3.

The prime candidate would seem to have been Joan Baez, who had traveled to the Gethsemani Abbey in December of 1966 and met with Merton. She had even turned one of his poems into a song, "The Bells of Gethsemani," which one can hear her sing on YouTube.[13] Up to now, though, we have heard nothing from her concerning Merton's death.

We were very pleasantly surprised, though, to learn that an equally famous folk-singing contemporary of Baez, Judy Collins, has done more than speak out. She has written a song about Merton's assassination, titled simply "Thomas Merton." It is on the track of her "Spellbound" album released early in 2022. In an interview with *American Songwriter* magazine, she states explicitly that she was moved to write and perform the song by reading *The Martyrdom of Thomas Merton: An Investigation*, learning there that a likely motivation for his killing was his opposition to the Vietnam War, just as she suspects was the case in the murders of Robert Kennedy and Martin Luther King, Jr. Merton's position on the war had been unpopular with many of his colleagues and fellow Catholics, she notes in the interview. [14]

---

[13] https://youtu.be/WwIGeGVXpSQ.

[14] Tina Benitez-Eves, "Judy Collins Looks Back on Her Times with New Album, 'Spellbound'," *American Songwriter*. February 2022. https://americansongwriter.com/judy-collins-looks-back-on-her-times-with-new-album-spellbound/.

Introduction

In *The Martyrdom of Thomas Merton*, we make it clear that the primary creator of the belief that Merton died from accidental electrocution by a faulty fan was the United States news media. We zero in on an initial report by John T. Wheeler, the Associated Press reporter who sent out a story with the dateline of Bangkok, just a few miles from where Merton died at a Red Cross retreat center where a Roman Catholic monastic conference was taking place. First impressions tend to be very strong, and the creators of false narratives in our news media know it and take great advantage of that fact. To this day, most of what people think they know about Merton's death can be traced to that first AP report.

We have done further research that shows that Wheeler was not completely alone in that initial reporting, and from examining that other reporting we have been able to get a clearer picture of the emerging cover-up. We had believed that the U.S. Embassy in Bangkok was involved in the cover-up and had suggested as much, but upon closer examination we see that all the most questionable things that supposedly emerged from the embassy were things that Merton's home Gethsemani Abbey—primarily its abbot, Fr. Flavian Burns—said that they were told by the embassy. Those assertions are not supported by anything tangible that we have been able to find that originated with the embassy, and in key instances, what we have from the embassy comports with known facts that contradict the electrocution story, contrary to what came out of the abbey. Furthermore, Abbot Flavian said other things related to Merton's death that seriously undermine his credibility.

We *did* place responsibility on the abbey for early complicity in the cover-up, along with the press, and the heaviest responsibility upon the abbey's leadership for continued perpetuation of, and expansion upon, the cover-up. We singled out four individuals as primary participants in that endeavor, Abbot Flavian; Merton's newly appointed secretary at the abbey, Brother Patrick Hart; the author to the abbey-authorized biography of Merton, Michael Mott; and popular writer and frequent visitor of Merton at the abbey, John Howard Griffin. Griffin was also the man first chosen to write that biography, but ill health prevented him from finishing it, and the torch was passed to Mott. As one can see from the subtitle of this book, we have pared three names from the list, leaving only Griffin, while adding a name that is completely missing from the first book, Abbot Flavian's predecessor and apparent continuing power behind the throne after stepping down, Abbot James Fox.

Fox met with Abbot Flavian Burns, his successor, on the day that Merton died, and, as we shall see, he bears a considerable amount of responsibility for the accidental electrocution story, right up there with the AP's Wheeler. Furthermore, Fox's stepping down as abbot while remaining a member of the abbey is very curious, something that is almost never done in the monastic world, for obvious reasons. Had he broken with his longstanding precedent and allowed, as Abbot Flavian did, the extended, abbey-financed flight from the coop as it were, ending in Merton's death in Thailand, it would have looked even stranger. Or, shall we say, it might even have looked incriminating.

John Howard Griffin was apparently the leading figure in the gathering and concealing of evidence about Merton's death. Griffin is best known as the author of the 1961 book, *Black Like Me*, important in its day for the Civil Rights movement, about his experience in the Deep South masquerading as a Black man and encountering a great deal of discrimination and overall shabby treatment. During 1969, Griffin routinely visited the abbey to meet with Brother Patrick and Abbot Flavian. Griffin spent time gathering documents and evidence from witnesses who had been at the scene of Merton's death. Secrecy was the hallmark of Griffin's work, and he tried not to leave any paper trail of his activities. Griffin was unable to hide all the evidence, though.

The abbey represents a consistent thread through the dominant accidental electrocution story, right up to the present day, evidence be damned. What follows is the text of a letter that Hugh Turley mailed to Abbot Elias Dietz of Gethsemani on November 29, 2018, more than eight months after the publication of *The Martyrdom of Thomas Merton*. At that point, Br. Patrick Hart was still alive, and his name was still at the bottom of the page of the statement on Merton referred to.

> Dear Fr. Dietz,
>
> The Merton Center has recently corrected their website so that they no longer state that Thomas Merton died in Bangkok by accidental electrocution.
>
> You can see from the enclosed pages that they now accurately state only that Merton died near Bangkok.
>
> The Abbey of Gethsemani web site still has Brother Patrick Hart's statement that "Merton died by accidental electrocution in Bangkok." This statement is 100% false.
>
> You can follow the lead of The Merton Center by simply saying that Merton died near Bangkok and say nothing about the cause. This would be a step in the right direction.
>
> Aren't you concerned that your community is continuing to promote falsehoods about Merton's death as we near the 50th anniversary? I continue to pray that you will tell the truth.
>
> Pax,
>
> Hugh Turley
>
> Encls: corrected pages from The Merton Center website

Abbot Dietz did not respond to the letter, and he made no change to the website page. Brother Patrick died on February 21, 2019, at the age of

93, and, at some point afterward, the abbey did make one small change to the page. It removed Br. Patrick's name from it.[15]

People make a big mistake when they think that members of a religious community who choose a cloistered life of prayer are not vulnerable to the sins that afflict mankind. There are sinners and saints in all walks of life. Thomas Merton, like the rest of us, was far from a perfect man, but in very important ways, it can be said that he imitated Christ in the virtues that he possessed. He remained obedient to a well-nigh insufferable abbot in the person of Dom James Fox, and he was patient with his brothers. As it turned out, we have been forced to conclude, Merton also imitated Christ in keeping close company with future betrayers. Unlike Christ, though, Merton almost certainly did not know who would betray him.

We should not be surprised that there should be fallen mortals at the Abbey of Gethsemani. Gethsemani is no different from other religious communities and our own families as well. When there was a scandal in St. Augustine's community, he wrote in a letter:

> However vigilant may be the discipline of my house, I am but a man and live among men: nor do I claim to for myself, that my house should be better than Noah's ark, where among eight men one was found reprobate, or better than the house of Abraham, when it was said, Cast out the bondwoman and her son; or better than the house of Isaac, to whom it was said respecting the twin children, Jacob have I loved, but Esau have I hated; or better than the house of Jacob, when his son defiled his father's bed; or better than the house of David, whose son lay with his sister, and where another son rebelled against his holy and gentle father; or better than they who were associated with the Lord Christ Himself, where eleven righteous men tolerated Judas, that perfidious thief; or lastly, better than heaven from which the angels fell.[16]

---

[15] https://monks.org/monks-pages/thomas-merton/. The Thomas Merton Center at Bellarmine University web site referred to is at http://merton.org/chrono.aspx.

[16] Augustine, On the Gospel S. John, *The Great Commentary of Cornelius à Lapide*, pub. Hodges, 1887, p. 7.

14

We should be realistic about man's fallen nature and not overly idealistic about our own reality. The betrayer Judas Iscariot teaches us that the choices and actions of evil men all play into God's divine providence, for He brings good from evil.

The goodness of Thomas Merton is manifest, in contrast to his accusers who have blamed him for accidentally killing himself. People may prefer to think that Catholic monks would not conceal evidence and invent stories about the murder of one of their own brothers, but as revealed in *The Martyrdom of Thomas Merton: An Investigation* and will reveal further in this book, the facts speak for themselves.

Merton's fame and success in generating sizeable royalties made him a very valuable, in fact, a well-nigh essential asset to the abbey. Abbot Fox kept Merton on a very short leash, virtually never allowing him even to leave the abbey except for trips to Louisville for medical attention. He even monitored Merton's mail. Fox justified his actions as protecting Merton from himself, what with the man having shown his weakness for the life of the flesh before becoming a monk. He was motivated, he—and later his defenders—explained, by concern for Merton's immortal soul. In fact, what apparently motivated Fox most was his fear that Merton might leave the monastery and take his financial bonanza for the abbey with him.

Just before Abbot Fox sent his letter of resignation to the Trappist abbot general in November of 1967, Merton had been persuaded to sign a trust agreement that, among other things, gave all his literary estate to the abbey in the event of his death.

To use the language of law enforcement, Merton continued to be a flight risk. From the moment he put his signature on that trust agreement, just looking at the matter from a cold, hard economic standpoint, he became worth a lot more to the abbey dead than alive. As long as he was alive, the proceeds for the abbey of his production would remain constantly in doubt, a bird in the bush, if you will. Were he to die, it would be a bird in the hand.

Officially, it was the new abbot, Flavian Burns, who granted Merton permission to travel. Abbot Flavian even suggested to Merton that he might find a more secluded place to live as a hermit in California. As we shall see, Merton had actually made the decision to leave the Abbey of Gethsemani, and he did not intend to return after his trip to Asia.

Following his sudden mysterious death in Thailand, Merton's body was buried at Gethsemani. His royalties and unpublished writing, photographs, drawings, etc. became the property of the abbey. The man who took charge of the mass of materials, always described as "Merton's secretary," had been Fox's secretary for the previous ten years, Brother Patrick Hart. He had been made one of Merton's secretaries only a short time before Merton departed on his trip. Contrary to the impression that has been cultivated in the wake of Merton's death, the two men were not at all close.

Finally, in our first book we characterized the poetry editor of the Jesuit *America* magazine, John Moffitt, who was one of the four people housed in the cottage where Merton died, as a sort of Hamlet character when it comes to coming to grips with what had actually happened to Merton. In this book, we flesh out that picture quite a bit by examining the series of letters that he exchanged with people at the abbey, particularly with Griffin, in the year after Merton's death.

CHAPTER 1

Thomas Merton and Abbot James Fox

Thomas Merton entered the Cistercian abbey of Our Lady of Gethsemani on December 13, 1941, just six days after the Japanese attack on Pearl Harbor. It is also the Feast Day of St. Lucy, which commemorates Lucia of Syracuse, an early-4th-century virgin martyr in Sicily under the Great Persecution, the last and most severe persecution of Christians under the Roman Empire. Merton had lodged in the abbey guest house after arriving three days before on December 10 from Olean, New York, where he had taught English at the Franciscan St. Bonaventure College.[17] He was a convert to Roman Catholicism who had been received into the Catholic Church on November 16, 1938, at Corpus Christi Church in New York City when he was a student at Columbia University.

---

[17] Thomas Merton, *The Seven Storey Mountain*, Harcourt, Inc., pp. 413-417.

At the time of Merton's entry, Frederic Dunne was the abbot at Gethsemani, a monastery of the Order of Cistercians of the Strict Observance (O.S.C.O.), better known as Trappists, practicing their religion in the oldest monastery in the United States. Dunne had become the first American-born abbot of the French-based Trappist order in the United States when he had become Gethsemani's abbot in 1935.

Recognizing Merton's writing ability and his scholarly background, Abbot Dunne encouraged him to translate some works from the Cistercian tradition and write historical biographies. Merton also continued his personal writing pursuits despite the cramped quarters in which he lived and the many other demands on his time required in the life of a monk. Later, learning of Merton's unique and tragic experience, Dom Frederic suggested that the young monk use his talents by writing his life's story.

The year 1948 turned out to be one of great significance for the monastery and for Merton. On August 4, Abbot Dunne died somewhat unexpectedly at the age of 74. Exactly two months later, on October 4, Dunne's suggestion to Merton came to fruition when *The Seven Storey Mountain* was published. It enjoyed enormous success.

Hardly anyone expected such great popularity for the book, but Gethsemani's own post-war experience showed that the time was ripe for it. The war had caused a great number of people to engage in soul searching, especially many of the young men who had lived through its horrors. The abbey had experienced such a rise in postulants that it had opened satellite monasteries in Georgia and Utah, with plans for more. The expansion had also put great strains upon the abbey's resources, and it was deeply in debt.

As it happened, the newly elected abbot, James Fox, had gone to Louisville to pay his respects to the archbishop when Merton received a check for $900, his first royalty payment for *The Seven Storey Mountain*. In August of 1948, $900 was a large sum of money. It would be worth over $10,000 today. When Abbot Fox returned from Louisville, Merton handed him the check, and the abbot told him that he wanted him to keep on writing.[18]

Thomas Merton and the new abbot were very different men from very different backgrounds. Merton was the son of artists, his mother from the United States and his father from New Zealand. They had met as art students in Paris and Thomas was born and spent most of his formative years in Prades, a small town in the south of France. He had a brother, John Paul, who was almost four years his junior. His mother died when he was six years old and his father, always struggling to make a living as an artist, had died when Thomas was attending a boarding school in England and was not quite 16 years old. John Paul had joined the Royal Canadian Air Force when the war broke out in Europe and was killed in a flight accident in 1943.

Merton had inherited his parents' artistic bent, but his had taken a strong literary turn. His life experience doubtless had something to do with his eventual vocation, but he was also greatly influenced by his extensive reading. Neither of his parents was known to have been particularly religious.

Fortunately, Merton's mother's family was well off, and they provided for him. He never had to think much about money. After his one wayward year at Cambridge, he entered Columbia University, where he flourished both academically and socially. His grandparents lived in nearby Douglaston in the borough of Queens.

By contrast, Dom James Fox, born Henry Vincent Fox, having been given the Catholic name of "James" upon joining the Trappist Order, as Merton was known among his cohorts as "Father Louis," came from a large Irish Catholic family in Dedham, Massachusetts.[19] His father was a shoe dealer and his mother a housewife, but she put great store in education, and she was a very devout Catholic. All the children thrived

---

[18] Roger Lipsey, *Make Peace Before the Sun Goes Down; The Long Encounter of Thomas Merton and His Abbot, James Fox*, Shambhala, 2015, p. 16.

[19] This profile comes from F. Dean Lucas, *Merton's Abbot: The Life and Times of Dom James Fox*, self-published, 2016.

academically. Altogether, there were nine of them. Two of them died at an early age. The one closest in age to him, Catherine Monica, died of a ruptured appendix at age 23. She had been a student at Radcliffe when Henry was a student at Harvard, both members of the Catholic Club at their respective institutions. Henry would become the president of his club in his senior year.

Two of the surviving sisters graduated from Radcliffe and obtained advanced degrees, and all three of them became nuns. One of his two brothers became a Jesuit priest. The other brother, after getting accounting and law degrees at Boston College, worked as an investigations officer for the U.S. Army, discharged in 1946 at the rank of captain. He would then work for the Internal Revenue Service in Baltimore and for the Office of Personnel Management in Washington over a period of 13 years. He never married and spent the last 30 years of his life at Gethsemani, though not as a monk.

In sum, all the Fox children pursued religious vocations. Dom James didn't start out that way, though. He never attended a Catholic school. Obviously highly intelligent and hardworking, he might have been the family's best student. Attending college with scholarship assistance, he graduated in only three years magna cum laude with a degree in history from Harvard in 1918. He then spent a semester at Harvard Business School, dropping out to join the Navy. Perhaps because of the general postwar demobilization taking place, he was able to leave the Navy after only one year and worked for a time checking corporate tax returns as a revenue agent for the Income Tax Division of the U.S. Treasury Department. After that, he worked briefly in different private sector jobs.

A letter that he wrote to a young man after his retirement as abbot provides great insight into Fox's general orientation at that stage of his life:

> At your age, i was ambitioning to become a 'millionaire.'...I had wonderful plans of becoming perhaps an Investment Banker, or Tax

20

Consultant – have a couple cars – yachts – to summer in Bar Harbor – to winter in Florida or Palm Springs...'[20]

It is impossible to imagine Thomas Merton ever writing or thinking anything even resembling that brief note. Not only the worldly ambitions expressed, but the manner of expression, right down to the capitalization and punctuation would have been utterly foreign to Merton.

The following quote comes from a monk who entered Gethsemani under Fox and was later in the abbey infirmary with him after Fox's retirement: "Dom James said, 'When I got out of Harvard, I wanted to get into something political to get power—money would come later.' He said his mother did not want him to go to Harvard. She knew a Catholic who had gone to Harvard and lost his faith. She was afraid he would lose his."[21]

What caused him to turn away from his youthful path of worldly ambition, Fox would write in a letter in 1976, was the death of the sister Catherine Monica, to whom he was very close. It took him another three years to make the move, but "Instead of continuing the 'grand pursuit of making money and of scaling the heights of fame and fortune' and living a life 'toiling in a race for power, prestige, passion and piles of stocks and bonds, from every one of which I am going to be separated someday,' he chose the opposite path."[22]

That's what he said for the 1943 *Harvard Class Report.* As his career in the Church took shape, though, one might seriously question how much that really was the opposite path.

He entered the Passionist Order of the Church in 1921 and transferred to the more secluded Trappists at Gethsemani Abbey in 1927. Apparently recognizing his administrative talent, Dom Frederic Dunne appointed him as the first superior of the new daughter house in Conyers, Georgia, in 1944. The new house was granted abbey status in

---

[20] Lucas, p. 254.
[21] Lucas, p. 22.
[22] Lucas, p. 24.

May of 1946 and Fox was elected as its first abbot in the following month. When Abbot Dunne died in 1948, Fox was the logical person to take his place as abbot of the Gethsemani Abbey.

Running the abbey and its growing branches apparently pretty much consumed him for the next two decades, just as he would have been consumed by running a business of comparable size as he might have ended up doing had he followed that "opposite path." There were endless financial, logistical, and personnel decisions that had to be made, in addition to the pursuit of what was supposed to be the monastery's primary purpose, the enrichment of the spiritual life of its residents and the larger religious community.

Merton captured the man well in a letter he wrote to Dom Gabriel Sortais, the newly elected Cistercian abbot general in France in 1952, saying that he feared that Fox was too much involved with day-to-day concerns, was overworking, and was neglecting his spiritual life.[23]

Fox's spirituality seemed to be primarily in the nature of lip service expressed in the form of clichés that Merton was not alone in finding nettlesome and tiresome. The one that everyone at the abbey got to hear ad nauseam was "All for Jesus thru Mary with a smile." Fox even had a stamp of it made in all capital letters in the following form to put above his signature:

ALL FOR JESUS
THRU MARY
WITH A SMILE

Robert Lipsey has an example of it from a book that Fox co-signed with Merton as the frontispiece of his own book about the two men. One can imagine that Merton would have even found Fox's shortening of the word "through" annoying.

---

[23] Lipsey, p. 46.

"Dom James has too few ideas, but he lives them," Merton once was heard to say.[24]

Fox was often described as "shrewd" by those who knew him, and a "pro at manipulation," powers that he put to good use in raising money from rich donors to the abbey.[25] The Gethsemani monk, Brother Alfred McCartney, also uses the adjective "shrewd," but specifically with respect to Fox's financial dealings.[26] McCartney also described Fox as a manipulator who was particularly good in charming rich women into donating money to the abbey, using either the hard sell or the soft sell as need be the case. He mentioned in particular Robert Kennedy's in laws, the Skakel family, who were big contributors to Gethsemani. Robert's wife, Ethel, was also among the many people with whom Merton corresponded.

Life under Abbot Fox was laborious and often tedious for all the monks, but it was especially so for Thomas Merton. Fox ran the monastery very much like a business venture with the goal of producing income. He dabbled in mail order businesses selling cheese, meats, fruitcakes, fudge, and other products. The monks were put to work baking bread and delivering their products. The monastery owned a dairy truck to pick up milk from local farmers to make cheese.

What Merton thought of this routine and of Abbot Fox is captured well in a letter he wrote to a friend in December of 1959 in which he decried Fox's obsession with the abbey's commercial ventures and his cocksure manner about everything, especially concerning religion, and his dictatorial nature.[27]

In his journal, Merton seriously questioned the point of monastic life as it had come to be practiced under this second abbot, which he described as basically false and "one hundred percent American."[28]

---

[24] Lipsey, p. 14.
[25] Lipsey, p. 28.
[26] Lucas, p. 313.
[27] Lipsey, p. 149.
[28] Lipsey, p. 123.

While the cosmopolitan and deeply philosophical Merton pegged Fox as a stereotypical superficial all-American type in that instance, elsewhere in his journal he zeroed in on Fox's home region, describing him as typical of the sanctimonious New England middle class.[29]

Though Merton described Fox's ideal of a monastery as "prosperous," his further ideal was apparently that its residents not share in that prosperity. The diet for the monks was simple. Breakfast was barley coffee and two slices of bread. Lunch was watery soup from the previous day's leftovers, potatoes and another vegetable, some fruit (usually stewed rhubarb). Dinner was another cup of barley coffee, possibly more rhubarb for fruit, and cheese. The monks did not eat the heavy Trappist black bread or the cheese that they made. Those products were sold to generate income. The monks would eat processed cheese and common commercial white bread.[30]

By contrast, Abbot Fox had a special diet, ostensibly for health reasons, that involved skipping breakfast and eating a steak with French fries for a mid-day meal every day.[31] By the time he had retired to the abbey infirmary, after a stint in his own specially constructed hermitage, he specified that the only vegetable that he would eat was potato, but now baked instead of fried.[32]

It should hardly be a surprise, then, that Merton regarded Fox as universally unpopular with the monks at the abbey, but more than the forced hardship, Merton believed that Fox's overbearing nature and the false religiosity accounted for it. [33] Though the oppressive atmosphere at the abbey might have been general, it probably fell most heavily upon and was felt most acutely by Merton. In a final letter to Merton, Fox admitted to Merton that he had been his nemesis.[34]

---

[29] Lipsey, p. 236.

[30] Edward Rice, *The Man in the Sycamore Tree*, Harcourt, Brace, Jovanovich, 1972, p. 67.

[31] Lucas, pp. 308-309.

[32] Lucas, pp. 258-259.

[33] Lipsey, p. 123.

[34] Patrick Hart, ed., *Thomas Merton Monk: A Monastic Tribute*, Cistercian Publications, 1983, p. 154.

We might contrast these observations with a statement we find by the author F. Dean Lucas in the acknowledgments section of his 2016 profile of Abbot Fox, which is heavily based upon interviews of the Gethsemani monks.

"To a person," he wrote, "none were critical of Dom James' handling of Thomas Merton; the comment I heard most often was that Dom James was his protector."[35]

The very fact that Lucas found it necessary to relay such a consensus suggests that there was something about that "handling" that needed defending, and Merton's determined effort to escape from it tells a different story.

While Fox made Merton's life difficult, Merton would remain obedient to his abbot and suffer injustice with heroic patience. Merton described himself as the "property" of the corporation in a 1967 letter to friend and publisher James Laughlin.[36] At the time of his death, royalties from his writing were helping to support five monasteries. Merton's requests to transfer from the Abbey of Gethsemani to the Carthusians were rejected by Abbot Fox. Fox then blocked Merton's appeals to Rome, while he told others that Merton was unstable and neurotic and that he must remain at Gethsemani for the sake of his eternal soul. The neurosis and instability charge might more fairly have been leveled at Fox. The thought of losing the income produced by Merton, including the loss of the most famous member of the monastery, at the very least, caused him a great deal of anxiety.[37]

Professor Higgins has described the conflict that existed between Fox and Merton as "fierce and long-lasting, a drama of near epic proportions."[38] As previously noted, Fox, as the abbot, was able to read Merton's incoming and outgoing mail. This may not have been an

---

[35] Lucas, pp. 8-9.

[36] Lipsey, p. 5.

[37] William H. Shannon, ed., *The Hidden Ground of Love: The Letters of Thomas Merton on Religious Experience and Social Concerns,* Merton letter to Sister M. Emmanuel de Souza e Silva, October 30, 1967, Farrar Straus Giroux, 1985, p. 200.

[38] Michael W. Higgins, *Heretic Blood,* Wipf & Stock, 1998, p. 48.

unusual situation in Cistercian monastic life, but it gave Fox a decided advantage in heading off Merton's efforts to transfer to another community. Fox's blocking of invitations for Merton to travel and participate in conferences apparently had the same veiled purpose.

Merton had wished to live as a hermit, and it was only after a long period that Fox gave him permission for a hermitage. Merton told his friend Edward Rice that the abbot thought he was going to build a wooden hut to sit in, but the novices built a solid cinder block house. Fox was irritated when he saw the structure and Merton was not permitted to complete it. It was not until the year before his fateful trip to Thailand that Merton was given an indoor toilet, kitchen, and a chapel. The hermitage was only heated by the fireplace and most of his meals were cold scraps that he brought up from the monastery. After visiting Merton one winter, Rice was upset by the conditions. He wanted to contact Fox but was advised by friends who knew both men that it would be pointless to interfere. Rice wrote, "A New York friend said after his death that in his opinion the Abbot had it in for Tom."[39]

Fox's "Retirement"

During 1967 there was speculation that Fox might retire. But in July of that year Merton wrote in his journal that Fox "can't and won't let go of power."[40] Merton's assessment was based on his living under Fox for almost two decades.

In September Fox told Merton that he had made his decision and planned to resign.[41] Merton speculated in his journal that Fox would direct the selection of his successor and that he would maintain control from the distance of his own hermitage.[42] Merton anticipated in a letter

---

[39] Rice, p. 71.

[40] Thomas Merton, *Learning to Love*, Volume 6, July 14, 1967, HarperOne, Kindle edition.

[41] *Learning to Love*, September 7, 1967.

[42] *Learning to Love*, September 11, 1967.

to Daniel Berrigan that the problem with Fox remaining at Gethsemani was that he would continue to influence things indirectly.[43]

The contrast between Merton's spartan hermitage and Fox's opulent getaway some five miles from the monastery, reached by jeep in about a half hour over a steep, rough track, says a great deal about the difference between the two men. When the abbey put it up for sale in 1984, they described it as "a beautiful lodge, constructed of fieldstone and steel, electric heat, fireplace, central air, bath, glass front, lounge, overlooking miles and miles of breathtaking scenery—with some good timber."[44]

It had been designed in the style of Frank Lloyd Wright by one of the abbey's brothers, who had worked with Wright. Fox moved in in May of 1968. A friend who later spent some time with Fox there described it as "a modernistic, extensively-glassed structure that made Merton's cabin look like a shabby shack."[45]

Although one of the rooms was a chapel, the house and the setting come across more as a vacation villa than a religious hermitage. Fox's choice of a retirement abode causes us to question once again whether his life's trajectory represented so greatly that "opposite path" from his youthful fancy.

Merton not only had doubts about the sincerity of Fox's retirement, but he also had misgivings about his choice of a location. In a letter to Dan Berrigan, he described the Fox hermitage as out among the rustic hooligans who make the beverage that the state is famous for and engage in other illegal and immoral activities.[46]

Dom James was able to enjoy nine years of peace at Cavalry Hermitage, as he called it, but on the Saturday after Easter in 1977, Merton's fears were finally realized. Just the sort of rabble that he had imagined, in the form of two local men, assaulted Fox and held him prisoner under threat of death for two and a half hours. Eventually, they

---

[43] *The Hidden Ground of Love*, p. 99.
[44] Lucas, p. 253.
[45] Lucas, pp. 230-231.
[46] Lipsey, p. 148.

left him tied up on his bed after shooting out the lights with Fox's own shotgun, which they took with them along with several other items.

Fox's initials on the stock of the shotgun made it easy to identify when the men tried to sell it and since Fox was well known in the community, the men were easily brought to justice. Fox was eighty years old at the time, and the trauma of the experience was enough to persuade him to move back into the abbey, where he spent the remaining ten years of his life in the infirmary. Of his ninety years, he had spent sixty-six as a monk.[47]

---

[47] Lucas, pp. 245-246.

CHAPTER 2

Thomas Merton's Brief Escape

In October of 1967, Merton's friend Jean Leclercq wrote to Merton and told him that a conference of Benedictine and Cistercian monastics would be held in Thailand at the end of 1968. Leclercq's letter could have been seen by Fox, who often read Merton's mail. That letter may have set in motion several events connected to Merton's ill-fated trip to Thailand.

The following month, on November 14, 1967, the Merton Legacy Trust document was finalized. It would serve as Merton's last will and testament. The original trustees were Thomasine "Tommie" O'Callaghan, who often hosted Merton upon his medical visits to Louisville along with husband Frank and their seven children, Merton's friend, James Laughlin, and Naomi Burton Stone. Laughlin, his publisher, and Stone, his literary agent, were both based in New York City.

In December of 1967, one month after the trust was created, Abbot Fox made his formal retirement announcement to the community. Fox, in restricting Merton's travel from the abbey, had always maintained that this was the "will of God." In January, when Flavian Burns was elected as the new abbot "the will of God" suddenly changed. Flavian would not only grant Merton permission to travel, he would even suggest that he look for a suitable place for a hermitage in California, where he could live apart from Gethsemani.

In January of 1968, Merton and Abbot Flavian received invitations to the monastic conference in Thailand in December. The abbot declined, but he granted Merton permission to attend the conference. During the summer of 1968, as Merton was preparing for his journey, Brother Patrick Hart was recalled from his assignment in Rome to act as Merton's secretary to handle correspondence for Merton while he would be away in Asia. Brother Patrick joined two other men who also were serving as secretaries to Merton, Br. Philip Stark and Br. Maurice Flood. After Merton's death, only Brother Patrick retained the title of Merton's secretary. Brother Patrick took over the management of Merton's literary assets.

Initially, Merton thought that he might try to schedule some speaking events on his trip to pay his travel expenses. He was told that this would not be necessary. Flavian gave Merton an American Express credit card and covered all his travel expenses. In addition to Thailand, Merton's itinerary included travel to New Mexico, California, Alaska, India, Tibet, and Japan.

The complete reversal of the long-time restrictions on Merton's travel gave the appearance that Fox no longer exercised any influence at Gethsemani. After Merton's death, Fox wrote in a letter to Joseph Steinke that if he had not resigned Merton would still be alive, because he would not have given him permission to travel. In so many words, Fox suggested that Abbot Flavian was responsible for Merton's death. Fox wrote further in a letter to one of the monks, "Jesus, mercifully, took him to Heaven before any 'harm' could come."[48]

It is hard to escape the conclusion that the real "harm" of Merton leaving Gethsemani, was not, as Fox implied, to Merton's immortal soul but, as Fox really saw it, to the abbey's bottom line. Merton would have taken all that royalty income with him to any new organization that he

---

[48] Lucas, p. 164.

might join, or it would have been his to use as he saw fit should he decide no longer to be a monk.

Merton Was Leaving Gethsemani

During the summer of 1968 Merton wrote to his friend Ed Rice to tell him that he was going to travel to Asia. In early September, Rice visited Merton for the last time at Gethsemani. Rice wrote, "My strongest impression at the time – and he said it quite clearly, too – was that he did not intend to return to Gethsemani."[49] Merton's decision not to return to Gethsemani is be found in his letters and his journal. In letters to William Ping Ferry, Merton wrote that was seeking a hideaway in California where he might live permanently. He wrote that his abbot was supportive of his settling in California when he returned from Asia in January.[50]

In his journal, on November 18, 1968, Merton wrote that he felt that he ought to leave Gethsemani due to the lack of quiet and the general turbulence there. He was thinking of living around the Redwoods in California or possibly in Alaska. Initially he thought that he may keep his official residence at Gethsemani that would serve as a legal address. Merton wrote that he saw no problem with simply leaving Gethsemani and ending his days there.[51] This entry was made in his journal twenty-two days before his violent death.

Brother Patrick wrote in his foreword to *The Asian Journal of Thomas Merton* that Abbot Flavian had suggested that Merton find a more secluded place to live upon his return from Asia. According to Brother Patrick, Merton told the abbot that he was a monk of Gethsemani and intended to remain one.[52] Merton's intention was only to remain a monk *of* Gethsemani and not a monk *at* Gethsemani. His clear intention was not to return to his hermitage at Gethsemani.

---

[49] Rice, p. 114.

[50] *The Hidden Ground of Love*, p. 239-241.

[51] Thomas Merton, *The Asian Journal of Thomas Merton*, New Directions, 1973, p. 149.

[52] Patrick Hart, Foreword to *The Asian Journal of Thomas Merton*.

Living away from Gethsemani would require a source of income for expenses. Merton could earn money as a speaker and through royalty income from his writing. Was the abbey willing to lose its valuable asset and famous resident?

Merton's late 1968 overt plans represented a significant change from a year earlier. In October of 1967 Merton had written that Abbot Fox was preoccupied with fear that he would go away and not return and that this would harm the "image" of Gethsemani and be bad for the business.[53] As the events unfolded Merton never found the home away from Gethsemani that he desired. His body was returned for burial at Gethsemani and the business of publishing books by Thomas Merton continued to produce profits for the abbey.

But by that time, the Merton Legacy Trust Agreement had insured that the abbey would not lose their prized asset if Thomas Merton were to die. Soon after Merton's death, the Merton Legacy Trust met at the abbey to begin their work to secure everything that Merton produced. Even Merton's final talk that he presented at the conference in Thailand was considered the property of the Abbey of Gethsemani. Abbot Flavian and/or Brother Patrick, Merton's secretary, always participated in the trust meetings. In January of 1969, Brother Patrick recommended, perhaps at the bidding of Fox, that the trust name John Howard Griffin as the authorized Merton biographer.[54]

In the spring of 1969, James Laughlin contacted John Moffitt, who was writing a book about the conference where Merton died. As noted, Moffitt, the poetry editor for *America Magazine*, had been one of the four people housed in the cottage at the Thai conference center at the fateful gathering. Laughlin was concerned about copyright ownership by the Merton Legacy Trust. Laughlin and Stone may have learned from Abbot Flavian or Brother Patrick that Moffitt was planning a book about the Bangkok conference that would be published by Notre Dame Press.

---

[53] *The Hidden Ground of Love*, p. 200.

[54] Br. Patrick Hart letter to John Howard Griffin, January 20, 1969, Griffin papers, Columbia University Library.

Moffitt was told that a share of royalties could be negotiated for use of any of Merton's material and that the trust would retain the copyright.[55]

The "Retired" Abbot Shows His Hand

When Michael Mott's abbey-authorized biography was published in 1984, it represented what the public was permitted to know about Thomas Merton's death as of that date. Until we published *The Martyrdom of Thomas Merton* in 2018 it remained, with all its shortcomings, the account that all subsequent writers on the subject relied upon.

Fortunately, there were some quick-thinking Benedictines present at the scene where Merton died, and they preserved a record of what they witnessed. We describe in detail in the earlier book what transpired, but here's a short summary.

Abbot Odo Haas, O.S.B., Archabbot Egbert Donovan, O.S.B., and Father Celestine Say, O.S.B., were the first to enter Merton's room and observe the body. They immediately recognized that Merton was dead. They did not touch anything before Say had retrieved his camera from across the hall and had photographed the scene to preserve the evidence.

The next two persons to arrive were Abbot Primate Rembert Weakland, OSB, and Prioress/Sister Edeltrud Weist, O.S.B., who was also a medical doctor. Dr. Weist examined the body and observed a bleeding wound on the back of Merton's head. She only declared Merton dead but not the exact cause of death. Dr. Weist wrote a handwritten report that included a drawing of the fan lying across Merton's lower right side on his abdomen. Her drawing was consistent with the two photographs taken by Fr. Say, which we were later able to obtain, getting a developed photograph out of one of the negatives that could not be developed with technology available at the time. The photographs show a burn where the fan switch box rested on the lower right side of Merton's abdomen.

---

[55] James Laughlin letter to John Moffitt, April 22, 1969, Moffitt papers, University of Virginia Library.

Dr. Weist was convinced that Merton suffered an electrical shock, however she could not determine if this was the actual cause of death.

Abbot Flavian Burns first disseminated the false story about a fan on Merton's chest in a letter allegedly written by Trappists at the conference where Merton died. In our earlier book, we make the case quite strongly that there was never any such letter originating from the Trappists at the conference, that it was a fabrication designed to embellish the press's accidental electrocution story.[56] Perhaps the best evidence that there never was any such letter is that the original copy of it seems to have disappeared. On December 19, 1968, a copy of that supposed letter was sent out to Merton's friends with a cover letter signed by "The monks at Gethsemani," as if the monastic community had signed on to the false story.

On February 1, 1969, James Fox sent his own six-page letter to monks who were away from the abbey purporting to explain what had happened to Merton while also memorializing him. In his account, he describes what he was told by the two men who came out to his hermitage to give him the news of Merton's death, Brother Patrick Hart and Abbot Flavian's secretary, Brother Lawrence Gannon. They told him that Fr. Flavian had first received notification from the State Department in Washington, D.C., that Merton had died. Later, they said, a phone call had been received from the American Embassy in Bangkok telling them that Merton had been electrocuted by a large fan in his room, although they were unsure as to whether he might have suffered a heart attack before grabbing the faulty fan or he might even have been trying to fix the fan. In the letter, Fox went on to say that Merton had been in his bare feet on a stone floor and the electricity had coursed through his body for hours, causing a deep burn mark on his bare chest. Interestingly, in the letter he twice misspelled "grabbed" as "grabed" and wrote "grabing" for "grabbing," so that it must be chalked up to Fox's poor spelling rather than to typographical error.[57]

---

[56] *The Martyrdom of Thomas Merton,* pp. 118-122, Chapter 21.

[57] James Fox, "To the Gethsemani Diaspora," Thomas Merton Center, Bellarmine University.

We have encountered nothing that we know originated from the U.S. Embassy in Bangkok that is consistent with this story. It agrees generally, though, with the story told in the almost certainly fabricated letter from the six Trappists, except that even that document has nothing about Merton "grabbing" the fan.

The false story that a fan was found on Merton's chest was repeated for a larger audience in *The Asian Journal of Thomas Merton*, published in 1973 and edited by two members of the Merton Legacy Trust, James Laughlin and Naomi Burton Stone, along with Brother Patrick. By that time those editors were long-since aware of the photograph taken by Fr. Say and the drawing by Sr. Weist that showed the fan was not found lying across Merton's chest. Brother Patrick also edited another book published in 1974, *Thomas Merton, A Monastic Tribute*. That volume repeated the false story by Fox that Merton's bare chest had been burned deeply. On the tenth anniversary of Merton's death Fox preached a homily in which he said, "An electric fan mounted on a five-foot metal stand, lay across his exposed breast, burning a deep red line into his flesh."[58]

When the police arrived, Fr. Say realized that the Thai police were doing a whitewash and not an actual investigation, so he did not tell the police about the photographs that he had taken, fearing that the police would confiscate their film and camera. The Benedictine monks, led by Fr. Say, acted to preserve the evidence. Without the prudent actions of the Benedictines at the scene the false stories that were spread by the Abbey of Gethsemani may have been the last word. In fact, they were pretty much the last word until 2018, when we published *The Martyrdom of Thomas Merton*.

Normally police investigators take photographs and draw a sketch of a crime scene. Rarely do private citizens act as these Benedictines had done in photographing and drawing a sketch of the scene of Merton's death. Those who appear to have devised a plan to place a fan on Merton's body to make it look like an accident could hardly have

---

[58] Lucas, p. 334.

foreseen the quick thinking of the first Benedictine responders on the scene who did what genuine police investigators should have done.

Fr. Weakland, to his credit, preserved the official death certificate and doctor's report. Weakland carried copies of these documents with him when he left the conference in Thailand. In 2012, when we contacted Weakland to ask him about Merton's death he sent those documents to us. We found additional copies at the National Archives with the Foreign Service Report on Merton's death and forwarded everything to the Thomas Merton Center at Bellarmine University for safekeeping.

In stark contrast to the actions of the Benedictines in pursuing the truth about Thomas Merton's death, Merton's home Cistercian community has ignored the evidence that we have uncovered.

Not only has the Abbey of Gethsemani exhibited hostility toward the truth, but they have also done so toward those who have revealed it. According to the Rule of Benedict, which is supposed to guide monastic behavior, visitors to the monastery represent Christ and have a claim on the welcome of the community. In 2019, Hugh Turley visited the Abbey of Gethsemani and he was told by the receptionist, Fr. Seamus Malvey, O.C.S.O., that Abbot Dietz would not see him. Malvey told Turley that he should not have come to Gethsemani and that he had been rejected. (See appendix 6, "Turned Away by the Abbey of Gethsemani.")

U.S. Embassy Preserved Documents

The U.S. Embassy in Bangkok sent a cable to the Abbey of Gethsemani informing them that Thomas Merton had died and that the official cause of death was "heart failure." The message also stated that Merton's body had been discovered at 4:00 P.M. (Bangkok time) with a standing electric fan on top of him and his body had an electrical burn.[59] The *New York Times* reporter Israel Shenker, learned of this cablegram from a spokesman for the abbey, but news of this early cable with its mention of "heart failure" as the cause of death was subsequently suppressed.

---

[59] Israel Shenker, "Thomas Merton Dead at 53; Monk Wrote of Search for God," *The New York Times*, December 11, 1968.

The only telegram that was preserved came from the U.S. State Department in Washington D.C. It stated only that Thomas Merton had died. Brother Patrick mentioned the cablegram from Bangkok in his postscript to *The Asian Journal of Thomas Merton*, but he falsely stated that the message from Bangkok was the same as the message from the State Department in Washington, the one that only said that Merton had died.

The American Embassy in Bangkok preserved several important official reports on Merton's death and mailed the official reports to the Abbey of Gethsemani. The embassy duly sent copies of these reports to State Department headquarters in Washington. We found them in the U.S. National Archives. The copies of these documents that were sent to the Abbey of Gethsemani, on the other hand, have disappeared.

In our previous book, we reported that the American Embassy was the source of the news that Merton's death was an "accident." But, as previously noted, we only had Abbot Flavian's word for that.

The U.S. Embassy in Bangkok, in fact, acted quite responsibly in immediately sending the abbey a cable with the official cause of Merton's death, assisting in the transfer of Merton's body to Kentucky, handling Merton's personal effects, and forwarding copies of the official reports to the abbey. The embassy report accurately stated that the cause of death was "Sudden Heart Failure (according to the death certificate)."[60] The embassy report did not, in fact, state that the cause of Merton's death was an "accident." Furthermore, the embassy translation of the Thai doctor's certificate by an embassy official added a correction stating that no autopsy had been performed, although the Thai doctor falsely stated that an autopsy had been performed at a hospital according to the law.[61] The American Embassy official acted responsibly to correct the false statement.

---

[60] Report of the Death of an American Citizen Thomas Merton, American Embassy Bangkok, Thailand, December 13, 1968, National Archives, College Park, Maryland.

[61] Luksana Nakvachara, Doctor's Certificate (cause of death), Samutprakarn Hospital, December 10, 1968, English language translation, National Archives.

CHAPTER 3

The Early News Reports

O n December 10, 1968, Brother Patrick and Brother Lawrence Gannon told James Fox that Merton had died and that Abbot Flavian wanted to meet with him.[62] Perhaps Abbot Flavian and Fox wanted to discuss what the abbey's statement to the news media should be. The meeting called between Fox and Abbot Flavian strongly suggests that the retired abbot was still participating in decision making at the abbey.

On December 11, 1968, *The New York Times* reported the first news of Merton's death. Its source was the Abbey of Gethsemani. The article by Israel Shenker stated:

> The Trappist Abbey of Gethsemani, at Bardstown, Ky., announced the death of its best-known member. A spokesman for the abbey said a cable with the news had arrived from the American Embassy in Bangkok....

---

[62] James Fox, February 1, 1969, letter.

Merton was found in his room at 4 P.M. badly burned by a shock he had apparently received from a standing electrical fan that toppled over on him. The cause of death was officially listed as heart failure.[63]

The early *New York Times* report, as we shall see, proved to be consistent with the report of the Thai police investigation that we now know, although it left readers with the impression that the electric shock must have caused the heart failure. What else could it have been, after all? Pointedly, though, the English-language *Bangkok Post* reported only that Merton had died of a heart attack, making no mention of any possible electrocution. It was a partner in error with Wheeler, though, in saying that the death had occurred at a conference in Bangkok.[64]

The abbey had been Shenker's source that heart failure had been the official cause of death, but then, in a bizarre turnaround, the Abbey of Gethsemani changed its story. Almost as soon as the original story was published in *The New York Times*, the abbey spokesman would say that the cable did not give any cause of death.

The original story from the Abbey of Gethsemani was published only in *The New York Times* proper. The New York Times News Service, though, sent a different story around the country:

> The Trappist Abbey of Gethsemani, at Bardstown, Ky., announced the death of its best known member Tuesday. A spokesman for the abbey said a cable with the news had arrived from the American Embassy in Bangkok. There was no indication of cause of death [65]

The story of the cable from the U.S. Embassy according to abbey spokesman, as we see, had been changed and no longer included any mention of an electric fan toppling over onto Merton, his body being

---

[63] "Thomas Merton Is Dead at 53," Israel Shenker, *New York Times*, December 11, 1968, p. 1.

[64] Dom. Jean Leclercq, O.S.B., "Final Memories of Thomas Merton," Vol. 9 (1969) of the Bulletin of AIM, web.archive.org/web/20081212155450 /http://monasticdialog.com/a.php?id=873.

[65] "Thomas Merton, Silent Speaker in Search for God, Dies," New York Times News Service, *Madison State Journal*, Madison, Wisconsin, December 11, 1968, p. 56.

found at 4 P.M., his body being badly burned, or that the cause of death was officially heart failure.

The syndicated story of United Press International (UPI) with a dateline of Trappist, Kentucky, reported the changed story from the abbey spokesman that the abbey was told the news of Merton's death in a cable from the U.S. Embassy in Bangkok and no cause of death was given:

> Thomas Merton, famed author and philosopher of the Gethsemani Abbey here, died Tuesday in Bangkok, Thailand, a monastery spokesman said. The abbey was informed of Merton's death by cablegram from the U.S. embassy in Bangkok the spokesman said. No cause of death was given.[66]

The morning edition of *The Courier-Journal*, published in Louisville, KY., reported the death of Thomas Merton on December 11, 1968. The story by a staff writer Joan Riehm stated simply:

> Thomas Merton, the Gethsemani monk with a worldwide reputation as an author and philosopher, died yesterday in Bangkok, Thailand...Spokesmen at the Gethsemani Abbey in Trappist, KY., near Bardstown, did not know the cause of death.[67]

The Associated Press Version of Merton's Death

Two other Kentucky newspapers near the Abbey of Gethsemani, *The Lexington Leader* and *The Lexington Herald*, using the Associated Press, would report that Thomas Merton was electrocuted by an electric fan. Notice that that AP story was quite different from that of the New York Times News Service, United Press International, and the local Louisville newspaper, although it is consistent with the original *Times* article by Israel Shenker, minus the "heart failure" as the official cause of death.

The headline in *The Lexington Leader* was, "Accidental Electrocution by Electric Fan Ends Multi-Faceted Life of Monk Merton." In Lowell, MA,

---

[66] "Famed Author Thomas Merton Dies in Bangkok," (UPI) *Jeffersonville Evening News*, Jeffersonville, Indiana, December 11, 1968, p.7.

[67] Joan Reihm, "Philosopher Thomas Merton Dies," *The Courier-Journal*, Louisville, Kentucky, p. 1.

The Lowell Sun headline was "Thomas Merton Dies in Electrocution Accident." The AP story by John T. Wheeler from Bangkok, widely published in newspapers across the United States, was the version of Merton's death seen by most Americans. Wheeler reported:

> Thomas Merton, the Trappist monk who wrote "The Seven Storey Mountain" and other best sellers was electrocuted Tuesday when he moved an electric fan and touched a short in the cord, local Catholic sources reported....
>
> Merton's body was found late in the afternoon on the floor of a room he was occupying during a visit to Bangkok. A doctor who was summoned said the monk's heart failed after the electric shock. A priest at the Church of St. Louis said Merton was not missed when he failed to show up for lunch.

Wheeler, who apparently did not know that Merton was not in Bangkok but in a Red Cross retreat center some 15 miles from Bangkok and that Merton had eaten lunch and was not found dead in his room until some hours later, nevertheless reported with great precision that Merton had been electrocuted when he touched a cord with a short in it while moving an electric fan.[68] If there really was such an anonymous priest, he clearly didn't know what he was talking about. He is also an odd source for information, since the Church of St. Louis is in Bangkok, and no indication was given that he was an attendee at the monastic conference. Considering the misinformation relayed by Wheeler and the fact that the conference was for members of monastic communities and not local priests, it is evident that he was not there.

---

[68] John T. Wheeler, "Thomas Merton Dies in Electrocution Accident," Associated Press, December 11, 1968. In actual fact, Fr. Celestine Say sat across from Merton at lunch and gave him the key to the cottage when he left with Fr. François de Grunne. (Celestine Say, letter to John Moffitt, July 1, 1969, Moffitt papers.).

John T. Wheeler – Associated Press correspondent

The actual source for Wheeler's mainly false information, which seems to have been crafted to sell the "accidental electrocution" story, continues to be a mystery.

Wheeler suppressed the news that there was a police investigation and only reported that a doctor said that Merton's heart failed after the electric shock. That statement was not true. The doctor, improbable as it may seem, said the exact opposite, that is, that the heart failure caused Merton to fall into the faulty fan postmortem, with his body then showing the burning effects of the bad fan.

No one witnessed Merton moving a fan and there is no evidence that he did. There was no evidence that Merton "touched a cord," and eyewitnesses said that Merton's hands were not burned, suggesting that he had not touched any part of the fan.

The AP report by Wheeler reveals the early participation of the news media in the cover-up of Merton's murder, and that *per se* is a very suspicious happenstance. From the very beginning, the cause of death was reported to be an accident without any reference to any investigation. One can almost believe that the story had been written in anticipation of the completion of the dastardly deed.

More evidence of the early participation of the news media can be seen in the withdrawal of the original true story published in *The New York Times* followed by the suppression of that story.

Comparing the original story in *The New York Times* by Israel Shenker with the Associated Press story by John T. Wheeler is instructive. The early report by Shenker had named the sources as the spokesman for the Abbey of Gethsemani, who said that the abbey received a cable from the U.S. Embassy in Bangkok. All the facts in Shenker's early report proved to be true, as far as it went, according to later revelations. Merton's body was discovered at 4 P.M.,[69] there was an electric fan on top of Merton's

---

[69] Egbert Donovan, letter to John Moffitt, December 5, 1969, Michael Mott papers, Northwestern University library.

body, and his body was badly burned.[70] And the official death certificate did, indeed, state that the cause of death was "heart failure."[71] No evidence supported the AP story, yet it became the accepted "truth" by the news media, historians, Merton scholars, and most importantly, by the Abbey of Gethsemani.

Perhaps the most unusual news report of Thomas Merton's death was from *The Kentucky Standard*, in Bardstown only 12 miles from the Abbey of Gethsemani. Unlike the major Kentucky newspapers, the local newspaper did not report Merton's death until December 12. Under the headline "Merton Trappist-Author Dies in Bangkok, Thailand," the newspaper reported: "Spokesmen at the Trappist monastery at Gethsemane [sic], Nelson County, said that it would be several days before they would know any information as to the cause of death, or arrival of the body in the United States."[72]

After an original false start in which they told the truth, relaying what they had received from a cable from the American Embassy in Thailand, a spokesman for the Abbey of Gethsemani changed their story, deciding to engage in the first principle of truth suppression, they dummied up. (See appendix 9.) They quite clearly decided to lie about what they had been told by the Embassy in Thailand while buying time to determine what their next step would be. We would see that step a little more than a week later.

Two days after Merton's December 17 funeral, *The Kentucky Standard* had its next article on Merton's death, and, in great contrast to its December 12 article, it was long and detailed. Ten paragraphs into its December 19 article we have this:

> Father Louis was accidently electrocuted while visiting in Thailand. His body was found late in the afternoon, December 10, in his room at

---

[70] M. Edeltrud Weist, Report on the first impressions after Rev. F. Thomas Merton's tragic death given by an eyewitness, handwritten note, Bangkok, December 11, 1968, the Merton Center.

[71] Tawil Chaiplab, Death Certificate No. 388/2511.

[72] "Merton Trappist-Author Dies in Bangkok, Thailand," *The Kentucky Standard*, December 12, 1968, p. 1.

45

Sawangke, Vivas, 15 miles south of Bangkok. He was lying on the floor with an electric fan on top of him. His body had several cuts and burns. Apparently he picked up a fan in the shower room to bring it into the bedroom.

The body was flown in an Army plane to Travis Air Force Base, near San Francisco Calif., on Sunday. An autopsy was performed in Oakland, Calif., before the body was flown by commercial plane to Louisville Standford Field arriving about noon.

One of the monks went to California to accompany the body home and to facilitate arrangements.

Considering that on December 12 the folks at the newspaper did not even know the correct spelling of "Gethsemani," indications are great that this article was composed by someone at the abbey and simply supplied to *The Kentucky Standard*. It is also quite inconsistent with the known record in several ways. There is no record of any monk accompanying Merton's body from California to Kentucky. No autopsy was performed in California or anywhere else, for that matter. There is no evidence that Merton was accidentally electrocuted moving a fan from a shower room. There *was* a severe burn on Merton's abdomen and there was also a bleeding wound on the back of his head, but it is inaccurate to say that his body had "cuts and burns."

The article had no byline. Along with its plethora of detail, the article also exhibits a familiarity with church protocol in its description of the funeral and it makes mention of an "abbey spokesman" and "Brother Patrick, Merton's personal secretary," further supporting the presumption that this article, with all its dubious "facts," was simply supplied to the newspaper by the abbey.

On the same day that it was published, December 19, the abbey sent out the almost certainly fraudulent six-Trappists letter to Merton's friends. That letter and the article in *The Kentucky Standard* were the first sources to suggest Merton might have taken a shower and they are the only sources to say that Merton's body had several cuts on it. No witnesses on the scene mention any cuts, no investigating Thai authorities record any, and there are none in evidence in the two photographs of the body that were taken by Fr. Celestine Say.

46

CHAPTER 4

The Gethsemani Abbey's Story Versus the Official Story

The story that Thomas Merton died by accidental electrocution may have first reached the public through the Associated Press, but, as we have seen, after a short delay that story was adopted and repeated by the Abbey of Gethsemani, and it remains their story to the present day. A spokesman for the abbey gave what is apparently an accurate account of the cable from the U.S. Embassy in Bangkok to Israel Shenker of *The New York Times*. Around noon, on December 10, a decision was made not to share the information from that cable with anyone else, not even with the monks at the Abbey of Gethsemani or Merton's friends when they were told that Merton had died. A few men at the abbey suppressed the news of the stated "heart failure" cause of death in the cable from the embassy in Bangkok.

The only full cable message on Merton's death to the abbey that it ever released was from the State Department in Washington. That telegram came on December 10, 1968, at 9:52 am (Eastern Time) addressed to Abbot Flavian Burns. A copy of that telegram, available at The Thomas Merton Center, states:

DEPARTMENT REGRETS TO INFORM YOU FOLLOWING MESSAGE RECEIVED FOR YOU FROM AMERICAN EMBASSY BANGKOK THAILAND: INFORMED BY ABBOTT WEAKLAND THAT THOMAS MERTON HAS DIED.

The telegram was sent by "Hobart Luppi, Dir. Special Consular Services, Dept of State."

In his postscript to *The Asian Journal of Thomas Merton*, Brother Patrick wrote that they had received an incredible cable from the American Embassy in Thailand that gave little more information than that Merton had died.[73] As we have seen from what the abbey told Israel Shenker of *The New York Times* about that cable, Brother Patrick mischaracterized it in this later account. The cable also said that Merton apparently had been shocked by a fan but that the official cause of death was "heart failure." Unfortunately, since the abbey never released that cable message, we don't know what else might have been in it. We can be virtually certain, though, that when Brother Patrick wrote "little more," what he really meant was that there was really nothing in it that would support the story that Merton had been electrocuted by a faulty fan.

The abbey would later receive the official written reports from the American Embassy in Bangkok confirming that the official cause of death was "heart failure." These documents, like that cable from Bangkok, were suppressed by the abbey as well. The deception has gone beyond simply suppressing the official death documents. We will see later how the official reports have been misrepresented as evidence that the cause of Merton's death was "accidental electrocution."

---

[73] Hart, postscript, *The Asian Journal of Thomas Merton*, pp. 258-259.

First Accounts of the "Accident"

During the Watergate Hearings Senator Howard Baker famously asked, "What did the President know and when did he know it?" The Abbey of Gethsemani has never revealed exactly when they first concluded that the cause of Thomas Merton's death was "accidental electrocution" and upon what that conclusion was based.

Abbot Flavian, Brother Patrick, and James Fox have given different and contradictory accounts of how the abbey learned that Thomas Merton was "accidentally electrocuted." Flavian would write many years later that he called the American Embassy in Bangkok and was told that Merton's death was an accident and nothing more.[74] Brother Patrick wrote that it was the other way around, that the embassy called Flavian and told him that "the death was caused by accidental electrocution." Whoever initiated the call, Abbot Flavian's account is consistent with what Paul Quenon says Flavian announced at the noon meal on December 10 and Brother Patrick's is not, that is, that the embassy had said that the death was from an accident, not from "accidental electrocution."[75] It's important to note, though, that neither account is exactly consistent with the abbey's earliest reports to newspapers, first, that Merton was found "badly burned" by a fan lying across his body and that the cause of death was from "heart failure," and then the quickly revised story that the abbey had not been told the cause of death.

James Fox wrote that at precisely 12:45 P.M, December 10, 1968, Brother Patrick and Brother Lawrence told him that the embassy had called Flavian. According to Fox, the embassy told Flavian about a large fan with a faulty insulation wire that Merton grabbed when he was fixing the fan, moving the fan, or having a heart attack causing the fan to fall with him.[76] These three versions of how the abbey learned about an "accident" cannot all be true. No real evidence that Merton was

---

[74] Paul Wilkes, editor, *Merton by Those Who Knew Him Best*, Harper and Row, 1984, p. 109.

[75] Paul Quenon, *In Praise of the Useless Life*, Ave Maria Press, 2018, p. 114.

[76] Fox letter Feb 1, 1969.

accidentally electrocuted has ever been presented, which reveals, along with the contradictions among them, the fanciful nature of the stories of Abbot Flavian, Fox, and Brother Patrick.

Deceiving the Gethsemani Community

The leadership at Gethsemani concealed the information in the cable that it received from the U.S. Embassy in Bangkok from its monks. Abbot Flavian did not tell the monks at the abbey what the abbey spokesman had told *The New York Times*. As we have seen, the abbey spokesman would later say that "no cause of death was given" in the cable from Bangkok. In his book, *In Praise of a Useless Life*, Br. Paul Quenon wrote that on December 10, Fr. Flavian walked to the reader's microphone and announced "that a message had arrived that Fr. Louis had had an accident and was dead...No further information was available, even the exact nature of the accident."[77] Without any official source and without any evidence that we know of, Flavian made the first announcement to the monks of Gethsemani that Merton had had an "accident".

If Abbot Flavian did speak to an embassy official, that person has never been named. We have seen nothing that supports the story that anyone at the embassy told Abbot Flavian that Merton's death was an accident. The embassy's Foreign Service Report on Merton's death did not state that the cause of death was an accident. Therefore, it is unlikely that the embassy would have called and told the abbot that Merton died because of an accident.

Other monks at Gethsemani remember Abbot Flavian coming to the dining hall to inform them of Merton's death. In a later homily, Brother Matthew Kelty told of his memory of Abbot Flavian coming to the microphone during the mid-day meal and announcing, "Brothers, I have sad news for you. Fr. Louis died in Bangkok. That is all I know. I'll let you know more when I learn it."[78]

---

[77] Quenon, p. 114.

[78] A Homily of Fr. Matthew Kelty, O.C.S.O. for the Thomas Merton Memorial Mass at the Louisville Cathedral, December 10th, 1998.

Brother Maurice Flood, Merton's secretary, had a similar recollection that at the end of the noon meal after the reader had finished reading and they were ready to get up and do the dishes, Father Flavian came to the podium and said that Merton was dead. Fr. Patrick Henry Reardon, currently a senior editor at *Touchstone* magazine, was also a monk at Gethsemani at the time, and his recollection is roughly the same as Quenon's. Reardon said, "The accident was very indefinite at first. Within days, however, and certainly when Merton's body actually arrived, the accidental electrocution was the only explanation I ever heard. I don't recall who first declared it."[79]

Quenon and Reardon's memory of the abbot saying that the death was "accidental" is consistent with Flavian's account in 1984. Flavian wrote that he called the embassy in Bangkok and was told "there had been an accidental death; no more than that."[80] Flavian added, "I asked for an autopsy because I wanted to have answers to questions I knew would be coming." There was no autopsy, but Flavian left the impression that there had been one because he said that he "asked for an autopsy." Without an autopsy and proper police investigation, Merton's death remains an unsolved death and likely homicide.

Flavian's statement that he asked for an autopsy marked the fifth story that an autopsy had been performed when there wasn't one. The Thai doctor's report and Thai policeman's note on the back of the death certificate falsely stated that Merton's body had been taken to the hospital for an autopsy, as prescribed by law. As we have seen, *The Kentucky Standard* reported that an autopsy had been performed in Oakland, California, before the body was flown to Louisville. As we shall see in the next chapter, a nun who was at the conference wrote shortly afterwards that the U.S. Army had performed an autopsy.

Quenon and Reardon are certain that "electrocution" was not stated initially. In 2018, during a public interview in Chicago to mark the 50th

---

[79] Fr. Patrick Henry Reardon email to Hugh Turley, January 17, 2022.
[80] Wilkes, p.109.

anniversary of Merton's death, Quenon said that, at first, they did not know "if it was a car accident, or a fall, or what."

Reardon's memory is that "adjectives such as 'moist,' 'damp,' and perhaps even 'wet' were used...in describing what all of us—without exception, in my memory—believed to be Merton's accidental electrocution." Reardon said, "To the best of my recollection, ALL of us believed that there was a large burn on Merton's chest. Whatever the truth of the matter was, I cannot name a single monk who believed otherwise during December of 1968." The evidence is irrefutable, though, that Merton was not wet, did not have a large burn on his chest, and the official cause of death was not accidental electrocution. We believe that the evidence is equally overwhelming that the actual cause of death was not accidental electrocution, either.

Someone successfully fooled the monks at the Abbey of Gethsemani into believing things about Thomas Merton's death that were false. We know that Fox wrote from early reports that he had received that there was a deep burn in Merton's chest. And on the tenth anniversary Fox would repeat this lie in a homily saying, "An electric fan mounted on a five-foot metal stand, lay across his exposed breast, burning a deep red line into his flesh." The photographic evidence of Merton's body prove that this was not true.

First the monks were not told that the abbey had received a cable from the embassy stating that Merton had officially died of heart failure and that he was found with an electric fan on top of him. Initially the monks of Gethsemani were kept completely in the dark. Later, their situation was even worse when they were told information that was not true.

More Contradictions by the Abbey

On the afternoon of December 11, Abbot Flavian sent telegrams to Merton's friends including Mark Van Doren, Dorothy Day, and Catherine

Doherty.[81] His message stated, "We regret to inform you of the death of Father Thomas Merton in Bangkok." No cause of death was mentioned. Another telegram was sent on the afternoon of December 11, from Brother Patrick to John Howard Griffin with the same message and no details or cause of death stated. Abbot Flavian did not disclose that the cause of death was heart failure according to the cable that the abbey had shared with the *The New York Times*. Abbot Flavian's telegrams did not even state that Merton's death was "accidental" as he had told the monks at their mid-day meal. Since the AP report with its "accidental electrocution" story was out all over the country by that time, one must wonder why Flavian bothered to send his completely uninformative telegrams at all. It can only be interpreted that the abbey was still in its holding-pattern mode after having initially given out too much information.

Matthew Kelty

The story about a fan killing Merton somehow became known at the abbey within a week. We might wonder about the mechanism by which the abbey learned that that was to be the story. The important thing seems to be that the song that the abbey was soon singing was the one first sung by John T. Wheeler at the AP, even with all the holes in his one article on Merton's death.

On December 18, the day after Merton was buried, Brother Matthew Kelty sent a "Dear Friend" letter to a limited number of his friends. Somehow in the week between Merton's death and his funeral on December 17, the monks had learned that the death may have been caused by a heart attack or an accident with an electric fan.

Kelty's letter began by stating that Merton's "death was confused. I mean we are not really sure what he died of: heart attack, accident with an electric fan?" It is an interesting admission by Kelty that the day after Merton's funeral the monks still did not know the cause of his death.

---

[81] Abbot Flavian telegrams to Mark Van Doren, Dorothy Day, and Catherine Doherty, December 11, 1968, The Thomas Merton Center, Bellarmine University.

Later in his letter, Kelty added, "rest content with the verdict that it was accidental death." Kelty's one-page letter, like Wheeler's Associated Press story, provided no evidence or any source for the verdict of "accidental death."

The "Monks'" Letter

On December 19, the day following Kelty's letter, the abbey sent out a letter signed "The monks of Gethsemani." This served as a cover letter for that curious six-Trappists letter, which was enclosed.

The short cover letter began by saying that the abbey was moved by the expressions of sympathy for Merton's death. The letter stated that another letter by six Trappists was enclosed in response to requests for details about Merton's death. But readers of the supposed Trappists letter had to have been greatly disappointed because it provided few details, named no witnesses, and only speculated that the death may have been caused by either a heart attack or by an electric shock. The letter gave no clue as to what authorities might be doing to learn more information or how anyone interested might go about learning any more information. The implication of the cover letter was that the monks at Gethsemani, amazing as it might seem, were fully satisfied by the six Trappists letter and therefore others should be satisfied, as well.

Since the six Trappist letter is suspicious in itself, it is hardly surprising that it should be accompanied by a peculiar cover letter. The cover letter stated that the enclosed letter was from the "six Trappist-Cistercian superiors" that were at the conference with Merton. The unsigned letter that was sent out ended with these words "Signed by the six Trappist delegates at the conference". Unless there was an original Trappist letter that the abbey suppressed and have since lost or destroyed, the author of the cover letter would not have known if "the six Trappist delegates" were superiors because there were no names or signatures on the letter that was sent out.

54

Calling the authors of the letter "six Trappist-Cistercian superiors" has another problem. After Merton's death there were seven and not six surviving Trappists at the conference. Only five of the surviving Trappists were superiors so the letter could not have been written by "six Trappist-Cistercian superiors."

The abbey's letter concluded by saying that a private funeral had been held on December 17th and that Thomas Merton had been buried. Expressions of prayers and sympathy were acknowledged as comforting. The letter indicated that the case of Merton's death had been closed. The six Trappist letter was to serve as the abbey's final word on the matter.

As noted, neither letter was signed by any actual person. The cover letter was signed, "The monks of Gethsemani" and the other letter closed simply with the words "signed by the six Trappist delegates at the conference." We think it is highly likely that both of those letters, at least in its final form, were written by the same schemer or schemers at the Abbey of Gethsemani.

In 1968, there were nearly 200 monks at Gethsemani, and it is inconceivable that they all got together and wrote the cover letter. It may have been appropriate for Abbot Flavian or Merton's secretary, Br. Patrick, to write the cover letter, but neither signed it. It appears that whoever wrote that cover letter did not want to put their name(s) on it. The fact that neither of these letters was signed is highly suspect, especially given the false information in the six Trappist letter.

Yes, in addition to its many other problems, it had provably false information. The letter stated that two Thai doctors arrived at the scene of Merton's death. There was only one Thai doctor at the scene, Dr. Laksana Nakvachara. The Trappist letter stated that "He was on his back with the electric fan lying across his chest." Photographs of Merton's body, exactly as it was found, prove that the fan was not lying across Merton's chest.

One might also reasonably ask why this group of people might have thought that it was their responsibility to attempt to tell the abbey what had happened and why and how they thought it was best to do it as a collective effort, with seemingly no one person in charge. Anyone with any experience working on committees will know how difficult it is to achieve a consensus among even a small group of people on matters that sometimes seem to be trivial. What this committee produced was clearly very unsatisfactory, and yet we are supposed to believe that every one of these six people signed off on it less than a day after Merton had died.

None of the six Trappists was a witness to the death scene, and none of them had any administrative responsibility for what went on at the conference or at the Red Cross conference center where Merton died. They were most likely strangers to one another, with the one thing they had in common being that they belonged to the same religious order as Merton. They were simply not the right people to be the primary source of information on Merton's death, and it showed.

The letter *did* reveal that there was a bleeding wound on the back of Merton's head, but it managed to distract readers from that possibly very important fact by saying first that there were cuts on his right side and arm. No witnesses reported seeing any such cuts, but the head wound had been widely noticed. An autopsy would have been the first order of business for any proper police investigation, with the head wound only highlighting the fact, but the ostensible letter from the six Trappists said nothing at all about any autopsy. We know now, of course, that none was conducted.

The Trappists' letter also failed to say anything about any Thai police investigation, which means that it did not tell anyone that the Thai police report made no mention of the wound to the head. What is most critical, the letter did not say that the Thai police had concluded, in the absence of an autopsy, that Merton had died of heart failure and was already dead when he fell into a floor fan in his room, which, by coincidence, happened to have, as the Thai police report stated, a "defective electric cord installed inside its stand" and somehow ended up lying across his supine body.

The letter writers also seemed to go to special trouble not to name any witnesses by calling them, "others," "they," "the nun," and by saying that Merton's body "was found," in the passive voice.

With all its shortcomings, this letter became, along with John T. Wheeler's AP report, a foundation document for the widely believed story that Merton had died from accidental electrocution by a faulty fan.

As we have pointed out, the Merton Center has no actual signed letter, and the current archivist at the Gethsemani Abbey tells us that if there ever was such a signed letter, they don't have it now.[82] One must wonder what reason there could possibly be for not retaining such an important letter, actually signed by those six Trappists. The best evidence suggests, then, that this almost certainly fraudulent letter with its curious "we the undersigned" closing that lacks any actual signatures, is the only such letter that there ever was.

It would be another week before the U.S. Embassy in Thailand would send the abbey the Thai Doctor's Report, Death Certificate, Foreign Service Report, and handwritten witness reports. Those documents would confirm that the official cause of death was "heart failure" just as the abbey spokesman had told *The New York Times* on December 10, 1968. But this would not be what the abbey would tell the public. The official documents were kept secret while the abbey feigned that those documents proved that the cause of death was "accidental electrocution." When we asked to see the abbey's copies of these documents, we were told that they had "lost" them.

---

[82] *The Martyrdom of Thomas Merton*, p. 261.

CHAPTER 5

The Asian Journal of
Thomas Merton and the Shower

The Trappists' letter did not become widely known to the public until it was included as an appendix to *The Asian Journal of Thomas Merton*, published almost five years after Merton's death. [83] Brother Patrick, Merton's belatedly appointed secretary, is the author of a postscript to the book. Like the writers of the Trappists' letter, Brother Patrick was careful not to name any witnesses. The most important thing about the postscript, though, is that it is the first time that anyone declared that Merton had just taken a shower before touching the faulty fan.[84] Neither any of the witnesses, the Thai police, the medical reports, nor any contemporaneous news accounts said anything about Merton having taken a shower. The notion that an electric fan killed a perfectly dry Thomas Merton is so absurd that

---

[83] Six Trappists letter to Flavian Burns, December 11, 1968, appendix VIII, *The Asian Journal of Thomas Merton*, pp. 344-347.

[84] Brother Patrick Hart, Postscript, *The Asian Journal of Thomas Merton*, pp. 257-259.

Brother Patrick, or someone exercising strong influence over him, apparently felt it necessary to invent the shower story to make it more believable.

Father Celestine Say, O.S.B., who was among the first three people to enter Merton's room and see his body, said that he looked like he might have been getting ready to take a shower.[85] Having entered the cottage, where his room alone shared the first floor with Merton, and with whom he shared a bathroom with a shower in the parlor between their rooms, Say had heard no sound from Merton or the shower from the time he entered the cottage about five minutes after Merton right up to the time the body was discovered some two hours later. Neither did he hear any sound from Merton's room.

Sister Marie de la Croix, O.C.S.O., who was an attendee at the conference, wrote shortly after the event in a five-page report that Merton had taken a shower, but she also says he then took a nap before touching the fan and being electrocuted, so the shower would not have been a factor in the electrocution.[86] At any rate, she was not a witness and is simply wrong about a number of things. She also wrote, for instance, that the United States Army had conducted an autopsy, the results of which were not yet available.

The letter from the Trappists was likely added as an appendix to the book that introduced Brother Patrick's shower story because the letter states that Merton, "could have showered." Brother Patrick began his shower story by stating that he had read the accounts of witnesses as well as the police and medical reports, strongly implying that he had supporting evidence, but, as we have noted, the evidence is all to the contrary. Brother Patrick admitted to us in 2017 that, in fact, he had no actual evidence that Merton had showered, saying only that the weather was hot and steamy and he "must have showered."[87]

---

[85] *The Martyrdom of Thomas Merton*, p. 126.

[86] "The Last Days of Thomas Merton," http://www.merton.org/ITMS/Seasonal/28/28-4Croix.pdf.

[87] Brother Patrick Hart, voicemail to Hugh Turley, May 31, 2017, 2:14 pm.

Changing the Trappists' Letter

The version of the Trappists' letter published by New Directions is not identical to the copy that the Merton Center has. It differs in what it adds and in what it leaves out. Taking the second point first, in describing how Merton's body was found, lying on his back on the floor of his room with the fan lying across his body, it leaves out the words, "in his pajamas." This is quite obviously not a matter of inadvertence. The editors of the book, Brother Patrick, James Laughlin, and Naomi Burton Stone, clearly made the conscious decision to cut those three words from the letter, thereby misrepresenting it in a very significant way. Putting it bluntly, they violated the commandment against bearing false witness.

The publishing company itself, New Directions, must also bear some responsibility for this historically crucial excision. The death scene photographs taken by Father Say confirm that Merton was wearing what appeared to be the bottom half of summer "shorty" pajamas, virtually ruling out the possibility that he had just stepped out of a shower. That short prepositional phrase, "in his pajamas," clearly had no place in a volume in which the shower story was introduced, and so it was cut out.

We can't be as completely certain about the circumstances around what the editors added as we can be about what they left out. We can only say that it is different from the copy available at the Merton Center in that it lists the names of "the six Trappists" at the end, though it does not show their signatures. Those names would have been easy to obtain from a published list of the attendees at the conference, and one must wonder if that is where the editors got them, instead of from the original letter. The heading is also a misrepresentation, because there were actually seven Trappists remaining at the conference after Merton's death. The name that was left off was that of Marie de la Croix.

That de la Croix's name, in particular, should have been left off is another reason to question the document's authenticity. One of the supposed signatories could not have failed to see that it was wrong for them to call themselves "the six Trappists" at the conference. That is Mother Christiana, the abbess of de la Croix's home monastery in

Seiboen, Japan. They happened to be the only two Trappistines at the conference and the only two people on the list from the same abbey. Mother Christiana could hardly have failed to notice that de la Croix was not included among the letter's supposed signatories.

Trappists Not Acknowledged

After the publication of our book, we noticed another possibly important omission from *The Asian Journal of Thomas Merton*. New Directions, like most publishing companies, is very legalistic and fussy about the matter of acknowledgements. We had wanted to use the long passage from Brother Patrick in which he told in a very authoritative manner how Merton had showered before encountering the fan, but the fee that they demanded—which is optional for the publisher to require—seemed higher than the usual going rate, so we went with a paraphrase instead.

In the acknowledgements of *The Asian Journal of Thomas Merton*, New Directions Publishing is meticulous in giving credit to everyone who gave them permission to use copyrighted material, but the six Trappists are not mentioned. Also, James Laughlin in the editor's notes for the book expresses appreciation to a long list of individuals and copyright owners. The six Trappists are not mentioned there, either.[88] It occurred to us, then, that New Directions had, in effect, commercially capitalized upon the supposed letter from these six Trappists without having obtained the permission of any of them to do so.

We wrote to New Directions and asked them if our assumption was correct. We also took the opportunity to ask them where the list of six names came from when there were actually seven remaining Trappists at the conference and what they might know about the apparent removal of the "in his pajamas" passage from the original letter.

Mr. Christopher Wait, permissions editor at New Directions, in response, agreed that we had made some interesting points, but since this happened "so long ago" and because they were really a very small

---

[88] *The Asian Journal of Thomas Merton*, pp. vi-xix.

operation that kept few records, he simply had no way to answer any of our questions.[89]

One may take this response at face value, or one may not, especially considering what the editors working for New Directions did to that "in his pajamas" passage. The publishing company, founded in 1936 by Laughlin, who is one of the book's editors, is well respected, and it seems to us that it would be routine for them to have such records in their filing cabinets, but perhaps not. However, were they really serious in answering our questions they might have made an inquiry to one of the three surviving editors of the book, Brother Patrick, who still resided at the Gethsemani Abbey.

The two editors of the book besides Brother Patrick, Laughlin and Stone, share responsibility for its false information, and we remind readers that they made up two thirds of the Merton Legacy Trust..[90]

One might well suspect that the normal procedure of obtaining permission for the publication of someone else's work was not followed because the folks at New Directions either knew, or suspected as we do, that the letter was not authentic and there was therefore no reason to obtain the permission of people who had not created it in the first place. Furthermore, they would have hardly wanted to alert any of these Trappists that they were publishing a letter in their name that they either knew or strongly suspected that they did not write.

---

[89] Christopher Wait, Permissions Editor, New Directions Publishing, email to Hugh Turley, May 7, 2018.

[90] One is tempted to believe that there is more wrong with *The Asian Journal of Thomas Merton* than the introduction of the spurious shower story in the postscript and the questionable six Trappists' letter with the "in his pajamas" removed. Ian S. MacNiven has revealed that the volume is largely the reconstruction work of James Laughlin, based on Merton's very sketchy notes. One is tempted to believe that the lapsed Presbyterian, Laughlin, a Trotskyite socialist politically, might have put his own slant on things and made Merton's religious leanings appear more heterodox than they really were. MacNiven says, though, that Merton's friend, Edward Rice, was the one who claimed that Merton "died a Buddhist" and that Merton's interest in Eastern religions was always "as a Catholic." See Ian S. MacNiven, "More than Scribe: James Laughlin, Thomas Merton, and *The Asian Journal*," *The Merton Annual*, 2013.

More Suspicions

There are a couple of more important reasons to regard the letter as a carefully crafted fabrication. Not only does the Trappists' letter say that the fan was lying across Merton's chest when it was across his pelvis, and that two Thai doctors arrived when there was only one, but it also has this passage: "Not long after [Merton] retired a shout was heard by others in his cottage but after a preliminary check they thought they must have imagined the cry."

That passage establishes in the mind of the reader that that was when Merton encountered the lethal fan and met his death. In fact, there were only two others in the cottage at the time, Father Say on the first floor with Merton, in a room separated from Merton's by a small parlor, and Father François de Grunne, O.S.B., who was in a room on the second floor over Say's. Actually, the rooms, at least on the first floor, were only temporary affairs separated by netting with sheets hung for a modicum of privacy. Only the doors and doorframes were permanent. De Grunne was the only one who claimed to have heard a shout or a "loud noise," as the Thai police reported. This occurred, according to Say, shortly after his arrival at the cottage, when de Grunne came downstairs, knocked on the door of the bathroom off the parlor where Say was brushing his teeth and asked him if he had heard a shout. Say had not. De Grunne then simply went back upstairs, and neither man checked on Merton.

The best evidence is that there was no such shout from Merton. In 1969, in a letter to Moffitt, de Grunne wrote that the only sound he had heard was from nearby houses and that he had not been particularly concerned about it.[91] Nevertheless, the "shout," as de Grunne initially responded to and the Trappists' letter passed on, and the Thai police's "loud noise," coming almost an hour later than when Say said de Grunne reported it to him, became the sound of Merton's death throes in the public imagination, and it has remained so ever since. (See appendix 3, "Thomas Merton's 'Death Shout.'")

---

[91] François de Grunne, letter to John Moffitt, July 6, 1969, Moffitt papers.

The Asian Journal of Thomas Merton was only the first of a series of books taken from Merton's journals that have been published posthumously and edited by Brother Patrick. *The Other Side of the Mountain*, Volume 7 of *The Journals of Thomas Merton*, was published in 1998.[92] In the introduction to that book Brother Patrick repeats almost verbatim what he wrote in that earlier postscript, with one important change. Earlier he had written that one of the monks discovering the body, Father Odo Haas, O.S.B., had experienced a "severe" shock when he tried to move the fan from Merton. This time he changed the word from "severe" to "slight."

In making that change he greatly weakened the case that Merton had died from the shock of that fan. But what he also did was to make the story consistent with the report of the best witness, Fr. Say, and with the Thai police report and the statement of Sr. Edeltrud Weist, as opposed to what is found in another very suspect document. Say, upon seeing Haas recoil from the shock asked him how strong it was, and Haas said that it was not very strong.[93] The Thai police report, for its part, says that Haas "jerked back" from the fan. Sr. Weist said that it was a "slight" shock. The only source for the shock being a strong one is a typed, unsigned document purported to be the statement of Haas given to the investigating police. In that statement Haas says that, not only was the shock a strong one, but it also "kept [him] from getting free of the fan" until Say could unplug it. (See appendix 4, "Key False Document in the Thomas Merton Death Case.")

By changing the shock description from "severe" to "slight," Brother Patrick also established at least a small precedent for making his writing accord more closely with the best evidence available. It is likely a matter of no small significance that Brother Patrick made his correction from "severe" to "slight" only after James Fox's death. Fox died on April 17, 1987, some 11 years before Brother Patrick made this important correction of the record.

---

[92] Harper, p. xix. We discuss this changed story about the Haas experience with the fan on pp. 176-177 of *The Martyrdom of Thomas Merton*.

[93] Say letter to John Moffitt, December 11, 1969, Moffitt papers.

We should also note that "severe shock" was as far as Brother Patrick would go originally in describing Abbot Haas's experience with the fan. He had in hand the purported Haas statement that said that he was stuck to the fan until Fr. Say could unplug it but chose not to use it, strongly suggesting that he knew that the statement was a fabrication.

The New Directions web site, it should be noted, similar to the Gethsemani Abbey site, continues to state, in spite of all the new evidence to the contrary that we have uncovered and published, that Merton was, "the victim of an accidental electrocution."[94]

---

[94] https://www.ndbooks.com/author/thomas-merton/.

CHAPTER 6

The Official Reports

Official Documents from Thailand

At the end of December 1968, the U.S. Embassy in Bangkok sent Abbot Flavian three historic documents related to Thomas Merton's death, a doctor's certificate,[95] the death certificate,[96] and the Foreign Service Report on the Death of an American Citizen.[97] The Thai officials concluded that *sudden heart failure* was the primary cause of Merton's death. These documents would support the report of Merton's death in *The New York Times* according to the cable that the abbey received from the U.S. Embassy.

---

[95] Luksana Nakvachara, Doctor's Certificate, (Cause of Death), Samutprakarn Hospital, December 10, 1968, English language translation, from National Archives.

[96] Death Certificate No. 388/2511, Samut Prakern Municipality, Thailand, from National Archives, http://merton.org/50th/Death-Certificate.jpg.

[97] Report of the Death of an American Citizen Thomas Merton, American Embassy Bangkok, Thailand, December 13, 1968, National Archives, http://merton.org/50th/Foreign-Service-Report.jpg.

The abbey concealed these documents. Instead, it chose to reinforce the "accidental electrocution" story that had been put out at the very beginning, based upon anonymous and highly dubious sources, by the Associated Press's correspondent in Bangkok.

In addition to the official reports the embassy also sent the abbey statements of witnesses who were at the scene where Merton died. These important official witness statements were also kept secret, and, along with the other official reports, they now seem to have disappeared.

The deception was successful for almost 50 years until we discovered the official reports. Archbishop Rembert Weakland, O.S.B., provided the death certificate and doctor's certificate to us in 2012. He had obtained these documents in 1968 when he presided over the conference in Thailand where Merton died. We found additional copies of these same reports and the Foreign Service Report at the National Archives in College Park, Maryland. All the documents have a stamp of authenticity from the U.S. Embassy in Bangkok.

In 2017, we sent copies of these documents to Dr. Paul Pearson, the Director of The Thomas Merton Center at Bellarmine University. Pearson told us he had never seen them before, and he noticed something peculiar. The doctor's certificate states that Merton's body was "brought to the hospital for the purpose of an autopsy." In fact, the body was not brought to the hospital, and no autopsy was performed. The abbey should have noticed this when they received this document.

Doctor's Certificate

The doctor's certificate exists in three versions, the one in the original Thai language and two others in English translation. Dr. Luksana Nakvachara completed and signed the doctor's certificate, dated December 10, 1968, the day of Merton's death. Dr. Nakvachara wrote in English on the Thai language document that the death had been caused by, "Fainting – due to acute cardiac failure and electric shock due to accidental falling against the fan to the floor." The doctor's certificate did not comment on a bleeding wound in the back of Merton's head, observed by witnesses.

Near the bottom of the English translation of the document that we found at the National Archives, it states:

> Remarks: The patient died outside Samutprakarn Hospital. The remains were brought to the Hospital for the purpose of a post mortem by medical doctors and investigation authority as prescribed by law.

Below these remarks, at the bottom of the State Department translation copy of the doctor's certificate one finds a comment from an anonymous American Embassy consular officer that states:

> * (CONSULAR OFFICER'S NOTE – *NOT PART OF TRANSLATION*): As will be noted from the copy of the original form, the comments under remarks are pre-printed on the form. In this case the remarks are not applicable even though correction was not made. The remains of Father Merton were released to the consular officer following post-mortem examination by Thai medical and investigating authorities at the place of death. (Emphasis added)

The post-mortem at the hospital prescribed by law—that is to say, the autopsy—was "not applicable" in the death of Thomas Merton, according to the U.S. Department of State. The anonymous consular officer said, in effect, that what is written on the doctor's certificate is not true.

When Abbot Flavian received this doctor's report, he may have been concerned that the document had been falsified to make it appear that an autopsy had been performed. This document could cause suspicion that the truth about Merton's death was being hidden and proper procedures were not being followed. For whatever reason, the abbey, as we have indicated, kept the very existence of this report secret.

The consular officer did say that Merton's body had a "post mortem examination by Thai medical and investigating authorities at the place of death." Whatever was done at the place of death—and was done there only—did not satisfy the eyewitness observers, many of whose letters we also discovered. They were deeply puzzled by the death scene and fully expected that a meticulous autopsy would be done to determine the cause of death.

Archbishop Weakland supplied another English translation of the doctor's certificate to us. His copies bear a stamp and signature of authenticity from the U.S. Embassy. Weakland's copy of the doctor's certificate is almost identical to the State Department translation, except for this note under the remarks:

> The patient died outside Samutprakarn Hospital. The remains were brought to the Hospital for the purpose of an autopsy by medical doctors and investigation authority in accordance with law.

Weakland's translation copy and the original Thai language document, it should be emphasized, do not include the consular officer's "correction" to the document, leaving the impression that a standard formal autopsy was performed at the hospital. It is quite clear that no autopsy was done in "accordance with law" by Thai authorities. Dr. Nakvachara signed the doctor's certificate that falsely stated Merton's body had been brought to the hospital for an autopsy. Proper official procedures were not followed in the case of Merton's death, even though paperwork made it appear that they were.

Death Certificate

The death certificate, dated December 11, 1968, declared that the cause of death was "Sudden heart failure." There are two English-version translations of the death certificate. The U.S. Embassy certified each as a true copy of the original. However, there is a police Investigator's note on the back of the National Archives version that does not appear on the one we obtained from Weakland. It states:

> (Reverse Page): The remains may be removed through the area of Amphurmuang, Samutprakarn Province and they may be allowed to pass through other areas as a post-mortem examination has already been made in accordance with the law.
>
> (Signed) Pol Lt. Boonchob Cheongvichit, Investigator December 11, 1968

The handwritten note on the death certificate agrees with the boilerplate on the doctor's certificate that an autopsy had been performed in accordance with the law. This additional note by a police officer that a regular autopsy had, in fact, been done strongly suggests that something beyond mere inadvertence is involved here. The record of all witnesses at the scene reveals clearly that the body was not taken to a hospital because it never left the conference center before the U.S. military removed it and took it to a nearby U.S. military hospital.

The death certificate did not say that the cause of death was "accidental electrocution." The abbey would keep the official death certificate secret and misrepresent what it said. Fox would later write, "as it turned out later from reports we received," Merton was in his wet bare feet when he touched a wire and was instantly electrocuted.[98] Much later, Brother Patrick would say in an interview, "After a very careful checking of the death certificate...the overwhelming evidence...was accidental electrocution by a faulty fan."[99]

The U.S. Embassy Report

The only U.S. government document that we have discovered regarding Merton's death is the Report on the Death of an American Citizen by the U.S. Embassy in Bangkok, Thailand, and it repeats the official Thai death certificate conclusion that "Sudden heart failure" was the cause of death. This contradicted the Associated Press report at the time that Merton had been electrocuted when he touched an exposed cord in a defective electric fan while attempting to move it.

The Foreign Service Report referenced the official death certificate and did not conclude that the death was an accident. The Foreign Service Report, like the other reports, was suppressed by the abbey.

---

[98] Fox letter.

[99] Kurt Remele, A Conversation with Brother Patrick Hart, *Merton Seasonal* (Autumn 1987), pp. 16-18.

On December 27, 1968, the U.S. Embassy in Bangkok sent Abbot Flavian a letter,[100] a copy of which we discovered in the collection of the papers of the authorized Merton biographer, Michael Mott, at Northwestern University. That letter refers to the enclosed copies of the doctor's certificate, the death certificate with a translation, letters from participants at the conference who found or examined Merton's body, and the embassy's own Report on the Death of an American Citizen. Those enclosures were not with the letter, however, and Brother Lawrence Morey, the archivist for the abbey, has informed us that he no longer has any of these documents.

The doctor's certificate states that "acute cardiac failure" caused Merton to faint and fall into the fan and receive a shock. The Thai police, after questioning the doctor, stated in their report that "heart failure" had "caused the dead priest to faint and collide with the stand fan."[101] Thai officials concluded that Merton had died of heart failure *before* he encountered the fan. Many writers, including the authorized biographer, Mott, have written what seems more plausible, that is, that a shock from the fan caused the heart failure, but it is not what the Thai authorities actually said in their written reports.

---

[100] Letter from John L. Hagan, American Consul General, U.S. Embassy in Bangkok, to Abbot Flavian Burns, December 27, 1968, Mott Collection, McCormick Library, Northwestern University.

[101] The conclusion of police investigation report on the death of Reverend Thomas Merton, author unknown, date unknown, The Thomas Merton Center, Bellarmine University.

CHAPTER 7

More about that Fox Letter

As we have observed, the December 19 story in the *Kentucky Standard* suggesting that the fan found lying across Merton's body might have killed him by electrocution was almost certainly composed by someone at the Abbey of Gethsemani. However, the first official signed statement from the abbey that bluntly stated that Merton was accidentally electrocuted by a fan was in that February 1, 1969, letter of James Fox, "To the Gethsemani Diaspora."

Recall, though, that Fox had not been the Gethsemani's abbot for more than a year at that point, having resigned in November of 1967. He seems not to have been the appropriate person to send out such a letter. Shouldn't this have been the responsibility of Abbot Flavian Burns, or perhaps Merton's secretary, Brother Patrick Hart, who seems to have taken on the duty of primary official abbey spokesman on Merton's death? Merton's concern that Fox would continue to play a strong behind-the-scenes role at Gethsemani was apparently borne out in this instance.[102]

According to Fox's letter, Brother Patrick and Brother Lawrence Gannon delivered the details about Merton's death from Abbot Flavian, who had been called by the U.S. Embassy in Bangkok. There is no evidence to support Fox's story that the details about Merton's death in Fox's letter, in fact, came from Brother Patrick, Brother Lawrence, Abbot Flavian, or the U.S. Embassy.

The letter began with Fox stating that he was about to prepare lunch at his hermitage at exactly 12:45 pm on December 10, 1968, when he saw his former secretary Br. Patrick and Br. Lawrence, the secretary to Abbot Flavian Burns, arriving in a jeep. The date, December 10, was Fox's birthday and he said that he thought that they may have been coming with a birthday surprise. Fox provided very specific details of his conversation with Brother Patrick and Brother Lawrence about the death of Thomas Merton. Some important details about Merton's death in Fox's letter would later prove to be false.

Recall that Fox quoted Brother Patrick that it was from a telephone call from the U.S. Embassy in Bangkok that they had learned that Merton had been electrocuted by a faulty wire in a fan that he had been attempting to move. But the discovery that a faulty wire had been installed in the fan was not known until after the police had taken the fan to their lab for analysis. In the afternoon of December 11, a Thai a police sergeant told Fr. Celestine Say about a "breakage in the cord." Thailand is 12 hours ahead of the Eastern Standard Time Zone in Kentucky. It would have been during the early morning hours in Kentucky on December 11, and not at 12:45 PM on December 10, when the faulty cord was officially first known by anyone in Thailand. The only person who could have known about the faulty cord earlier would have been the person or persons who tampered with the fan. Fox would have us believe that the abbey was told about the faulty cord even before the Thai police had discovered it. For the record, that police report stating

---

[102] Thomas Merton, *The Other Side of the Mountain: The Journals of Thomas Merton, Vol. 7: 1967-1968,* Harper Collins, 1999, Kindle ed. p. 44.

74

that "the fan had a defective cord installed inside its stand" did not arrive at the abbey until August 7, 1969, many months after Fox wrote his letter.

The official Thai death certificate, doctor's certificate, and embassy report sent to Abbot Flavian on December 27, 1968, made no mention of any "faulty wire" or of an "accidental electrocution."

Fox mentioned the "reports received" as evidence for the "facts" that he shared. That he should have access to the reports that were sent to Abbot Flavian is more evidence that Fox was working closely with Flavian more than a year after he had officially resigned. Only a few people had access to the official reports, and Fox informed us in his letter that he was among them.

Fox did not say what reports were received, and as we have noted, no official reports were ever released by the abbey. Fox wrote that "a very large segment" of Merton's "bare chest had been burned deeply by the electricity." There are no reports that Merton's chest was burned, and the photographs of Merton's body discovered in 2017 prove that there were no burns on Merton's chest. Fox gave vital false information about Merton's death to the recipients of his letter, which would later be passed on with new false embellishments as part of a book for a wider audience.

Fox's letter is more than likely the origin of another popular, though much less important, error, that is, that Merton entered the Abbey of Gethsemani, on December 10, the same date that he died. Fox talked about what an amazing coincidence that was and also that it happened to be his own birthday.

Numerous people have repeated this error that Merton died 27 years to the day that he entered Gethsemani on December 10, 1941. As we have noted, Merton entered Gethsemani on December 13. Merton wrote in his autobiography, *The Seven Storey Mountain,* that he entered Gethsemani on December 13, the Feast of St. Lucy. Merton did not write that he entered the abbey on December 10, the feast of Pope St. Melchiades. Though a good deal less pernicious, Fox's mistake about the day that Merton entered Gethsemani has been almost as popular as the false "accidental electrocution" story about how Merton died.

It makes for a good story, and it does bear some small relationship to the truth. Merton arrived at the abbey from Olean, New York, on December 10 and was lodged in the abbey's guest house. He was not accepted into Gethsemani as a monk until three days later, though.

Fox's six-page letter also informed the monks about other things that go beyond the death of Thomas Merton. Fox announced that he had written to Merton on October 6, 1968, and that he had received a reply from Merton dated, October 20. Fox presented himself as on very close terms with Thomas Merton, saying that they had been so for a long time.

The reality is that there were long years of conflict between Fox and Merton.[103] Fox tried to repair his image by conceding that they had had mere differences of opinion about monasticism, but it hadn't damaged their deeper friendship at all.

Returning to the subject of Merton's death, the letter included a story by Fox that a monk (unnamed) had told him that it was ironic that Merton was killed by "the big electric fan" because he had complained about machines. This unverifiable story by Fox was obviously meant to reinforce the story that Merton had been killed by a fan.

Fox further pushed the "accidental electrocution" story by comparing electricity to fire, and then he wrote that it was prophetic that Merton used the word "burnt" in the epilogue of his book, *The Seven Storey Mountain*. Fox concluded his letter by comparing Merton's death to a line from scripture, "The coming of the Son of Man will be like lightning." Fox repeated this metaphor in his aforementioned homily 10 years after Merton's death, reminding his listeners that lightning is electricity.[104]

Of course, Fox did not mention the cable that the abbey had received on December 10 that stated that the official cause of death was "heart failure." He also did not enclose copies of any of the "reports received" that he said supported his stories that a fan had killed Thomas Merton

---

[103] Monica Furlong, *Merton: A Biography*, Harper and Row, 1980, p. 166.
[104] Lucas, p. 335.

and that electricity burned his chest deeply. Fox did enclose his final letter to Merton and Merton's reply as evidence of their supposed intimate friendship.

Although it is clear that much of what Fox says he was told in that meeting in which he was informed of Merton's death is not true, it doesn't take much reading between the lines to see that the meeting was pivotal in the way in which the abbey dealt with the death publicly. Something had to have happened at the abbey to cause them to go from telling Israel Shenker at *The New York Times* simply and factually what was in that cable from the U.S. Embassy in Thailand to saying that they had been told only that Merton had died. When that call came in from Shenker, Fox, out in his hermitage miles away from the abbey, was not yet in on the act. When the story was to be, as John T. Wheeler of the AP had fashioned it, that Merton was electrocuted by a faulty fan, it was a serious misstep to report that the official cause of death was heart failure. The Wheeler story would not be in the newspaper until the next day, but someone at the abbey recognized that a misstep had been made, and because it was a delayed recognition, and because of his pivotal importance in the cover-up along with John Howard Griffin as we reveal throughout this book, that someone had to be James Fox.

A question remains as to when Fox was informed of the death by the secretaries. The fact that Abbot Flavian told the monks at the noon meal that the death had been an accident suggests that Fox had already told him that that was what the story was to be, having been informed of the death before the 12:45 pm time that he reported in his February 1 letter. However, the Shenker article, faithfully reporting what was relayed from the U.S. Embassy through the abbey, mentions a fan that had "badly burned" Merton and the "heart failure" cause of death practically in the same breath, so there is a very good possibility that Flavian had reached a logical conclusion from that when he told the monks that Merton had died of an accident.

Suspicions confirmed?

More evidence that Fox continued to exercise his influence at the abbey after his "retirement" is in a January 3, 1969, letter from Brother Patrick to Naomi Burton Stone. In his letter, shortly after Merton's funeral, Br. Patrick told Stone that Fox had suggested to Abbot Flavian that she might be chosen to write the official biography of Thomas Merton.

Br. Patrick told Stone that, just between them, he had a recent conversation with Fox. Fox was concerned about what may be in Merton's journals and diaries pertaining to their relationship. Br. Patrick told Stone that this was a delicate situation but that he had assured Fox that nothing offensive would be published by the trustees. Furthermore, Br. Patrick informed Stone that he had reminded Fox of a specific clause in the Merton Legacy Trust Agreement, Article II, C, b that stated nothing would be published without "written consent of a representative of the abbey." He reminded Stone that nothing should be published regarding Merton and Fox without "first consulting us here."[105]

The Letter in *A Monastic Tribute*

The letter that Fox wrote in 1969, later appeared in the volume, *Thomas Merton/Monk: A Monastic Tribute*, and was reprinted several times by different publishers: Sneed & Ward in 1974, Hodder and Stoughton, London, 1975, The Catholic Book Club, London 1976, Knopf Doubleday, 1976, and an expanded edition by Cistercian Publications in 1983. *Thomas Merton/Monk: A Monastic Tribute*, edited by Brother Patrick, contained articles by those who knew Merton. Fox's letter was given the title, "A Spiritual Son," with a footnote that stated, "This letter was written several weeks after Fr. Merton's death and circulated in mimeographed form. It was revised and expanded in 1973 for publication here – Editor."

---

[105] Br. Patrick Hart letter to Naomi Burton Stone, January 3, 1969, Friedsam Library, St. Bonaventure University

In 1974, when the volume was first published, Brother Patrick, Abbot Flavian, and Brother Lawrence should have recognized that Fox's story about what he knew on December 10 contradicted Flavian's story. Recall that at that time Flavian was telling the monks of Gethsemani that he only knew that there had been "an accident" and nothing more.

Recall further that on December 10, Fox would have people believe that he had already been informed that Merton "had been electrocuted by a faulty wire" while the newspapers, using the abbey as their source, were reporting that the cause of death was not known.

When Fox's letter was published for a larger audience in 1974, one would have had to have been a keen observer, indeed, to have seen the contradictions. By 1974, the "accidental electrocution" story had long taken root and Merton's friends and colleagues seemed to be satisfied. With the death reports from Thailand having been kept secret, no one, including, to our knowledge, Merton's friends, questioned the patently absurd story that a household appliance, a common floor fan, had somehow killed Thomas Merton.

Only a few people knew about the cable from the embassy that stated Merton had died from "heart failure." These few people, who just happened to be the leaders at Gethsemani Abbey, would have known that the official reports from Thailand did not support Fox's statement that Merton's "bare chest had been burned deeply." They also would have seen Say's photograph, so they had to have known with certainty that there was no burn on Merton's chest.

The official reports sent to the abbey by the U.S. Embassy on December 27, 1968, confirmed the December 10th cable from the embassy. A few people had to have known that Fox's account as it was published in 1974 was essentially false. Brother Patrick, especially, as editor of Fox's letter that was published in the book had to know that what Fox had written about Merton's death was not true. Brother Patrick may not have been in charge of spreading false information about Merton's death, but he was clearly a key participant in it.

As the editor, Brother Patrick could have made corrections to Fox's original letter to make it more truthful when the letter was published for a larger audience. Instead, he added a new layer of falsehood to further buttress the notion that Merton had been accidentally electrocuted by the fan. By his actions, Brother Patrick at the very least revealed himself to be a willing salesman of the faulty product that his former abbot was selling.

Wet Feet

In Fox's published letter, only the first two sentences concerning the message from the State Department in Washington and the phone call from the American Embassy in Thailand saying that "Fr. Louis had been electrocuted by a faulty wire in his room" are given as a direct quote from Brother Patrick. All the following precise details of the event in Thailand in the original quote of Brother Patrick are then just roughly characterized. The published letter was prefaced, though, with that statement that the new version was a "revised and expanded" version of the original. What wasn't said was that it was done with pernicious intent, which appears to have been the case.

Both versions of Fox's letter are also in direct contradiction to what, as we have noted, Abbot Flavian would later say publicly about that telephone call from Thailand, both with respect to who initiated it and the information that it contained. Abbot Flavian wrote, "Eventually, I got through to the embassy in Bangkok and they confirmed it and they said there had been an accidental death: no more than that."[106]

There is no reason to believe either Flavian or Fox and their contradictory changing stories about Thomas Merton's "accidental electrocution." Flavian, as the abbot, would have known about the cable from the U.S. Embassy that said the official cause of death was "heart failure." Flavian also received the official death certificate and Embassy Report that stated the cause of death was "sudden heart failure."

In his original letter, Fox was very specific about the details that Flavian "was told by the embassy" in Bangkok. Fox quoted Br. Patrick's *exact words,* prefacing his quote with, "Said Brother Patrick and

---

[106] Wilkes, p. 109.

seconded by Brother Lawrence." In his revised letter Fox also quoted Brother Patrick's *exact words*, only the quote was shorter, leaving out the comments about a "heart attack," "grabing [sic] the fan," and "fixing the fan." There is no evidence to support either account by Fox.

Fox wrote that Brother Patrick and Brother Lawrence arrived at 12:45 pm, "when they should be eating their dinner." If they had been eating their dinner with the other monks, they would have heard Abbot Flavian announce that Merton had died in an accident and no details were available.[107] These men could not have delivered a message from Flavian to Fox about a faulty wire in a fan if Flavian did not know about a faulty wire.

The treachery of Fox is more obvious as his letter continues. In the original letter sent to the Gethsemani Diaspora Fox wrote, "As it turned out later by reports received, Fr. Louis had been in his bare feet standing on a stone floor and thus the electricity went right through him."

The revised letter added water to the mix: "As it turned out, according to reports we received later, Fr. Louis had been in his *wet* bare feet, standing on the terrazzo floor." (Emphasis added)

Fox's addition of "wet feet" to his letter as revised in 1973 conveniently corresponded with the false shower story in Brother Patrick's postscript to the *Asian Journal of Thomas Merton* published that same year. In 1973, five years following Merton's death, Fox may have become confident that he could say whatever he wanted about Merton's "accidental electrocution" without worrying that the official reports from Thailand, witness accounts, and the negatives of Say's photographs, all of which contradicted him, would ever see the light of day.

Fox's loyal subordinate, Brother Patrick, as we have noted, had assumed the title of "Merton's secretary," only a couple of months before Merton departed for Asia. Brother Patrick enjoyed that title until his death in 2019. Brother Patrick would follow Fox's example of telling people that the official reports said "accidental electrocution" without ever showing those reports to anyone. In a 1984 interview, Brother

---

[107] Br. Paul Quenon, *In Praise of a Useless Life*, Ave Maria Press, 2018, p. 114.

Patrick told Kurt Remele that "after very careful checking of the death certificate...the overwhelming evidence is rather that it was accidental electrocution by a faulty fan."[108] That is not at all what the death certificate said, but no one dared to challenge the credibility of "Thomas Merton's secretary."

In his review of *The Martyrdom of Thomas Merton: An Investigation*, Michael W. Higgins noted that we had placed primary blame for the falsehoods emanating from the abbey about Merton's death on Brother Patrick Hart and to a slightly lesser degree on Abbot Flavian Burns.[109] He is right about that, but upon further inquiry we see that the first and perhaps the primary false weaver of a false narrative about Merton's death was its "retired" abbot, James Fox. There is not the slightest evidence that we have seen that Merton caught hold of a faulty wire, that his feet were wet, or that there were burns on his chest, as Fox fashioned the story. Had there been any such evidence, we can be certain that the abbey would have shared it far and wide.

The deceitful actions by Fox to blame Merton for accidentally electrocuting himself invites a closer examination of the final letters exchanged between Fox and Merton. Fox wanted people to believe that he was Merton's friend. This is why he wrote in his final letter to Merton, "You never had—nor will you ever have—one who has been a more faithful and loyal friend and brother than myself." Merton would have known that the statement was as untrue as the grammar was bad. A true and loyal friend would hardly have made up the false story that Merton's feet were wet.

Fox's letter to Merton, from its inception, may well have been aimed at a larger audience than Merton. It seems quite likely that he intended all along to share his letter to make himself appear to have been Merton's friend. As Merton's abbot for 19 years, Fox knew that he could count on Merton to send him a polite and respectful reply, and Merton

---

[108] Kurt Remele, "A Conversation with Brother Patrick Hart," *Merton Seasonal* (Autumn 1987), pp. 16-18.

[109] Michael W. Higgins, Review of *The Martyrdom of Thomas Merton: An Investigation, The Merton Annual*, Vol. 32, p. 280.

did. Fox used both letters to his advantage in fashioning himself as Merton's well-wisher. He used the letters to elevate himself while he made Merton appear careless around electricity and water.

Similar to others' description of Fox, Merton's characterization of the man as being crafty, calculating, and secretive would never have been more apt.[110]

---

[110] Thomas Merton, *Learning to Love: Exploring Solitude and Freedom,* *(Journals of Thomas Merton, Book 6)* HarperOne, Kindle ed., 1966, p.111.

CHAPTER 8

Trouble for the Abbey?

John Moffitt

I n February of 1969, John Moffitt contacted Abbot Flavian and offered
to give him information that he had about Thomas Merton's death.[111]
Moffitt had been one of the four men staying in the cottage in
Thailand where Merton had died. Moffitt included with his letter a copy
of an article that he had written about the conference where Merton
died. In his article, "New Charter for Monasticism," Moffitt mentioned
Merton's death briefly, calling it a mystery and saying that what really
caused Merton's death would probably never be known. [112]

Moffitt wrote that a Thai physician said the cause of death had been a
"heart attack." This statement must have caught the attention of the
abbot because he knew from the cable received from the embassy and
from the official documents that heart failure was the official cause of

---

[111] Br. Patrick Hart letter to John Moffitt, February 18, 1969, Moffitt papers.

[112] John Moffitt, "New Charter for Monasticism," *America*, January 18, 1969.
P.63

death. Moffitt's statement was nearly consistent with the official Thai reports; a "heart attack" and "heart failure" are not the same thing by strict medical definition. Since the abbey was concealing the official cause of death, they may have been worried about what Moffitt had written.

Moffitt's was the first report, outside of Thailand, that a Thai physician had officially declared that Merton died because of a problem with his heart. Moffitt called the death "a mystery." This contradicted the December 11, 1968, Associated Press report from the "anonymous Catholic source" that Merton was accidentally electrocuted when he touched a short in a cord while moving a fan. Moffitt's article in *America* would be only the second published report in the U.S. that Thai officials did not conclude that Merton died by "accidental electrocution." *The New York Times* was the first to report, ever so briefly, that the official cause of death was "heart failure."[113]

Moffitt speculated that the heart failure "may have resulted from electrocution." Moffitt wrote, "What really caused Merton's death may never be known." Moffitt gave no source or any details for his electrocution speculation. He also failed to mention that there had been no autopsy, which is a major reason for the open-ended speculation about the cause of death right up to the present day. He did not provide the name of the Thai physician or any of the witnesses who found Merton's body. Moffitt knew the two monks, François de Grunne and Celestine Say, who stayed with him in the cottage where Merton died, but he said nothing about them or what they had witnessed.

It was only five days after Fox had mailed out his letter to the Gethsemani diaspora, on February 6, that Moffitt sent a copy of his *America* magazine article to Abbott Flavian with an offer to share his information about Merton's death. Brother Patrick responded to Moffitt and told him that Abbot Flavian had received his article published in *America*. He told Moffitt that he was handling correspondence related to

---

[113] Israel Shenker, "Thomas Merton Dead at 53; Monk Wrote of Search for God," *The New York Times*, December 11, 1968.

Merton and that his letter had been turned over to him. Brother Patrick wrote that he was interested in anything Moffitt could share about Merton's "strange death."[114]

In July, *Catholic World* published another article by Moffitt that stated Merton's death happened "illogically."[115] John Howard Griffin eventually contacted Moffitt in August to introduce himself.

Father Celestine Say

Father Celestine Say, O.S.B., was a crucial witness lodged in the cottage where Merton died. Say, with Abbot Odo Haas, O.S.B. and Abbot Egbert Donovan, O.S.B., were the first to reach Merton's body, at about 4:00 P.M. At the suggestion of Haas, Say took two photographs to preserve the suspicious scene. When the police did not appear to be doing a serious investigation, Say did not tell the police about the photographs. Say returned to his home in the Philippines with his film.

At the end of February or early March, a friend of Fr. Say who was visiting the United States hand delivered a photograph of Merton's body to Abbot Flavian. It must have been a shock to the abbot to learn of this photograph. The picture did not show the fan across Merton's chest as the six Trappists letter had said, and there was no burn on Merton's chest as Fox had written. The scene did not look like an "accidental electrocution." Merton was found lying perfectly straight on his back with his arms at his side and a fan diagonally across his pelvic area. It is impossible to escape the conclusion that the scene in the photograph appears to be staged.

On March 18, Say wrote a letter to Abbot Flavian to introduce himself as the person who had taken the photograph of Merton's body. Say told Flavian that he had been staying on the ground floor of Merton's cottage, next to Merton's room.

---

[114] Patrick Hart, letter to John Moffitt, February 18, 1969, Moffitt papers.
[115] "Thomas Merton: The Last Three Days, *The Catholic World*, July 1969.

Say gave an account of some of the details that he had witnessed and named the other Benedictine witnesses who were the first on the scene, including François de Grunne, Odo Haas, Egbert Donovan, Rembert Weakland, and Edeltrud Weist. Say also told Flavian that Abbot Joachim Murphy and Prior Anselm Parker dressed Merton's body. Say briefed the abbot about the strange behavior of de Grunne. He explained how the police arrived with a doctor who concluded that the death was due to "heart failure." Say wrote that the doctor "thought [heart failure] a better diagnosis than electrocution to avoid complications in the police report." [116]

Say's March 18 letter to the abbot stated clearly that the Thai doctor thought that "heart failure" was "a better diagnosis than electrocution." Advocates of the "accidental electrocution" cause of death would not want it known that the doctor thought that "heart failure" was a better diagnosis. We have discovered only four of Say's letters, but as we see, they were extremely revealing. We found two letters from Say to Moffitt and only one of the two letters from Say to Griffin in Moffitt's papers. It appears that Abbot Flavian did not share the important March 18 letter that Say sent him because it was not among Moffitt's papers at the University of Virginia.

At the end of his letter to Abbot Flavian, Say wrote that the police were not "too eager about an autopsy," and he then asked Flavian if "the cause of death had been determined prior to his burial?" That final question may have triggered concern because it implied that the cause of death was not known. Abbot Flavian probably wondered if Say had doubts about the cause of Merton's death.

Moffitt and Say were likely to have been seen as potential risks to the press's and the abbey's "accidental electrocution" narrative.

---

[116] Celestine Say, letter to Flavian Burns, March 18, 1969, the Merton Center.

Edward Rice

Edward Rice, Merton's friend, was another person who got the abbey's attention early in 1969. A preview of Rice's biography of Thomas Merton, *The Man in the Sycamore Tree*, had been published in the February issue of *The Sign*. John Howard Griffin wrote to Brother Patrick about this development. Brother Patrick expressed his disappointment that Rice could not be stopped from writing a biography because it would not be the official biography. He told Griffin that he did not think the trustees approved of Rice, so he would be prohibited from reading Merton's letters and private journals.

Rice had his own photographs of Thomas Merton that were published in his book. Both Griffin and Brother Patrick agreed that they did not like Rice's photographs. Brother Patrick said that Rice's photographs "did not capture Merton."[117] What was probably most objectionable about Rice's photographs was that they were not the income-producing, copyrighted property, of the Merton Legacy Trust. Rice's book also painted an unflattering description of James Fox.

---

[117] Brother Patrick Hart letter to John Howard Griffin, February 19, 1969, Griffin papers.

CHAPTER 9

John Howard Griffin

T he writer, John Howard Griffin, would seem to have as much in common with Thomas Merton as Fox and Merton were on completely different wavelengths. Indeed, Griffin and Merton had had an association of several years out of choice, out of friendship, if you will, not because they were thrust together because of the positions that they held.

Griffin, the second of four children, was a man with a rather remarkable background. He was born in Dallas, Texas, in 1920 to parents very similar to Merton's and raised in Fort Worth. His mother was a classical pianist and longtime piano teacher, and his father though professionally a wholesale grocery salesman was also an Irish tenor and radio personality. His artistic family imbued him with a love not just of music, but of literature. He had intrepidly gone off to France at the tender age of 15 in search of a classical education. He attended the Lycée Descartes, a secondary school in Tours, France. His widow has written that he "completed studies in French and literature at the University of Poitiers, and then studied medicine at the École de Médecine." As an intern at the Asylum of Tours, she reports further, he conducted experiments on the use of music as therapy for the criminally insane. He also received certificates, she tells us, in musical study from the Conservatoire de Fontainebleau, studying under renowned teachers. There he became a musicologist, specializing in the Gregorian chant. In that capacity he would later spend time as a musicologist at the Benedictine Abbey of Solesmes where he did more study of the Gregorian chant.[118] That experience would provide the setting for his first novel, published many years later in 1952, entitled *The Devil Rides Outside.* He had become a Roman Catholic the previous year.[119]

World War II began while he was in France, and he worked with the French resistance army as a medic and helped evacuate Austrian Jews. Escaping France, according to his biographer Robert Bonazzi he joined the U.S. Army Air Force in 1941, serving for four years, 39 months of which were spent overseas. He was sent to the lonesome outpost of the Solomon Islands where he worked as something of an ethnographer with the local population. The experience would dramatically affect his health in a delayed-reaction fashion. Leaving the Army in 1946, he slowly began to go blind, the after-effect, according to his authorized biographer writing in 2018, of a severe concussion that he had received from a Japanese bomb.[120] He would be completely blind from 1947 until 1957,

---

[118] Elizabeth Griffin-Bonazzi, Texas State Historical Association, January 1, 1995, https://www.tshaonline.org/handbook/entries/griffin-john-howard. From the account of Robert Bonazzi, his biographer and later Griffin's widow's husband, these educational claims are great exaggerations. He tells us that Griffin "audited literature classes at the University of Poitiers and attended the École de Médecine de Tours in 1938." He would have been only 18 years old at the time. He says nothing about any study at or certificates from the Conservatoire de Fontainebleau. See Bonazzi's *Reluctant Activist: The Spiritual Life and Art of John Howard Griffin*, TCU Press, 2018, p. 39.

[119] Bonazzi, p. 74.

[120] Bonazzi, pp. 43-44. Curiously, other accounts say his wartime concussion was suffered in an "accidental bomb explosion." See William Jolesch, AP writer, "Blind Novelist Watches Supreme Court Session," *The Herald Sun* (Durham, NC), October 21, 1956. Another AP story without a byline is more specific about the supposed accident, saying, "He suffered a concussion when a B24, loaded with bombs, exploded." "Once Sightless Author Seeing World with Awe," *The Pomona* (CA) *Progress Bulletin*, January 11, 1957. In still another account, the B24 is there, but it's the airplane's crash landing that caused Griffin's injury leading to

when his sight miraculously returned.[121] During his period of blindness, however, he would write five novels, only two of which, *The Devil Rides Outside* and *Nuni*, based on his South Sea experience, were published. Like Merton, he kept a journal, which at his death in 1980 had reached 20 volumes.[122]

In 1954, Griffin would suffer paralysis in both legs and numbness in both hands. That ailment was eventually diagnosed as spinal malaria, which had an eight-year incubation period, and then it was successfully treated with small doses of strychnine.[123]

Readers may well notice that these writing activities of Griffin that we have described hardly add up to a livelihood. Indeed, his financial situation would seem to have been precarious for many years. During the period of his blindness, he was apparently heavily dependent upon his parents. We learn from his widow that in the immediate years after emerging from his blindness, 1957 through 1960, he worked as a journalist, writing syndicated features for the International News Service and King Features.[124]

His primary source of income during this period seems to have been working for the Fort Worth-based *Sepia* magazine. The magazine may be

---

his loss of sight. See Irvin Farman, "Mansfield Veteran's First Novel Attracting Widespread Response," *Fort Worth Star-Telegram*, September 12, 1952. A 1980 obituary says he was injured in an "air accident" and then again when the hospital in which he was recuperating was bombed. See Jordan Sollitto, "Author's Journey Tested Racial Climate," The *Los Angeles Times*, September 15, 1980. In his own account, Griffin wrote only that "bomb concussions (plural) had damaged my vision." "Now I Can See," *The San Francisco Examiner*, May 19, 1957.

[121] His widow dates the commencement of his total blindness, however, to 1946. See Griffin-Bonazzi, Texas State Historical Association. But Griffin still had some vision in the spring of 1947 according to his own *San Francisco Examiner* series and to the biographer Bonazzi, p. 61. To show how slippery the facts about Griffin's blindness can be, the Harry Ransom Center of the University of Texas that houses many of Griffin's documents, says that the blow to the head that he suffered in the war caused him to be "struck blind while walking down the street one day in France." https://norman.hrc.utexas.edu/fasearch/findingaid.cfm?eadid=00050&kw=john %20howard%20griffin.

[122] Griffin-Bonazzi, Texas State Historical Association.

[123] Bonazzi, p. 91.

[124] Elizabeth Griffin-Bonazzi.

described as somewhat short of respectable. Its owner, George Levitan, a Jewish man from Michigan, had moved to Fort Worth and had made his fortune salvaging and selling used plumbing parts. In 1950 he purchased the Good Publishing Company, which had started up in 1946, from its local founder, a Black man by the name of Horace J. Blackwell. Good Publishing produced several magazines, *Bronze Thrills, Jive, Hep, Soul Confessions,* and *Sepia.* The magazines targeted a Black audience, publishing lewd romance stories, sexual sagas, and bawdy pictures. Titles of *Sepia* articles included: "Exposed: Men Who Dress Like Women," "Why Hollywood Stars like Negros," "The Inside Story of Black Pimps," "Women Learn the Art of Teasing in School for Strippers" and "Are Chorus Girls Immoral?"

The April 1957 issue of *Sepia* had a malicious racist smear against the newly popular singer Elvis Presley under the headline, "How Negroes Feel About Elvis." The magazine relayed a supposed rumor about something Elvis had said that was still being repeated in the 21st century. What Wikipedia has to say about that episode on its *Sepia* magazine page is worth repeating in its entirety for what it tells us about Griffin's primary employer and the magazine that turned him into a national celebrity and something of a civil rights icon:

> According to African American author Joyce Rochelle Vaughn in the preface of her book *Thirty Pieces of Silver: The Betrayal of Elvis Presley*[125] an aunt who raised her had forcibly told her to never listen to Elvis Presley's music because *Sepia* magazine had run an article in early 1957 in which he had been quoted as saying, in Boston, that the "only thing Negroes can do for me is buy my records and shine my shoes." She then decided, forty years later, to undertake a full study and complete unmasking of falsely reported news surrounding his life and career. According to Ms. Vaughn, the truth about the invented slur lay in white liberals making money exploiting statements and falsifying others because so many whites during the era openly made stupid remarks against black people. So when a black radio station decided to play Elvis' music and black people started acknowledging that they listened to and bought Elvis' records, white liberals went into panic mode and the slur was invented. *Jet* magazine sent its most prestigious writer, the late Louis Robinson, to the set of *Jailhouse Rock*, to raise the matter with the then 22-year-old Presley and, after interviewing

---

125 Justice Payne Publishing, 2017.

African American musicians like BB King, who knew Presley since his teen years, as well as Presley himself, he cleared him of all charges but the damage was done, the slur continuing to be utilized as late as in the first two decades of the 21st Century by people not well informed on the matter.

The false story about Elvis Presley in *Sepia* deceived Black readers and promoted racial unrest. Two years later Levitan would sponsor John Howard Griffin's adventure of "going undercover' as a Negro in the Deep South.

At this point, a more critical examination of Griffin's background, and particularly the primary source for it, the 2018 "authorized biography" by Robert Bonazzi, is in order. As we have seen, Bonazzi's story of how Griffin sustained the severe concussion that supposedly produced Griffin's delayed-reaction blindness is contradicted by other sources, including, apparently, Griffin himself. We should also point out that Bonazzi's account, while the most dramatic, also appears to be the least plausible. After the serious fighting that had taken place on the main island of the Solomons, Guadalcanal, the area where Griffin was stationed had been well neutralized by early 1943. Bonazzi tells us, though, that from his job embedded with the Solomon Islanders, Griffin was transferred in 1945 to Morotai, some 2,000 miles to the west to work as a radio dispatcher where he happened to be on patrol "during the anticipated invasion."

At that point in the Pacific War, the Japanese were well past invading anywhere. Their invasion of Morotai had taken place early in 1942, shortly after the attack on Pearl Harbor. The Americans had retaken it with a massive attack in 1944. It is difficult to avoid the conclusion that Bonazzi has the Army Air Force making a rather odd personnel move to put Griffin somehow in the line of Japanese fire. In fact, Bonazzi's account of Griffin's four years of military service is very sketchy, and when he is specific, his account is replete with such peculiarities. According to Bonazzi, Griffin was shipped out to Guadalcanal in 1942 as a radio operator. The major naval battle at Guadalcanal did not take place until November of that year and the American authorities did not declare the island to be secure until early February of 1943. The job that

Griffin supposedly had there, playing music as a sort of disc jockey for the occupying forces, was far removed from any military activity, the sort of thing that takes place securely behind the fighting lines. After a year of that, Bonazzi tells us, Griffin volunteered as a "language specialist" in 1944 and spent a year in a village on one of the Solomon Islands.

The very telling term that Bonazzi scrupulously avoids using is "military intelligence." Griffin's work in the village which involved, among other things, befriending grand Chief John Vutha is classic intelligence work. It's hardly the sort of thing that one would usually get into as casually as Bonazzi describes it. What is more likely is that Griffin was given some preparation for it before he was shipped to the Solomon Islands and that would have been his purpose for going there in the first place.

Returning to the climactic event of Griffin's military tour as Bonazzi recounts it, the unconscious Griffin was discovered in a trench the morning after the attack, and he did not regain consciousness "until days later." Already, according to Bonazzi , Griffin realized that he had "lost most of his eyesight."

At this point Bonazzi's narrative turns really bizarre. For some reason, Griffin withheld this information from his doctors, and the doctors remained ignorant of Griffin's loss of sight. One might well conclude that that Japanese bomb had also blown away some of the man's ability to reason. Doctors are there to cure our ills. If Griffin, upon regaining consciousness, found that he had lost a good deal of his vision and it was getting worse daily, would he not have been greatly alarmed and would he have not had every reason to let the doctors know in hopes that they might do something about it? Instead, Bonazzi tells us, Griffin "played the role of the fully-recovered man." Then Bonazzi contradicts himself, telling us that the doctors released him, even though they didn't believe him, upon Griffin's assurance that he would see a civilian eye specialist, although he had just finished telling us that Griffin had successfully concealed his vision problems from the military doctors. Bonazzi also leaves the impression that they released him from the Army by telling us in the very next sentence that, "Griffin's separation papers were dated December 15, 1945, and he was shipped out to San Francisco." No one there in the South Pacific would have had the authority, least of all military doctors, to release him from military service before the appointed time.

Griffin's subsequent actions, per Bonazzi, are even more incredible. But first we must note another contradiction. "He lived most of 1945 at his parents' home in Fort Worth," he tells us in the very next paragraph. Something's wrong here. That was supposedly the year of all his major military action in the Pacific, and Bonazzi just got through telling us that Griffin, "shipped out" from there in the middle of the last month of 1945. He also tells us that Griffin never claimed the medals that he had earned nor filed for any service benefits, having rejected war, and declaring himself to be a pacifist.

Pacifist or not, these actions make absolutely no sense for a war-wounded veteran who might be facing a lifetime of disability as a result. Besides the Veterans' Administration hospital attention that he supposedly passed up on, Griffin also eschewed the very generous education benefits of the GI Bill, which went into effect in 1944. His studies in France had been interrupted by the war. His widow's article for the Texas State Historical Association notwithstanding, he was not even close to having a college degree and his career prospects would appear to have been bleak, especially if he was losing his sight. According to Griffin's authorized biographer, Bonazzi, though, he decided to return to France to study the Gregorian chant at a Benedictine monastery there, relying completely upon the generosity of his parents, who were not exactly wealthy.

These seem to be very much the actions of a person who was little concerned about where his next dollar was coming from. The impression that this is someone whose career skids had been greased for him by powerful people beyond his family is greatly enhanced by the over-the-top article that appeared in his hometown newspaper a month before the publication of his first novel in 1952. Right off the bat they tell us, "The New York Times had declared, '...It's our bet that the book out of Texas that will make history this fall is one by a young, blind war veteran, John Howard Griffin, whose novel, 'The Devil Rides Outside,' has mightily impressed everyone who has seen advance proofs." They tell us that no less a personage than the New York critic Clifton Fadiman writing in the Book-of-the-Month Club News called it, "A staggering novel...Griffin's intense psychological analyses...recall Dostoyevsky or Pascal. The pure doctrine of asceticism has rarely been so effectively demonstrated in 20th Century fiction. Griffin's baroque excesses are easy to ridicule, but—at least to this reviewer—they seem the excesses of an intense temperament and possibly of a notable literary talent."[126]

After writing that four motion picture companies had requested copies of the manuscript to consider bidding on the rights to make a movie of it, the article continues in this gushing tone for column after column.

Despite the best efforts of the national tub thumpers, nothing much came of the book. No movie was made of it, and to anyone who has taken the time to read it, it's easy to see why. The book is wordy in the extreme, lacks dramatic tension, and seems to go nowhere. Usually, in the case of books written in the first person as this one is, the reader naturally comes to like the narrator and to identify with him. It's difficult in this instance. The young American man who first lives at the monastery for a few cold and miserable months while studying manuscripts and observing the daily routine comes across as rather shallow and sex-obsessed. At the first opportunity, he has a liaison with a local matron, and because he later boasted about it, the scandal got around the small town and the talk forced her to leave the community. Later, when she surprisingly returns to seek medical attention, he fears that it is because she is pregnant, so we surmise that the sex they had was irresponsibly unprotected. He seems almost relieved to learn that her medical condition turns out to be terminal cancer. In another instance, when he is asked to escort to the train station a flirtatious Parisian woman nearer his own age with whom a couple of the local ladies have set him up for a group dinner, he arranges for the town's

126 Irvin Farman, "Mansfield Veteran's First Novel Attracting Widespread Response," *Fort Worth Star-Telegram*, September 12, 1952.

licentious and talkative cab driver to drive them around while he has sex with her in the back seat.[127]

The central character of the book, other than the narrator, is a rather haughty and complicated upper-class woman who is his hostess after he escapes the physical ordeal of the unheated monastery. Her concerns—indeed her obsessions—seem to be so uniquely Catholic and small-town French that one must wonder what anyone could have possibly seen in the manuscript that could interest a general American movie audience for more than a minute.

In short, there seemed to have been something very artificial about the big build-up that *The Devil Rides Outside* was given. Griffin's second novel, *Nuni*, based upon his Solomon Islands experience, was even more boring, and although the major publisher Houghton Mifflin put it out, it went nowhere. Like his first novel, *Nuni* is semi-autobiographical, but the protagonist, the sole survivor of an airplane crash living among primitive South Sea islanders, doesn't actually marry one of the native women as Griffin did, but he does purchase a pre-pubescent girl.[128]

Griffin's Claim to Fame

Griffin's big splash came after he had miraculously regained his sight in early 1957. Supposedly, the strong medication that he had been given to clear up his malaria-induced paralysis had had the delayed beneficial

---

[127] Like the author himself, his first-person character is a chain smoker, as we gather from the frequent mention of his enjoyment of or craving for cigarettes, but at least Griffin doesn't have him lighting up after his backseat conquest. The character, also like Griffin, has a relapse from a previous bout with malaria. Although the story is derived from Griffin's experience at the monastery in 1947, the young man has no problem with his eyesight, though.

[128] Griffin-Bonazzi tells us in her Texas Historical Association article that the Vatican gave him permission to marry a second time. We have not seen the question addressed as to whether that second marriage was legal in the eyes of Texas law or if they even knew of the existence of that other wife. Apparently, Griffin simply abandoned her.

side effect of clearing up the artery blockage that was responsible for his blindness.[129]

In his famous book, *Black Like Me,* Griffin described how, in 1959, he met with his "old friend," George Levitan, the owner of *Sepia* and convinced him to fund a daring project in which Griffin would darken his skin with drugs, dyes, and a sunlamp. He would then travel for four weeks in the South as a "black man" to experience life as a Negro. In 1960, *Sepia* published the series of seven articles about Griffin's "experience." That series would eventually elevate Griffin's status to that of a civil rights hero.

CBS Television got wind early of the series and on March 23, 1960, broadcast an interview of Griffin with the newsman Mike Wallace. The program aired at the same time as Griffin's first installment in *Sepia,* (April 1960) was available at newsstands. Griffin became an instant celebrity and interviews with others soon followed, including Dave Garroway, the original host and anchor of the NBC Today Show. The first three articles were titled, "Life as a Negro: Journey into Shame." The seventh and last installment was titled, "White Man Turned Negro Is Praised and Damned."

Once the national opinion molding apparatus declares something to be reality, all critical thinking is suspended. From the moment Griffin's story was anointed by the national press, it was accepted as true and,

---

[129] Ernest Sharpe, Jr., "The Man Who Changed His Skin," *American Heritage,* February 1989. https://www.americanheritage.com/man-who-changed-his-skin#5. Curiously, in his biography of Griffin, Bonazzi makes no mention of this medical explanation of the sight restoration. He tells us only that after the first glimmering of sight return an unnamed specialist prescribed a blood-circulation stimulant, but without any particularly hopeful prognosis, since the cause of the initial loss of sight was unknown. Bonazzi does tell us that the miraculous return of Griffin's sight was covered by the national press, including *Time, Newsweek,* and the AP and Griffin fulfilled other requests to write about it himself. Bonazzi, pp. 109-110. Further complicating the story of Griffin's sight restoration, one Griffin obituary suggested that it resulted from "a series of treatments to relieve scar tissue from the nerves of his brain" in 1956. That article also said that Griffin's diabetes was a contributor to his blindness. See Donna Darovich and Doug Clarke, "John Griffin FW Author Dead at 60," *Fort Worth Star-Telegram,* September 9, 1980.

before long, the book, *Black Like Me*, became assigned reading in school classrooms nationwide.

Americans have never questioned the veracity of Griffin's *Black Like Me* story. It is hard to verify because he names hardly anyone. One person he *does* name in the book is Sterling Williams. Williams was a Black shoeshine man in New Orleans who allegedly gave Griffin advice on how to change into being a Negro. The dermatologist who gave Griffin dangerous medications that could have harmed his health was anonymous. During the days it took for Griffin to transform into a Black man in New Orleans he stayed at the home of an anonymous friend. These people and others who took part in the noble experiment to advance civil rights never received any credit.

Griffin's description of his transition into a Negro is reminiscent of Lon Chaney, Jr., in his role as Larry Talbot, *The Wolf Man*. Griffin said that when he looked at himself in the mirror for the first time, what he saw was a total stranger, an angry looking "very dark Negro" who resembled the previous John Howard Griffin "in no way."[130]

For Griffin to state it hardly makes it true. How could he "in no way" resemble himself in a mirror? The truth is that he would have looked like his old self in every way except for the color of his skin and his shaved head. Facial recognition software would have identified him with no trouble. Griffin's eyes, ears, nose, and mouth would have still looked the same. The shape of his head, chin, cheeks, eyebrows, and forehead wouldn't change. It is hardly credible for Griffin to say that he did not resemble himself in any way by simply darkening his skin and shaving his head.

Griffin was able to get away with his story because he got so much help in selling it by the national molders of public opinion. In the beginning, his story about the process to become a black man took four days using medication and a sunlamp. Later in his book, he could change from white to black almost instantly. All it took was an isolated place, in

---

[130] *Black Like Me*, New American Library, 2003, p. 10. *Black Like Me* was first published by Houghton Mifflin in 1960. This and subsequent page references are to the New American Library version.

a dark alley or behind a bush, damp sponge, cleansing cream, and some Kleenex for making himself white again and just dye for making himself black. He could be a Negro by day and a white man by night.[131]

Griffin could change his appearance as if he were Clark Kent changing into Superman in a telephone booth. One might think that in applying and removing dyes while in an alley or in some roadside brush Griffin might miss a spot on his neck or behind his ear. What originally took Griffin days with a sunlamp, suddenly could be done in minutes. Could Griffin really emerge from an alley or some bushes in blackface and pass himself off as a black man? But people believed Griffin because CBS, NBC, *The New York Times*, and all the other voices of authority said that it was true.

The writing of *Black Like Me* is so different from the writing in the two novels that one is tempted to believe that it is not the work of the same person. The people come across as cardboard characters, with the whites universally blinded by their racial prejudice, without redeeming qualities, and the Negroes painted as the purest blameless victims. But then, consider who his initial audience was, the average reader of *Sepia*. The writer of that series could hardly have been thinking of producing a work of art meant for sophisticated readers. Furthermore, it could hardly be clearer that *Black Like Me* was intended to be a political polemic.

Hardly surprisingly, although Griffin's opus was heavily promoted and well-received in most of the country, the locals in the Fort Worth area did not take very kindly to Griffin's portrayal of white Southerners. In the late summer of 1960, Bonazzi tells us, Griffin moved his young family and elderly parents to Morelia, Mexico, "to avoid the racist threats."

By Bonazzi's account, Griffin, as an American, was a passive victim of the anti-American sentiment that swept over Mexico in the wake of the abortive Bay of Pigs invasion of Cuba in 1961, although he does say that the U.S. Embassy did ask him to report on the political activity in his

---

[131] *Black Like Me*, p. 126.

area. The previously cited *Fort Worth Star-Telegram* obituary paints a somewhat different picture, and the relevant passage bears repeating in its entirety:

> When Communist student riots shook Mexico in 1961, Griffin was asked by the American Embassy there to research the incidents in Mexico, where he had lived since writing *Black Like Me*. He learned the riots were planned and financed by the Russian Embassy there. He published the names of the embassy officials, the amounts they paid students, the hotels where they stayed, and the license number of their car.
>
> As a result of the attacks on his family resulting from his work, Griffin and his family returned to the United States.[132]

It goes without saying that such actions by a private American citizen, performed presumably without remuneration, would have been highly unusual.

As much as Griffin and Merton would seem to have had in common, we can see from this brief profile of Griffin that there was one very important difference between them. In our previous book we wrote:

> Merton's peace activities alone probably would not have targeted him for assassination. The combination of being a moral authority and critical of the news media in a way that was far ahead of his time made Merton a genuine threat. More than anything else, it was Merton's love of the truth that brought him into confrontation with powerful enemies.[133]

As we have seen, Griffin's entire career was very closely aligned with the most powerful elements of the society, particularly those engaged in the molding of American public opinion. Griffin even tells us that as he

---

[132] Darovich and Clarke. Bonazzi went a bit farther in describing Griffin's cooperation with the U.S. authorities in tying the agitators to Soviet agents in the 2009 book that he edited, *Available Light: Exile in Mexico: Essays and Photographs of John Howard Griffin* (Wings Press), than he did in his 2018 biography. In that account as with the obituary, Griffin's sleuthing skills come across as quite extraordinary for a mere civilian.

[133] Hugh Turley and David Martin, *The Martyrdom of Thomas Merton: An Investigation*, p. 215. For a survey of Merton's critical writing on the American press, see David Martin, "Is the American Press the Enemy of the People?", January 18, 2018. https://www.dcdave.com/article5/180118.htm.

embarked upon his big venture as a fake Black man in the Deep South, he had a lunch meeting with three FBI men from the Dallas office.[134] Even though, as his biographer Bonazzi wrote, Griffin left military service as a pacifist, we have seen nothing in his writing, public or private, taking issue with the country's prosecution of the very unpopular Vietnam War.

We have also found that when it comes to important facts about Griffin's life, even regarding how and when he lost his sight and how he regained it, the truth seems to be quite elusive. There are competing stories for both strange phenomena.[135] We should expect the most comprehensive and recent source of information on Griffin's life, that is, the work of his biographer Bonazzi, to be the most reliable, but in what we have examined so far, that doesn't seem to be the case. It gets a lot worse for Bonazzi when we compare his account of Griffin's military experience with the official Army Separation Report. (See appendix 5.)

We have noted that Bonazzi's account of military career is extremely sketchy. We learn from Bonazzi only that Griffin spent most of his time in the Pacific in the Solomon Islands, first at Guadalcanal, then for a year on the island of Nuni among the primitive natives, and then was sent west to the island of Morotai in Indonesia where he suffered the serious concussion from the Japanese bombing that eventually resulted in his blindness.

Here is what we find in the "Battles and Campaigns" block of his discharge report: Bismarck-Archipelago, Central Pacific, Eastern Mandates, New Guinea, Northern Solomons, Luzon, Western Pacific, Air Combat Borneo. The Solomons are there, but lots of other places are there as well. Morotai, where Griffin supposedly suffered his blindness-inducing concussion, isn't listed. Although in Indonesia, it was a staging

---

[134] *Black Like Me*, p. 4. That FBI Dallas office would play a crucial role in "investigating" the assassination of President John F. Kennedy some four years later. In contrast to Griffin, Merton was under surveillance by the FBI and by the CIA. See Robert Grip, "The Merton Files: Washington Watches the Monk," *The Merton Seasonal*, Vol. 11, Winter 1986.

[135] It is also of some interest that in most of the photographs we have seen of Griffin during his blindness period he is wearing what we can best describe as opaque welding goggles. They would appear to turn even one with 20/20 vision into a sightless person.

area for the assault on the Philippines, so it could possibly be subsumed under Luzon as part of that campaign, though.

We had observed that it seemed odd for Griffin to have been shipped so far away from the Solomons near the end of the war, but Borneo and Luzon, in the Philippines are even farther. We just don't know when he was there and what he was doing there. For a mere radio operator or mechanic, it looks like he really got around, and Bonazzi gives us no clue as to what he might have been doing in those places.

Bonazzi does state quite confidently that Griffin spent 39 months overseas.[136] Doing the subtraction on his arrival and departure dates for his overseas service, we come up with just a few days more than 32 months. He says that Griffin spent four years in the Army, but his entry date was March 9, 1942, and his discharge date was October 27, 1945. That comes to a little more than three years and seven months. And remember, Bonazzi stated that Griffin's separation papers said he left the Army on December 15, 1945. He is not so specific about Griffin's entry into the Army except to report erroneously that it was in 1941. We might wonder about what Griffin might have been up to in that unaccounted for time between his return from France and his entry into military service. Bonazzi strongly implies that Griffin mustered out of the Army in San Francisco, but we see from his separation papers that it was at Fort Sam Houston, which is in San Antonio.

The really big news in the separation papers might well be in that box #34, "WOUNDS RECEIVED IN ACTION." The entry says "None." Similarly, in #33, DECORATIONS AND CITATIONS, there is no Purple Heart. One can do the research online and discover that there is some controversy as to whether a concussion qualifies a soldier for a Purple Heart, but one would think that a concussion of the severity described by Bonazzi in his Griffin biography would certainly have measured up. As we have seen, though, several different explanations have been offered as to what caused the concussion or concussions (as Griffin wrote) that brought on the blindness, and even without the official military records,

---

[136] In *Available Light: Exile in Mexico*, Bonazzi wrote that it was three years and that he was wounded. p. 45.

Bonazzi's seems the least likely. It might not be the least likely explanation for what caused the blindness, though. The BBC reported in 2009 that "illness struck him blind" and a 2021 YouTube presentation says in an authoritative voice that "shrapnel caused him to go temporarily blind."[137]

The Penn Jones Connection

Chapter 18 of *The Martyrdom of Thomas Merton* is entitled, "Penn Jones: Covert Agent?" In the pages ahead in our chronological account of Griffin's work in managing the story of Merton's death we will examine the use that he made of his long-term associate and neighbor in Texas, Penn Jones, Jr., and the follow-up "investigation" that Jones made in a trip to Thailand with a side-trip to the Philippines to interview Fr. Celestine Say. Jones never told Say that he was working for Griffin, on behalf of the abbey; only later, as we will see, did Griffin let it slip that Jones was his agent. We might question, though, whether that characterization of Jones is exactly accurate. That means that Jones was working for Griffin, which suggests that Griffin would have paid for his trip. What is much more likely is that Griffin and Jones were being financed by the same people, and we're not talking about the Gethsemani Abbey.

In our chapter we compared Jones, in his well-known work as an early "skeptic" of the conclusions of the Warren Commission in the assassination of President John F. Kennedy who, through time, "mellowed" and revealed himself as something less than a real critic, to journalist Christopher Ruddy in the case of the death of Deputy White House Counsel in the administration of President Bill Clinton. We concluded our chapter this way:

---

[137] Kevin Connolly, "Exposing the Colour of Prejudice," October 25, 2009, http://news.bbc.co.uk/2/hi/americas/8318628.stm; Yesterday in History, "What Happened When a White Man Became Black in Mid-20th Century America," December 17, 2021,
https://www.youtube.com/watch?v=hfcBxGpuBhY.

As noted, we have found no evidence that Jones ever did anything in the wake of Merton's death that is worthy of being called any sort of an investigation. There is only the unwarranted inference made by Robert Bonazzi and second hand by James Douglass that if Jones, the JFK researcher, found no evidence of murder that alone "proves" that Merton's death was an accident.

Few people ever suspect journalists would act as agents to cover-up state-sponsored secret assassinations. One of the few people who was astute enough in 1968 to have suspected such things would have been Thomas Merton.[138]

In his review of our book, the noted scholar of the JFK assassination, Phillip F. Nelson, told the public a lot more about Penn Jones:

The person Jones was arguably closest to was Gary Mack (born Lawrence Alan Dunkel) who had started out as conspiracy theorist but eventually became a "debunker" of some theories, finally settling in as a "conspiracy-light" advocate who believed that Lee Harvey Oswald was the assassin but believed that he did not act alone. Yet, after that conversion, he would spend the rest of his life refuting any and all suggestions of evidence pointing toward conspiracy. That movement was cemented when he joined the staff of the Sixth Floor Museum, located in the Texas School Book Depository Building in the early 1990s, eventually becoming the director of the museum.

Among Penn Jones' other close friends or associates were Hugh Aynesworth, a Dallas reporter and strong supporter of the Warren Commission's most ludicrous findings, and many other similarly-deluded researchers including Dave Perry, also a close associate of Gary Mack, who tried, unconvincingly, to discredit Dr. Charles Crenshaw's testimony about having received a telephone call from the new president Lyndon Johnson while attempting to save Lee Harvey Oswald's life. Jones was also similarly connected to Bud Fensterwald, who many truth-seeking researchers believe was a CIA operative. Another associate of Jones was Gordon McLendon, a Dallas-based wealthy owner of major radio stations in some of the largest cities in the country, whom many researchers have connected to CIA operative David Atlee Phillips and wealthy oilman (and suspected financier behind JFK's assassination) Clint Murchison and Bobby Baker, Lyndon Johnson's conduit to Mafioso throughout the country. McLendon had also known and associated with Jack Ruby.

---

[138] Turley and Martin, p. 242.

Moreover, Jones was also very closely connected to Mary Ferrell, whom researcher Harrison Edward Livingstone described at length in his 1993 book *Killing the Truth: Deceit and Deception in the JFK Case*. Livingstone summarized his opinions (with which many other long-time researchers agree) by calling her the "gatekeeper" and the head of a "sophisticated private intelligence operation . . . a *de facto* secret society in Texas, run by powerful people there, to protect the name and reputation of Texas and to protect those who were involved in the murder of John Kennedy." (Livingstone, pp. 386–396).[139]

James W. Douglass, author of *JFK and the Unspeakable: Why He died and Why It Matters,* asked Bonazzi about Merton's death. Bonazzi told Douglass that his friend Penn Jones had travelled to Bangkok to investigate Merton's death and that Jones found no evidence of murder.[140]

Griffin wrote the preface to Volume I of Jones's early Kennedy assassination book *Forgive My Grief.* In that preface we find the following passage:

Why had they been so eager to drop all of the loose ends, to declare within hours of his death that Oswald was guilty, guilty alone; and then slammed the doors on the historic tragedy?

One investigates the simplest crime far more profoundly than that.[141]

And why, we might wonder as we read further in this work, was Griffin so eager to tell the world that his "friend," Thomas Merton had died from accidental electrocution—the conclusion of the early AP report based only on anonymous "Catholic sources"—when he was in possession of evidence that so clearly contradicted that conclusion?

---

[139] Nelson, "The Mysterious Death of Thomas Merton," March 22, 2018, https://www.lewrockwell.com/2018/03/phillip-f-nelson/the-mysterious-death-of-thomas-merton/.

[140] James W. Douglass, Keynote Address to the ITMS meeting, June 13, 1997, *Merton Annual,* 1998, p. 82.

[141] Penn Jones, Jr., *Forgive My Grief, Volume I: A Critical Review of the Warren Commission Report on the Assassination of President John F. Kennedy,* Midlothian Mirror, Inc., 1966, unnumbered preface page, https://archive.org/details/ForgiveMyGriefPennJonesJr/Forgive_My_Grief_01/.

CHAPTER 10

Secrecy

Men loved darkness rather than light because their deeds were wicked.
-John 3:19

The Need for Secrecy

The Merton Legacy Trust convened shortly after Merton's death. They would meet at the Abbey of Gethsemani, often with Brother Patrick or Abbot Flavian present. The trust was created to direct all income from everything written by Thomas Merton to the Abbey of Gethsemani in the event of Merton's death. Eventually, at the suggestion of Brother Patrick, they would select John Howard Griffin as the authorized Merton biographer.[142]

The timing of Griffin's original connection to the abbey and to Merton is of some interest. Merton's writings, until the 1960s, had been almost all spiritual in nature. In 1960, however, he wrote to a fellow Catholic priest and confidant that he felt that he had been wrong to be so

---

[142] Br. Patrick letter to Griffin, January 20, 1969, Griffin papers.

apolitical in his writings and that times called for taking a political stand.[143]

In October of 1961, Merton's essay "The Root of War" was published in *The Catholic Worker*. The essay gained Merton the attention of a lot of people, including the activist priests Daniel and Philip Berrigan. During the following year Merton wrote around one hundred letters opposing nuclear war. Merton felt it was the duty of Christians to oppose war. The intelligence community would almost certainly have taken note.

In late 1961, John Howard Griffin, was getting publicity as the author of *Black Like Me*. Griffin first visited the abbey as he put it, "to spend a few days in a Trappist silence" in 1962. According to Griffin, some of the monks suggested that he meet Thomas Merton, and they met briefly for a few minutes. Griffin wrote that at the time that he met Merton, they "had read one another's books."[144] Merton confirmed that he read *Black Like Me*, in March of 1962.[145] It is interesting that Griffin seems to go almost out of his way to make it appear that the fact that Thomas Merton happened to be living at the abbey, more than 800 miles from his own home where he had chosen to spend his silent time, was little more than a coincidence. He would have us believe that he was content upon that first visit only to meet and talk with Abbot James Fox.

In 1963, Griffin wrote Abbot Fox and asked permission to begin "a photographic archive of Merton's life and activities," explaining that he had already done that on a number of people, from the unknown to the famous, including in the latter group the French Catholic philosopher Jacques Maritain and the Belgian Nobel Peace Prize winner Dominique Pire. To his considerable surprise, Griffin reports, not only did Fox agree to it, but he asked Griffin to take photographs of Merton that could be

---

[143] Lipsey, p. 159.

[144] John Howard Grifffin (Robert Bonazzi, editor), *Follow the Ecstasy: The Hermitage Years of Thomas Merton*, Orbis Books, 1993, p. 1. The year of the first visit comes from Bonazzi, *Follow the Ecstasy*, p. 263.

[145] Thomas Merton, *Turning Toward the World: The Pivotal Years*, March 24, 1962.

used for publicity, including Merton's "official" portrait.[146] Griffin eventually bought Merton a camera and cultivated his interest in photography. More than their common American, French background and social and political interests, or even Griffin's interest in the Catholic monastic life and the fact that they were both converts to Catholicism, photography became the big link between them.

We might wonder how Griffin became such a skilled photographer. The biographer Bonazzi provides more questions than answers. In his forward to Griffin's *Follow the Ecstasy* he simply states that Griffin was both a professional photographer and musicologist, famous for his portraits of a number of notable people.[147] We admit that it is speculation on our part, but his photographic skills might have been a part of specialized military training. In support of this possibility, we offer the following passage from a recent book by the son of another WW II veteran who worked in the same South Pacific theater of operations as Griffin:

> We have seen how Tom [O'Loughlin] kept two kinds of photos from the war; a set printed on thin paper and probably done by an official ship's photographer, and some much nicer prints, which may have come from a camera Tom had, or at least had the use of, during the Nashville's cruises, photos he would have had printed in Sydney or elsewhere.
>
> We also know that Tom had attended Bomb Disposal School in Southeast Washington, DC, before graduating from Midshipmen's school at Columbia. It is possible that he also received additional training, which was connected to intelligence. The Naval Photographic Laboratory was within walking distance of the DC Fire Academy where Tom trained. MacArthur and other commanders needed photographic interpretation experts. Tom would be assigned to the Seventh Fleet where aerial photography would become crucial in preparing for landings on enemy held islands.
>
> A second indication is found on Tom's separation affidavit when answering the question, what would be the most appropriate assignment would you be re-activated in a national mobilization? He

---

146 Thomas Merton and John Howard Griffin, *Wholeness: The Visual World of Thomas Merton*, Houghton Mifflin Company, 1970, p. 36.

147 *Follow the Ecstasy*, p. viii.

answered 1. Afloat: Officer on a Cruiser or 2. Ashore: Intelligence officer.[148]

If Griffin's photographic skills had a similar origin it would explain all those different places he turned up during his period of service and much else, and it would be just the sort of thing that Bonazzi would have wanted to avoid mentioning.

The plot thickens with the "Notes on Photography" section of the 2009 posthumously published Griffin book that Bonazzi edited.[149] There, Griffin tells us that his interest in photography greatly intensified just at the time in 1947 when he was going blind, aiming his camera based upon sound alone, and even continuing to practice the art to a degree even after he had gone completely blind, as unbelievable as that might be. Perhaps the most telling part of that section, though, is when he informs us that his interest in photography began when he was the subject of stories (plural) by military magazines or was photographed for articles by other magazines. He mentions Jim Hansen of *Look* and Shel Hershorn of *Life* as two photographers who had been generous with their assistance. We can gather that the Hershorn encounter came from a series of 1958 articles about Griffin by *Life* alluded to in a frontispiece Griffin family photograph by Hershorn. Since this was even before Griffin's Deep South adventure that resulted in the *Sepia* series that became *Black Like Me*, this outsized interest in Griffin suggests as does the press promotion of his books that there was more to Griffin than meets the eye. That Griffin should have been the subject of military magazine articles only adds to the mystery surrounding the man. At the very least, it suggests a longtime coziness with the same molders of public opinion who were in the forefront of the planting of the "accidental electrocution" explanation for Merton's death.

---

[148] John OLoughlin, *McDuff Lives! The Life and Untimely Death of Thomas F. O'Loughlin, Jr.*, ScreamingOspreys.com, 2021, pp. 30-31.

[149] *Available Light: Exile in Mexico*, pp. 103-109.

Griffin, the "Investigator"

Following Merton's death, Brother Patrick and Griffin exchanged letters at the end of December 1968 and early in 1969. It should be noted that none of the letters that were preserved contain any discussion of the cause of Merton's death. A letter from Brother Patrick, dated January 28, informed Griffin that the abbey had received Merton's personal effects from Thailand. The abbey had also received the official Thai reports about Merton's death, but they were not discussed in the letters, which is odd given their later interest in what had happened.

In January of 1969, Brother Patrick passed information from Naomi Burton Stone, a member of the Merton Legacy Trust, to John Howard Griffin.[150] Soon after Merton's death Griffin was in contact with all three members of the Merton Legacy Trust, Tommie O'Callaghan, James Laughlin, and Naomi Stone.

After Griffin was selected to be the official Merton biographer, he assumed an active role in "investigating" Merton's death. According to Griffin, his role was to gather the questions about Merton's death "for no other reason than to allay the suspicions or clarify the contradictions."[151]

John Howard Griffin was very sensitive about leaving anything significant in writing. Griffin might have been responding to a suggestion by Brother Patrick that he preserve his correspondence for the historical record when Griffin wrote that no matter how justified or historically important, the thought of anyone having access to his letters was "profoundly repugnant."[152] This could well explain why most of the letters that were preserved by Griffin lack any substance.

Griffin and Brother Patrick were both concerned with the narrative about Merton's death, but there is little on the subject that they kept in their letters. That is likely because they destroyed their confidential letters. In fact, on one occasion Griffin wrote to Brother Patrick, "I have

---

[150] Br. Patrick letter to Griffin, January 2, 1969, Griffin papers.
[151] Griffin letter to John Moffitt, August 11, 1969, Moffitt papers.
[152] Griffin letter to Br. Patrick, February 14, 1969, Griffin papers.

greatly appreciated your confidential letter, Brother Pat, and have destroyed it."[153]

Griffin had the same agreement with John Moffitt who corresponded with him about the details of Merton's death. Griffin wrote to Moffitt, "Thanks so much for your confidential letter which I have read and then burned."[154] In one letter to Griffin, Moffitt added, "p.s. No need to burn this. It's just the same sort of 'confidentiality' that we agreed on from the start."[155]

When Griffin first contacted Moffitt on August 11, 1969, he shared his desire to keep their discussion confidential. He advised Moffitt to contact him at his home or through Brother Patrick Hart at the abbey. Griffin told Moffitt that he would like to meet with him in New York where he would feel free to talk, "more so than committing things to paper."[156] Moffitt wrote to Griffin, "About keeping things confidential: At this point I should like everything (emphasis Moffitt's) I write to you to be kept so, as I shall keep everything you write to me."[157]

Naomi Stone also participated in the secrecy to avoid leaving written records. On July 5, 1969, she wrote to Griffin, "Thanks for your good letter which I have destroyed." Griffin had written to Stone about Say's negatives that had been sent to Flavian. She told Griffin that the monks should be "a little careful about what they say." Stone advised Griffin not to tell Tommie O'Callaghan about Say's negatives because O'Callaghan would want them placed in the Bellarmine archives. Before writing to Griffin, Stone contacted him by telephone for a private conversation.[158]

Another method used to avoid leaving a written record was to use tape cassettes. Griffin told Brother Patrick that he was taping his questions for him instead of putting them in writing. Griffin wrote that, "since some of this is quite confidential, the tapes can be erased and

---

[153] Griffin letter to Br. Patrick, July 24, 1969. Griffin papers.

[154] Griffin letter to Moffitt, November 5, 1969, Moffitt papers.

[155] Moffitt letter to Griffin, December 28, 1969, Moffitt papers.

[156] Griffin letter to Moffitt, August 11, 1969, Moffit papers.

[157] Moffitt letter to Griffin, August 15, 1969, Moffitt papers.

[158] Stone letter to Griffin, July 5, 1969, Griffin papers.

reused without fear of someone's taking a peek."[159] John Moffitt was also encouraged by Griffin to use cassette tapes to be more efficient.[160] Griffin recommended tape cassette recorders for Moffitt to purchase in order that they could exchange cassette tapes.[161]

In-person meetings were also employed to prevent written records. Griffin, though he lived far away, visited the abbey virtually monthly in 1969. He scheduled his visits with Brother Patrick and Abbot Flavian. One meeting planned for May 28, 1969, was supposedly to discuss Griffin's book project. Their meetings must have included a discussion of Celestine Say and the photograph of Merton's body that Say had sent to Abbot Flavian. A decision must have been made that Griffin would contact Say to obtain the negatives of his photographs. This is apparent because on June 2, a few days after his meeting with Flavian and Brother Patrick, Griffin contacted Say. He got in touch with Say again on June 4.[162] The timing of Griffin's meeting at the abbey followed by his contacting of Say is a strong indicator of when Griffin learned about Say and his photographs.

Griffin told Say, "I have in my hands, thanks to your kindness, the photograph you made of Thomas Merton shortly after his death."[163] Griffin asked for the negatives and reassured Say that he was working with Abbot Flavian. Griffin also asked Say to provide him with the details of Merton's death because he was the official biographer. Following his meeting at the abbey, Griffin also dispatched his friend Penn Jones to travel to the Philippines to interview Say and to investigate the scene of Merton's death in Thailand. Abbot Flavian and Brother Patrick must have briefed Griffin when they showed him the photograph and they gave him Say's contact information.

After another face-to-face meeting at the abbey in early August, Griffin initiated contact with John Moffitt to find out what he knew and

---

[159] Griffin letter to Br. Patrick, August 19, 1969, Griffin papers.

[160] Griffin letter to Moffitt, September 3, 1969, Griffin papers.

[161] Griffin letter to Moffitt, October 6, 1969, Griffin papers.

[162] Griffin letter to Say, June 2, 1969, Griffin papers.

[163] Griffin letter to Say, June 4, 1969, Griffin papers.

what he thought about Merton's death. Moffitt had sent Abbot Flavian some articles that he had written that mentioned Merton's death. Moffitt's knowledge of the scene and the accounts of eyewitnesses interested the people promoting the "accidental electrocution" narrative.

Journalists often conceal the truth by suppressing information. Griffin knew that Moffitt was a journalist, so he was curious about any information that Moffitt might have left out of his articles. Griffin put it to Moffitt this way, "I hoped that you would share with me in the minutest possible detail anything that you possessed in the way of recollections – the things for example, that could not be included in the brief articles."[164]

Eventually Griffin traveled to New York to meet privately with Moffitt.[165] Griffin also had in-person meetings with Merton Legacy Trustees, Naomi Stone and James Laughlin.[166] In 1973, Stone, Laughlin, and Brother Patrick would co-edit *The Asian Journal of Thomas Merton*, that included the likely manufactured six-Trappists letter and introduced Brother Patrick's false story that Merton had taken a shower.

Secrecy extended beyond the circumstances of Merton's death. Fr. Dan Walsh, Merton's former professor and long-time friend, had delivered the homily at Merton's funeral Mass. In 1969, Walsh asked Brother Patrick for the contact information for Merton's aunt in New Zealand and his former guardian in England. Brother Patrick told Griffin, "I told Dan nothing. Gave no addresses. But more about this when we meet." [167]

Tommie O'Callaghan, a member of the Merton Legacy Trust, was not let in on some of the secrets that were being kept. Griffin told Brother Patrick that Say's negatives should be "deeply hidden." He said that, as a matter of principle they should not be destroyed, but they should not be available to just anyone, either. Griffin advised Br. Patrick, that Stone said that O'Callaghan should not even be told about the existence of Say's

---

[164] Griffin letter to Moffitt, August 11, 1969, Moffitt papers.

[165] Griffin letter to John Moffitt, November 5, 1969, Moffitt papers.

[166] Griffin letter to Br. Patrick, October 23, 1969, Griffin papers.

[167] Br. Patrick letter to Griffin, October 4, 1969, Griffin papers.

negatives. Naomi thought that O'Callaghan would want Say's negatives to be given to the Bellarmine archives. Griffin then told Brother Patrick that he had many things to discuss with him and Flavian on his next visit to the abbey.[168]

Griffin told Brother Patrick that O'Callaghan had expressed her concern that things were being hidden at the abbey that she, as a trustee, should know about. He told Brother Patrick that he was sure O'Callaghan was acting without the approval of Naomi Stone or James Laughlin. Griffin advised Brother Patrick to "be as bland and dumb as possible for the time being." Griffin told Brother Patrick that he played dumb with O'Callaghan "just sending her the vaguest answers."[169] A few months later Griffin told Brother Patrick that if it was not convenient for him to stay at the abbey that he would stay at a motel in Louisville, "but not at [O'Callaghan's] – too much strain."

On August 19, 1969, Naomi Stone wrote to Griffin that she had destroyed the carbon copy of his August 10, letter to O'Callaghan. She told Griffin that O'Callaghan was "a hazard" they would have to live with. Stone wrote that she disliked the need to keep information from O'Callaghan but that she and Laughlin agreed this was essential.[170]

It is impossible to know for certain what O'Callaghan thought was being hidden. It is conceivable that she read Moffitt's story in *America* that said that the Thai physician said that Merton's death was caused by a heart attack. Maybe she wanted to see the official reports from Thailand. The death certificate that did not state "accidental electrocution" and the reports that falsely stated that an autopsy had been performed may have caused O'Callaghan to ask more questions. Perhaps she read the report in *The Kentucky Standard* about an "autopsy performed in Oakland, California," and she wanted to see that autopsy report.

---

[168] Griffin letter to Br. Patrick, July 24, 1969, Griffin papers.
[169] Griffin letter to Brother Patrick, July 24, 1969, Griffin papers.
[170] Stone letter to Griffin, August 19, 1969, Griffin papers.

O'Callaghan's intuition was accurate that things were being hidden by the abbey. We have mentioned many of them before, but here is a more complete inventory:

- The cable from the U. S. Embassy in Bangkok dated December 10, 1968, that stated that the official cause of Merton's death was "heart failure"
- Thomas Merton's death certificate
- Thai doctor's certificate of cause of death
- Foreign Service Report on the death of Thomas Merton
- Handwritten witness statement of Abbot Odo Haas
- Written statements of witness Fr. Celestine Say
- Written statement of witness Fr. François de Grunne
- A letter from Celestine Say sent to Abbot Flavian on June 26, 1969, with his negatives
- Say's negatives of the photographs of Merton's body as it was found
- Say's letter to John Howard Griffin in September of 1969
- Reports from specialists in forensic medicine
- Report of Penn Jones, John Howard Griffin's investigator of Merton's death

Some of these documents have been discovered outside of the abbey. Others are still missing.

As we said earlier, an abbey spokesman said that a cable was received by the abbey from the U.S. Embassy in Bangkok on December 10, 1968, stating that the official cause of death was "heart failure" according to *The New York Times*. This cablegram has never been produced and was never mentioned again.

The first publication of these historic Thai documents concerning Merton's death was in our book, *The Martyrdom of Thomas Merton: An Investigation*. Four years after our book was published the secular news media, the Catholic news media, and academia continue to suppress the news of the discovery of these important documents. Those same people still call Merton's death an "accidental electrocution" although it has never been the official cause of death. Scholars like Michael W. Higgins in his review of our book commended our research in "acquiring official documents" but didn't bother to tell his readers what those documents were, what their significance was, nor that we had made them available for public scrutiny.[171]

Statements of witnesses who were present at the scene were sent from the U.S. Embassy to the Abbey of Gethsemani on December 27, 1968. John Howard Griffin told Moffitt that he and the abbey had the handwritten reports of Odo Hass, François de Grunne, and several accounts by Celestine Say, but these reports have remained secret.[172] A clear distortion of the handwritten statement from Odo Haas, even more egregious than the six-Trappists letter, was later circulated as a typewritten and unsigned statement. Chapter 4 of our first book is a dissection of this document. The document's purpose was clearly to plant the story of the witness Haas being frozen to the fan by its "powerful" shock when he attempted to remove it from Merton's body. (See appendix 4.)

The letter Celestine Say sent to Abbot Flavian on June 26, 1969, with his negatives remains hidden. Only the envelope and the negatives have been found.

The negative filmstrip of the photographs of Merton's body, exactly as it was found, was kept hidden for almost 50 years until we discovered it in the papers of John Howard Griffin at the Rare Book and Manuscript Library at Columbia University. Griffin advised Abbot Flavian and Brother Patrick that the negatives should never be published or available to anyone. The negatives are now available at the Columbia and Bellarmine University libraries. The abbey refused to grant us permission for even drawings of these important pictures to be published in our previous book. As was the case with our previous book,

---

[171] Michael W. Higgins, Review of *The Martyrdom of Thomas Merton: An Investigation, The Merton Annual,* vol. 32, 2019, p. 279.

[172] Griffin letter to John Moffit, August 18, 1969, Moffitt papers.

the abbey refuses to grant us permission to publish even drawings of these important pictures. (See appendix 7.)

Griffin told Brother Patrick on September 28, 1969, that he had received a nice letter from Say. The only letter from Say that Griffin preserved is dated June 25, 1969.[173] Griffin may have destroyed the letter that he received in September.

John Howard Griffin sent his investigator Penn Jones to interview Celestine Say in the Philippines and to visit the scene of Merton's death in Thailand. The report that Penn Jones gave Griffin, including the photographs that he took, are missing.

Griffin, Brother Patrick, Flavian, and Moffitt may have discussed the bleeding wound on the back of Merton's head at their in-person meetings. They surely knew about this wound because it was mentioned by witnesses. The head wound was even mentioned in the six-Trappist letter. If they discussed Merton's head wound in writing or on cassette tapes those letters and tapes may have been destroyed.

---

[173] Griffin letter to Brother Patrick, September 28, 1969, Griffin papers.

Chapter 11

Griffin with the Cover-Up Reins

Spring, 1969

On May 7, Merton Legacy Trustee Naomi Burton Stone wrote to John Moffitt thanking him for sending her a copy of the Bangkok talk by Thomas Merton. She told Moffitt that no one can know if Merton was electrocuted, had a heart attack, or what. Stone thanked Moffitt for his offer to assist the biographer when someone was named, implying that the Merton Legacy Trust had not yet appointed anyone.[174] However, on April 23, John Howard Griffin had already tentatively agreed to be the authorized biographer.[175]

---

[174] Naomi Burton Stone letter to John Moffitt, May 7, 1969, Moffitt papers.
[175] Griffin letter to Naomi Stone, April 23, 1969, Griffin papers.

The Authorized Biographer

The Merton Legacy Trust Agreement provides for any potential "competent" biographer to have access to Merton's notebooks, journals, and diaries. Griffin had never written a book review, article, or anything concerning Thomas Merton at the time that he was appointed to be the authorized biographer in 1969. It appears that the selection of Griffin as the Merton biographer was for a reason other than his being either a competent biographer or an experienced student of Merton's works.

By June of 1969, Griffin began introducing himself as the authorized Thomas Merton biographer. From the beginning, contacting witnesses who were at the scene of Merton's death seemed to become Griffin's primary concern. Celestine Say was one of the first of Griffin's contacts. As we mentioned earlier, Griffin must have learned about Say and obtained his contact information at the end of May during his meeting with Abbot Flavian and Brother Patrick at Gethsemani.

Brother Patrick, on the record, recommended that the Merton Legacy Trust select Griffin to be Merton's biographer. Fox contacted Griffin in June to suggest that Griffin portray him favorably in his biography of Merton. Fox enclosed a copy of his February 1, 1969, letter to the Gethsemani diaspora to provide Griffin with some evidence of his "close personal friendship" with Merton. [176]

Griffin's Inquiry into Merton's Death

On June 2, after Griffin's meeting with Flavian and Brother Patrick, Griffin wrote to Say and introduced himself. Griffin began by telling Say that the abbey had a report that "stated [Merton] had showered." This was almost certainly a false statement. There is no official report that Merton showered. In 2017, Brother Patrick told us that there "was no evidence that Merton had showered." This was likely a bluff by Griffin to draw Say into thinking that Merton may have taken a shower. He asked

---

[176] James Fox letter to John Howard Griffin, June 6, 1969, Griffin papers.

Say about the physical scene and the details of what he had witnessed. Griffin asked Say if he had any contact information for François de Grunne.

Griffin's first letter was a false start. Griffin was at the abbey and probably shared his letter with Flavian and Brother Patrick. They quickly realized that Griffin had forgotten to ask Say to send him the negatives of the photos that he had taken of Merton's body. On June 4, Griffin wrote to Say again, telling him that he had Say's photograph of Merton's body that Abbot Flavian had given to him. The abbey superiors were working closely with Griffin, so he probably had also read Say's March 18th letter to Flavian. Say's letter made it clear that he was an important witness. Say's question if an autopsy had determined the cause of Merton's death prior to the burial would have been a concern to the abbey leadership. By this time, they had to have been keenly interested in knowing exactly what Say had witnessed and what his thoughts were about Merton's death.

Griffin praised Say for taking the important photograph. He stressed that the photograph must be protected and remain unpublished. Griffin beseeched Say to kindly send him the negative strip and openly copied his letter to Abbot Flavian. Say decided that he would not send the negatives to Griffin, and instead he sent them by registered mail to Abbot Flavian on June 26, 1969.

Brother Lawrence wrote a note on Say's envelope from the Philippines to Abbot Flavian that said, "Brother Patrick is concerned about these negatives. They are for H. Griffin as you know." Say's photographs were a problem because they did not support the story that Merton died by accidental electrocution. The note from Br. Lawrence to Abbot Flavian stating that Say's negatives were for John Howard Griffin is interesting. Griffin was not a Trappist monk at the abbey, and yet he had unlimited access to confidential materials about Merton's death that the abbot and Brother Patrick were keeping secret. Griffin appeared to be a good deal more than just Merton's biographer.

The day before Say mailed the negatives to Flavian, he mailed a letter to Griffin, dated June 25. Say was replying to Griffin's two letters earlier in the month. He informed Griffin that he was sending the negatives to Abbot Flavian as a gift. Say told Griffin specifically how he took the photographs of the scene before anything had been disturbed.

In the three-page single-spaced letter, Say wrote a detailed description of the cottage where Merton died. He told Griffin that Merton left the dining area with de Grunne at "twenty to 2 pm" and that he left shortly after them. He provided the details of what he witnessed in the cottage and the times of these events. He said that Merton was not wet. Say was precise that he saw Haas recoil from a shock when he touched the fan and that Haas later told him that the shock was "not too strong."

Griffin would later write a different account of what Say had said. Griffin would write to John Moffitt, "Fr. Say seems quite definite in his times: Tom and Fr. de Grunne left the lunch at 2:10 p.m. to go for the rest." Griffin moved the time forward by 30 minutes. Griffin would say that Haas received a shock so strong that he could not release his hands from the fan until Say unplugged the cord. Griffin had to know that what he was telling Moffitt was not the truth. Griffin was not aware that Moffitt had been doing some investigating on his own and that Moffitt would know that Griffin was not telling him the truth.

While Griffin was writing to Say, he dispatched his friend Penn Jones on a mission to the Philippines to interview Say. Jones would also travel to Thailand to photograph the cottage where Merton died and investigate further. Jones told Say simply that he was a journalist and that he believed that Merton was assassinated and that it was connected to the Kennedy and Martin Luther King assassinations. It appears that Jones was trying to draw Say out, to discover if Say had any suspicion that Merton had been assassinated.

Moffitt Seeks Answers

Moffitt was also seeking answers about how Thomas Merton died. Moffitt was perplexed, like the eyewitnesses, about how the fan had curiously come to rest on top of Merton. Moffitt thought that Merton may have fallen, but there was no explanation for how he fell. Merton scholars have accepted various explanations that Merton fell because he slipped in a bathtub or shower or on a wet floor. There is absolutely no evidence to support those theories.

Moffitt had his own rather bizarre hypothesis that Merton suffered a heart attack and then somehow pulled the fan down on top of himself while at the same time breaking the fan to somehow rearrange the wiring causing a shock.

But the combination of events essentially made no sense, so Moffitt would get in touch with several eyewitnesses to try to get a clearer picture of what had transpired. On June 22, he wrote Say asking him for the details that he recalled when Merton died.[177] Say sent letters with the details of what he had witnessed to both Griffin and Moffitt. Since Moffitt was getting information directly from Say, he would later notice that the times of events that Griffin told him later were not true and that Griffin had to know that they were not true.

On July 1, Say enclosed a copy of the photograph of Merton's body in his letter to Moffitt. He told Moffitt that the official biographer John Howard Griffin had requested the negatives, but that he had sent them to Abbot Flavian. Moffitt knew then that Griffin and Flavian had a copy of the photograph and the negatives. At that time, Griffin and Flavian did not know that Moffitt had the photograph. Griffin first contacted Moffitt in August. It was not until two months later that Moffitt revealed to Griffin that he had the "not-to-be-shown photograph."

Say was confused by Merton's death. He was unsure if Merton had died from a heart attack or by electrocution. He told Moffitt that no autopsy had been performed. Say also informed Moffitt that a journalist named Jones had told him that Merton's death may have been connected to the Kennedy and King assassinations. Say told Moffitt that this connection seemed almost unbelievable to him. Moffitt would not learn that Jones was Griffin's agent until six months later.

---

[177] Celestine Say letter to John Moffitt, July 1, 1969, Moffitt papers.

In July, another article by Moffitt, "Thomas Merton: the last three days," was published in *The Catholic World.* Moffitt wrote that he wanted to report what he knew about "the accident." He reported that the Thai doctor had concluded the death had been "heart failure." Moffitt then speculated that Merton may have had a heart attack and grabbed the fan for support, pulling it on top of himself. Moffitt reported that Merton had been found in his shorts with a fan lying on his body. He wrote that Merton's right side had been burned, a fact that was inconsistent with the six-Trappist letter and Fox's letter that had said that the fan had been on Merton's bare chest and that his chest was burned.

Moffitt did write that when Merton's body was discovered a monk touched the fan and received a shock. He *did not* say that the monk became stuck to the fan until it was unplugged. With Say's letter and the photograph in hand, Moffitt knew more than he had reported in his *Catholic World* article. Moffitt knew the names of the witnesses who discovered Merton's body, but he kept them to himself.

François de Grunne wrote to Moffitt apparently in response to a request for more information about the sound that he reportedly heard and when he heard it. De Grunne was a dubious character who changed his story several times about what he had witnessed. He said that he heard a shout in the cottage around 2 pm. He also said that he heard a cry around 3 pm, and he told others that "he had heard this thump." Later, he said that he only heard "a sound" and eventually he said that he did not hear any sound inside the cottage. Many of the participants at the conference knew that de Grunne reported hearing "a shout." Edeltrud Weist wrote in her report that de Grunne, "heard a shout about 3 pm." The police report stated that at 3 pm de Grunne, "heard a loud noise coming from the lower story which sounded like a heavy object falling onto the floor."

On July 6, de Grunne wrote to Moffitt that he did not hear any significant noise in the cottage. He wrote, "I simply heard a sound but there was much noise coming from a neighboring house, my attention was not specially stirred up." Obviously, de Grunne had not heard any shout or loud noise of something falling at 3 pm, because Say, who was also in the cottage, would have heard it, too. Moffitt wrote "NO" in the margin and underlined the shout at "3 PM" in his copy of the statement by Edeltrud Weist, because he knew that there was no evidence to support de Grunne hearing a shout in the cottage at that time.

On August 7, when the report of the Thai police investigation arrived at the abbey, Brother Patrick brought the report to Griffin who was working at Merton's hermitage. Brother Patrick would have had the approval of his superiors to share the Thai police report with someone who was not a member of the Gethsemani community. Griffin, it is clear, had taken the leading role investigating what witnesses knew or suspected about Merton's death. Griffin wasn't just working closely with Abbott Flavian and Brother Patrick. He was directing them. Later we will learn that Griffin told Moffitt that Gethsemani was reluctant to share certain documents with Moffitt without getting the approval of Griffin.[178] Where did the layman Griffin get the authority to direct the Cistercian monks at the Abbey of Gethsemani about sharing documents related to Thomas Merton's death? And who, we might wonder, was directing Griffin?

---

[178] Griffin letter to Moffitt, October 24, 1969, Moffitt papers.

CHAPTER 12

More Griffin-Moffitt Exchanges

August 1969

Moffitt's interest in Merton's death got the attention of the Abbey of Gethsemani, no doubt, because they were concealing information that did not agree with the "accidental electrocution" story. Following the success in obtaining Say's negatives, Griffin turned his attention to Moffitt. Just as Griffin was curious to know if Say had any suspicions about Merton's death, he was also curious about Moffitt.

To keep their secrecy, the confidential matter of the problem they might have with Moffitt was not discussed in writing. Rather, Griffin told Brother Patrick that he would return to the abbey from August 3 to August 10 when matters could be discussed privately.

Griffin was at the abbey when the police report arrived on August 7 with a cover letter to Abbot Flavian Burns that was dated July 30, 1969. Griffin would eventually share the police report with Moffitt.[179] The

---

[179] Moffitt letter to Griffin, November 25, 1969, Moffitt papers.

police report is discussed in detail in Chapter 2 of *The Martyrdom of Thomas Merton: An Investigation.*

While Griffin was staying at the abbey, Brother Patrick received a letter from Moffitt dated August 8. Moffit told Brother Patrick that he did not think that Merton's death had been as it was alleged to have happened. Brother Patrick, Merton's secretary and spokesperson for the abbey on Merton's death, did not respond to Moffitt. Instead, Brother Patrick handed Moffitt's letter over to Griffin to let him respond to Moffitt's concerns. This represented a change in who was in command, a passing of the torch. In February, when Moffitt wrote to Abbot Flavian about Merton's death, that letter was handed over to Brother Patrick. At that time, Brother Patrick told Moffitt, "Since I have been taking care of the correspondence in regard to [Merton], your letter was turned over to me for reply."[180]

Griffin had access to everything, the official reports from Thailand, the handwritten witness statements, Say's letters to Abbot Flavian, Say's photograph, Say's negatives, and correspondence like Moffitt's letter to Brother Patrick.

On August 11, Griffin wrote to Moffitt, introducing himself as the official Thomas Merton biographer. He told Moffitt that he was working at Merton's hermitage and Brother Patrick had given him the letter dated August 8. Griffin told Moffitt that his letter resonated with Brother Patrick and with him. He said that he was looking forward to reading Moffitt's article in *The Catholic World* and that he was interested in resolving any questions, contradictions, and suspicions about Merton's death.

Griffin wrote that he had wanted to establish contact with him because Moffitt was one of the individuals who had stayed in Merton's cottage. He stated that he was already in contact with Fr. Celestine Say, Fr. François de Grunne, and Sr. Marie de la Croix and that he was eager to learn Moffitt's thoughts. He told Moffitt that Say had been extremely

---

[180] Patrick Hart, letter to John Moffitt, February 18, 1969, Moffitt papers.

frank in his police interview and subsequent letters.[181] Griffin may have been referring to the letters that Say had sent to Abbot Flavian in March and June, as well as a letter that Griffin received in June.

Griffin's mention of Say's interview report is highly significant, because later Griffin would later change his story and tell Moffitt that there was no report from Say. Say's report is among those that the abbey claims to have lost and is unavailable to researchers.

Griffin told Moffitt that, as the biographer, he had special access to materials that he could not share. Griffin told Moffitt that there were reports from "specialists in forensic medicine."[182] This implied that there had been an autopsy, but since there was no autopsy, this amounted to a sixth false claim that there had been one, adding to the five others mentioned in chapter 4. No forensic medicine reports related to Merton's death have ever been produced.

Griffin told Moffit that it was his desire that they investigate Merton's death together and that everything that they share should be strictly confidential. He asked Moffitt for the details about Merton's death that he had not included in his articles. Griffin suggested that since Moffitt had questions about Merton's death that they both may have found some of the same contradictions.

He sought to impress Moffitt that there was a sizeable amount of confidential information that he couldn't share. Griffin also stressed that it was his responsibility to dispel any suspicions and clear up any contradictions about Merton's death.

To gain Moffitt's confidence, Griffin told him that he shared Moffitt's interests, and that he was "certainly not yet satisfied that things actually happened the way they are alleged to have happened." Griffin was parroting what Moffitt had written to Brother Patrick. This skepticism by Griffin was short lived, and he was soon telling Moffitt that Merton's death was by accidental electrocution, based on the confidential information that he had.

---

[181] Griffin letter to Moffitt, August 11, 1969, Moffitt papers.
[182] Griffin letter to Moffitt, August 11, 1969, Moffitt papers.

It is peculiar that Griffin should see the initial duty of the authorized biographer to be the allaying of suspicions surrounding Merton's mysterious death. This assignment must have had the approval of whoever gave Griffin full access to the Merton death documents, confidential letters and other materials that have remained secret. Accidental electrocution as the cause of death was authorized by someone, and Griffin seems to have been assigned to safeguard it.

August 15, 1969

Moffitt sent a copy of his article from *The Catholic World* to Griffin and said that he was delighted to receive Griffin's letter. He agreed that everything that they write to each other should be kept confidential. In future correspondence, Moffitt and Griffin would sometimes mention letters being "burned."[183]

Moffitt told Griffin that he thought it was interesting that the accounts by Say and de Grunne were very different. Without being specific, Moffitt told Griffin that someone had written that Merton may have been the victim of an assassination related to the Kennedy and Martin Luther King assassinations. Moffitt was probably referring to what Say had written to him about the journalist named "Jones" from Texas. At this time, Moffitt would not have known that it was Griffin's own friend, Penn Jones, who told Say that Merton may have been assassinated.

August 18, 1969

Moffitt did not express any opinion about the story that Merton may have been assassinated. By telling Griffin that someone else had said that Merton had been assassinated, Moffitt may have been interested to get Griffin's reaction. Griffin's response came swiftly, telling Moffitt that

---

[183] Moffitt letter to Griffin, December 28, 1969, Moffitt papers.

Jacques Maritain, Fr. Stanley Murphy, Fr. Dan Walsh, and Penn Jones with Merton

John Howard Griffin's associate Penn Jones visited Thomas Merton's hermitage and later travelled to the Philippines where he told Fr. Celestine Say that Merton may have been the victim of an assassination related to the Kennedy and Martin Luther King assassinations.

he'd heard the assassination story and he "completely and immediately discounted it." Griffin very likely did not know that the assassination story that he totally dismissed had originated from his agent Jones. The purpose in sending Jones to the Philippines appears to have been to determine if Say suspected that Merton was murdered and to determine how much trouble he might stir up based upon that belief and what he knew of Merton's curious death.

Griffin told Moffitt that Merton's friends, including monks at the abbey, were not satisfied that Merton had died as they had been told.[184] He did not say exactly who those people were or why they were not satisfied. It is highly unlikely that Griffin would know what Trappist monks living in silence were thinking, since they would not have been talking to him. It appears that Griffin was trying to draw from Moffitt any reasons that he may have had to doubt the "accidental electrocution" story.

Griffin, characteristically, told Moffitt that he was glad that they both agreed to keep everything confidential and said that he would only discuss Merton's death with Moffitt and "the forensic medicine men." This was the second time Griffin said that there were "forensic medicine men."

In his letter Griffin told Moffitt that he had access to all the documents related to Merton's death. Griffin told Moffitt that he had the following documents:

- Several personal and detailed accounts by Fr. Say.

(Griffin did not specify to Moffitt what these detailed accounts were. Three letters by Say were known to be at the abbey in August of 1969, one sent to Flavian 3/18/69, a letter sent to Flavian with the negatives 6/26/69), and a letter sent to Griffin 6/25/69.)

- The police report
- Statement to the police by François de Grunne
- Statement to the police by Odo Haas

---

[184] Griffin letter to Moffitt, August 18, 1969, Moffitt papers.

134

- Statement of Celestine Say
- Statement by Sr. Edeltrud Weist
- A commentary in French by Sr. Marie de la Croix
- All the official papers, inventories etc. from the American Consulate in Bangkok

Griffin did not tell Moffitt what those official papers included. We know that the embassy sent the abbey the Thai death certificate, doctor's report, U.S. Foreign Service Report, and an official inventory of Merton's personal effects.

Later in his letter Griffin mentioned "the death photos" without specifying the source. There was only one photograph by Say that was developed at that time. Griffin had recommended that Abbot Flavian request additional photographs and evidence from the Thai police. Say had written to Griffin on June 25, 1969, "The police took a good number of shots of both Merton and the room, and I had to sign that the things were as they were in the pictures, being a witness. Perhaps you might ask to see them in the police files, should you pass by Bangkok. You (sic) print you have with you shows the fan's position before it was moved. The police snaps show the position after they had replaced the fan. Sister Edeltrud, a doctor, removed the fan to examine Merton." We don't know if Abbot Flavian ever followed through with Griffin's suggestion that he try to get the additional photographs from the Thai police.

Griffin wrote that Merton's shorts looked "neatly arranged" and that he thought that the shorts should have been stained by the burn on Merton's abdomen. Griffin seemed to suggest that the shorts had been put on Merton. This false story that Merton was found naked and that shorts were put on the body would be repeated by the biographer Michael Mott and others as part of the concocted shower story.

Griffin did not tell Moffitt that he had the negatives of Say's photographs, which Moffitt happened to know about already. As noted, Moffitt knew that Griffin had requested the negatives but that Say had sent the negatives to Abbot Flavian. Moffitt may have noticed that Say's photograph and negatives were not on Griffin's list and suspected that Griffin was not sharing everything that he had.

There were other reasons why Moffitt may not have trusted Griffin. Griffin may have impressed Moffitt with his access to documents, but as we said earlier, Griffin tried to mislead Moffitt about the times of the events.

Griffin agreed with Moffitt that there were considerable discrepancies between the accounts of Say and de Grunne. Griffin wrote that Say was very specific about the times. Griffin then attributed to Say times of events that were false, telling Moffitt that Merton and de Grunne had left the lunch hall at 2:10 pm and that Say left at 2:30 pm. Moffitt drew a "?" and an arrow on Griffin's letter because he knew this was not true.

Moffitt was at the lunch with Merton, and after lunch Moffitt went on a bus excursion sightseeing in Bangkok. The lunch was at 1:00 pm and Moffitt would have known almost everyone finished lunch around 1:30, and well before 2:30 pm.[185] Moffitt also had received a letter from Say telling him that Merton and de Grunne left the dining area at 1:40 pm.

Griffin told Moffitt, "Fr. Say is deeply suspicious of de G. I have read a good deal from de G and he sounds like a perfectly stable person to me – in fact I was most impressed."[186] Griffin's praise for de Grunne would not sway Moffitt, because he knew that Say was much more reliable than de Grunne.

In the margin of Griffin's letter Moffitt had drawn six question marks "?" indicating things that he did not think were true. Griffin wrote, "Odo Haas says that the current was so strong when he attempted to remove the fan that he could not free himself until Fr. Say unplugged the cord." Griffin had to know that that was not true because Say had written to him on June 25 that Haas "recoiled" on touching the fan and later told Say that the shock was "not strong."

---

[185] Say letter to Moffitt, December 1969, Moffitt papers.

[186] Griffin letter to Moffitt, August 18, 1969, Moffitt papers.

Moffitt also knew the account as related by Griffin was not true, because Say had written to him in July, telling him that Haas recoiled on touching the fan. The reasons were mounting for Moffitt to lack confidence in the information that Griffin was telling him. That leads us to the very likely origin of the obviously fabricated unsigned, undated Haas "statement." Griffin had to put up or shut up.

As we explain in our chapter on the subject in our earlier book, whoever composed it could not have been on the scene in Thailand or he would not have gotten so many known details wrong. The document's other errors point very strongly toward a particular individual, and it is not Griffin. Unlike the professional writer, Griffin, the person who wrote this document is loose with capitalization and spelling. The statement's writer has "osb" in lower case after "Odo Haas." This abbreviation for "Order of Saint Benedict" is always capitalized, as surely as the first person, singular, "I," is capitalized. The city in Korea in which Haas's abbey is located is misspelled right up at the front and then spelled correctly at the end. In the concluding paragraph, in speaking of Fr. Rembert Weakland, the writer first calls him "Abbot Primat," and then correctly "Abbot Primate" in the next sentence. Most tellingly, the work comes across as the work of a single imperious individual who would not be inclined to submit his handiwork to anyone else for review.

The virtual clincher that the composer of the Haas document was Fr. James Fox is to be found in a passage from a February 1969 letter from Merton Legacy Trustee Tommie O'Callaghan to John Howard Griffin: "It was definitely electrocution as the priest who found Tom, lifted off the fan and was immediately 'hung' on the current, until his companion unplugged it. So, thats [sic] settled and somehow I'm glad we know for sure-before it was a bit dubious."[187]

O'Callaghan is giving Griffin this information as though it would be news to him. It does not show up in the public record until it appears in that typewritten "statement" by Haas that Griffin eventually shares with John Moffitt many months later. Clearly, someone at the abbey told that

---

[187] Griffin papers, February 19, 1969. (O'Callaghan's punctuation is almost as bad as Fox's.)

to O'Callaghan to mollify her. Her main contact at the abbey was Brother Patrick Hart, but he was little more than the messenger boy of Fr. James Fox.

Moffitt's article in *The Catholic World* concerned Griffin and the abbey because it suggested that Moffitt knew specific details about Merton's death. Griffin told Moffitt that his account "showed that he had some rather complete reports also." They may have wondered if Moffitt had any of the official Thai reports. Griffin clearly wanted to know how much Moffitt knew.

In 1970, the times of events in Thailand as related by Griffin would reappear in the draft of Brother Patrick's postscript that Brother Patrick sent to Moffitt to look over. In response, Moffitt told Brother Patrick that the times were wrong and why they were wrong. And even though Brother Patrick said that the 3 pm time of death was based on what the abbey had been told by the embassy, Moffitt convinced Brother Patrick to change the time of death to 2 pm. Brother Patrick changed the time of death to one hour earlier but still said, quite falsely, that this was, "based on what the abbey was told by the embassy." We will say more about this in Chapter 16.

August 22, 1969

A few days later, on August 22, Brother Patrick wrote to thank Moffit for sending him the article in *The Catholic World* and suggested that maybe they should just accept that Merton's death was a mystery.

Brother Patrick wanted to know if Moffitt's publication about the Bangkok Conference would be available soon. He told Moffitt that the *Asian Journal of Thomas Merton* was due to be published by June of 1970. They had hoped that Moffitt's account would be published first. The *Asian Journal of Thomas Merton* was later delayed until 1973.

The publishers of Brother Patrick's account of Merton's death clearly wanted to see what Moffitt would write first. Moffitt's book *A New Charter for Monasticism* was published by Notre Dame Press on January

1, 1970. That same month, Brother Patrick would send Moffitt a draft of his foreword and postscript for the *Asian Journal of Thomas Merton*.

August 31, 1969

On August 31, Moffitt responded to Griffin's statement that de Grunne was "a perfectly stable person." Moffitt told Griffin that even the day before Merton's death, de Grunne was acting suspiciously and distraught. Moffitt wrote that Fr. Jean Leclercq had been his overnight guest on August 27, 1969. Leclercq told Moffitt that de Grunne "as a person was not complete" and that he was mentally unstable. By contrast, Leclercq told Moffitt that Say could be trusted "implicitly."[188]

Griffin had told Moffitt that Haas had been "stuck to the fan" and Moffitt knew that this contradicted what Say had told him. Moffitt wanted to see some evidence. This would present a problem for Griffin. Moffitt asked Griffin to show him the handwritten statement from Haas that said that he had been stuck to the fan.

Moffitt requested several of the reports on Merton's death that Griffin told him that he had. Moffitt asked to see the reports of Celestine Say, Odo Haas, Edeltrud Weist, François de Grunne, and the police report. In return, Moffitt offered to send Griffin accounts that he had from witnesses.

September 3, 1969

Griffin replied, saying that he agreed with everything that Moffitt had said in his previous letter. Therefore, he said, in effect, that he now agreed that Say was more reliable than the unstable de Grunne. What is more important, Griffin agreed that Moffitt should see the documents that he requested.

---

[188] Moffitt letter to Griffin, August 31, 1969, Moffitt papers.

But Griffin's actions did not match his words. He did not send any documents to Moffitt. Griffin said that the developing solution was too weak, so that the photographs of the documents were unreadable. Photocopying machines were available to copy documents in 1969. Griffin would not have needed to use a camera and then develop the film with chemical solutions in a darkroom to copy documents. Nevertheless, Griffin wrote that he would re-photograph the documents on September 15th. Griffin delayed giving Moffitt the requested documents. It would not be until the end of October that he would send some of the documents to Moffitt.

Griffin changed the subject in his letter of September 3 to the topic of Merton's shorts, calling it "troublesome" that the shorts "were not even marked by the wound." Griffin had an unusual interest in the shorts that Merton was wearing when he died. Moffitt's interest was not in the shorts but how the electrified fan came to be lying on Merton's body.

September 11, 1969

Griffin was apparently overconfident that Moffitt would not present any challenge to the "accidental electrocution" story. In a rare mention of John Moffitt in the letters that he saved, Griffin, in his letter confirming his impending September 15-21 visit to the abbey, told Brother Patrick, "Splendid correspondence with John Moffitt – He does not know very clearly what happened and a lot of his speculations were easily taken care of. He built a structure that could not have been."

In truth, Moffitt knew a lot more about what happened than Griffin thought. Moffitt was holding back from Griffin information that challenged what Griffin was telling him. Moffit wanted to see some of the secret documents that Griffin claimed to have, so he kept his cards close to the vest.

CHAPTER 13

Griffin and Moffitt, Late 1969

October 1969

A month later Moffitt had still not received any copies of the documents that he had requested. Moffitt wrote to Griffin again on October 4 and mentioned that he had the "not-to-be-shown" photograph from Say. It must have been a shock to Griffin and to the abbey to learn that Moffitt not only had the photograph, but he knew that Griffin had it too. Moffitt then quoted at length from the July 1 letter that he had received from Say, including the passage in which Say wrote that Haas had recoiled when he touched the fan. Then Moffitt wrote that it appears that Haas's "hands were not stuck to" the fan.[189]

Moffitt was prepared to reject the claim from Griffin that Haas had been stuck to the fan. The evidence from Say seemed to make that clear. Griffin had not yet provided any evidence from Haas for it. If Haas had been stuck to the fan, it could be argued that Merton had been stuck to the fan, as well, until he died.

---

[189] Moffitt letter to Griffin, October 4, 1969, Moffitt papers.

On October 6, Griffin made a slip-up and revealed that the statement by Haas had been handwritten, like the statement of Weist, and not typewritten. Griffin told Moffit that he did not think that they would find anything other than normal explanations. He said the best thing to do would be to give Moffitt copies of the witness statements in their own *handwriting*. Griffin wrote, "For example, Odo Haas in his *handwritten* testimony for the police states that his hands were stuck to the fan and the shock was great enough to make it impossible to release it."[190] (Emphasis added)

There is other evidence that the statement by Haas was handwritten. John Hagan, the American Consul General, in his letter to Abbot Flavian, December 27, 1968, said that he had enclosed letters "from those who found or examined the body." Flavian in a letter to Moffitt in December 1969, wrote that he had read and re-read "the handwritten reports of those who found Father first." Haas was one of those who found Merton first. On October 6, Griffin wrote that the testimony of Haas was handwritten, so both Griffin and Flavian indicated that they had a handwritten statement by Haas.

The only known handwritten statement that has surfaced was by Sr. Edeltrud Weist. The typewritten Haas document—which we believe we have established beyond reasonable doubt is fraudulent—was substituted for the handwritten Haas statement. This fake document was given to John Moffitt and later to Michael Mott when he replaced Griffin as the authorized biographer.[191]

---

[190] Griffin letter to Moffitt, October 6, 1969, Moffitt papers.

[191] Mott really ran with the information, writing that Haas was "...given an electric shock that jerked him sideways. He was held to the shaft of the fan until Father Celestine managed to unplug the fan at the outlet...," *The Seven Mountains of Thomas Merton*, Houghton Mifflin Company, p. 565. Interestingly, Mott does not cite the Haas document for that assertion, nor does he cite it anywhere else. That is likely because that document also says that "[Merton] was dressed only in his shorts." The shower story had not yet been invented when the Haas document was composed. Mott, knowing better, speculates that the naked body was likely dressed for modesty's sake before Say took his photograph of the body. Compounding his falsehoods, for his assertion that Haas was stuck to the fan, rather than Haas, he references a letter from Fr. Say to Abbot Flavian, which

Griffin said that he gave authorization for the likely Fox-composed fake statement to be sent to Moffitt, demonstrating the complicity of the two men in the attempted deception of Moffitt.[192] It is quite likely, then, that they also conspired in the creation of the false six-Trappist letter and the later removal the words, "in his pajamas," from the published version of the letter. Recall that the duplicitous Fox added the word "wet" to his own letter when it was published to make it appear that Merton's feet were wet and wrote falsely that the fan burned Merton's chest.

Brother Patrick's draft postscript for *The Asian Journal of Thomas Merton* repeated false information from Griffin about the times of events. The postscript also drew "facts" from the fake Haas document that the "fan was running" and that Haas received "a severe shock." As we said in chapter 5, Brother Patrick would write in 1998 that the shock Haas received had, in fact, been slight, but that was well after Fox's death in 1987, and Brother Patrick was free to write as he wished.

In a letter on October 24, Griffin arranged a meeting with Moffitt in New York during November. Griffin told Moffitt that he knew that he had received the "supplementary materials" from Gethsemani. According to Griffin he had authorized the Abbey of Gethsemani to put those materials at Moffitt's disposal. Griffin said that the abbey had received Moffitt's request "but had been reluctant to decide until getting my [Griffin's] opinion."

Griffin would sometimes use the official stationery with the Abbey of Gethsemani letterhead. This was the same stationery used by Fox, Brother Patrick, and the other monks. Griffin's letters on the Gethsemani letterhead may have impressed upon his recipients that he was speaking for the Abbey of Gethsemani. Who would have authorized Griffin to do this?

Griffin made the decision that the abbey would send some of the Merton death documents to Moffitt. Other materials remained secret.

---

cannot be true, because Say consistently maintained that Haas recoiled from the fan and Haas told him that it was only a slight shock when asked.

[192] Griffin letter to Moffitt, October 24, 1969, Moffitt papers.

Moffitt had asked for the reports of Say, Haas, Weist, de Grunne, and the police report. Moffitt only received the report of Weist, the fake Haas document, and the police report. Griffin took credit for the abbey sending the fake Haas document to Moffitt. If Griffin had the authority to release documents to Moffitt, he probably also had authority to withhold documents.

Moffitt did not save the cover letter from the abbey that accompanied the documents that he received, but we know that they were mailed to Moffitt by Brother Patrick. In another letter, Griffin explained to Moffitt why some documents were not included with those sent by Brother Patrick.[193]

As stated earlier, several important documents related to Merton's death that were at the abbey are missing. It is unfortunate that Griffin, who admitted to burning letters, was granted access to key documents concerning Merton's death, Merton's journals, and also to the fireplace at the hermitage. We might remind readers that we found Say's negatives, the property of the Abbey of Gethsemani, in the papers of John Howard Griffin at Columbia University after they had been missing for almost a half century.

Moffitt, exhibiting well-warranted suspicion of Griffin, marked seven things that did not ring true in the Haas document:

- He underlined the time "3 pm" because this was not the correct time that de Grunne told Say that he heard a shout. There was no shout.
- Moffitt wrote the words "not exact" in the margin where Haas said that de Grunne had gone "to get a key" to unlock Merton's door. Merton's door was secured with a latch and did not require a key.
- There was a question mark in the margin where it stated that the fan was "on the face or the head" of Merton. Moffitt knew this was wrong from the photograph taken by Say.

---

[193] Griffin letter to Moffitt, November 5, 1969, Moffitt papers.

- Moffitt underlined where it said that Say advised Haas to take photographs. It was the other way around.
- He underlined where Haas stated that the fan was still running. Say stated that it was not running.
- Moffitt underlined where Haas stated that he went to get Rev. Weakland. Say said that Abbot Egbert Donovan went to get Weakland.
- And probably most important, Moffitt underlined that, Haas stated "a strong electric shock...kept me from getting free of the fan." Say said that Haas recoiled from a shock and later told him that the shock was not strong. (See appendix 4.)

Moffitt marked only seven errors.[194] There were more. The document stated that four people including de Grunne entered Merton's room. De Grunne was not there, leaving only Say, Haas, and Donovan. De Grunne had continued to the main building after informing Haas and Donovan about Merton's troubled condition in his room. Moffitt might also have noticed that the statement had been typed with no signature and remembered that Griffin had told him that it was a handwritten statement. "What's with this fake document?" Moffitt might well have wondered.

November 1969

On November 5, Griffin told Moffitt that he had received his confidential letter which he had "read and then burned." We do not have a copy of the destroyed letter, but the response by Griffin provides some clues as to what may have been in Moffitt's letter. Since Griffin confirmed their plans to meet in New York during November, this had probably been discussed in the burned letter.

Griffin also responded to Moffitt's requests for the interview reports of Celestine Say and François de Grunne. In August, Griffin had told Moffitt that he had these documents. Moffit had asked for copies of these

---

[194] Moffitt copy of likely fake Haas document, Moffitt papers.

documents on August 31. Griffin's first excuse in September was that he "photographed the documents at Gethsemani," but unfortunately his developing solution was too weak. He promised to try again on September 15. On October 4, Moffitt asked again, and he did receive some documents at the end of October, but not the reports of Say and de Grunne.

In November, Griffin offered Moffitt new excuses for not sharing the reports of Say and de Grunne. Griffin contradicted what he had previously told Moffitt and said that "there was no statement from Fr. Say," adding that this surprised him.[195] Griffin had been very specific in August that "Father Say was extremely frank in his interview."[196] We don't know what was in Say's interview, but it most likely did not support the "accidental electrocution" story, explaining why it would be suppressed. In place of Say's interview, Griffin told Moffitt, "Fr. Say said a lot more to my investigator than he did to either of us in his letters."[197] But then Griffin did not tell Moffitt what it was that Say told his investigator. No report by Penn Jones on his trip to Asia has ever surfaced.

Griffin told Moffitt that Brother Patrick did not send him de Grunne's statement to the police because, "it said nothing at all."[198] This was another contradiction by Griffin, who had informed Moffitt on August, "I have read a good deal from de G and he sounds like a perfectly stable person to me – in fact I was most impressed."[199] It doesn't make sense that Griffin "was most impressed" by "nothing at all."

When Griffin first contacted Moffitt in August he wrote that there were unanswered questions and contradictions and that he had the responsibility to check them out thoroughly to allay suspicions and

---

[195] Griffin letter to Moffitt, November 5, 1969, Moffitt papers.
[196] Griffin letter to Moffitt, August 11, 1969, Moffitt papers.
[197] Griffin letter to Moffitt, November 5, 1969, Moffitt papers.
[198] Griffin letter to Moffitt, November 5, 1969, Moffitt papers.
[199] Griffin letter to Moffitt, August 18, 1969, Moffitt papers.

clarify the contradictions.[200] Now Griffin himself had become the source of contradictions, more, in fact, than when Griffin first contacted Moffitt.

Griffin had clearly had enough of Moffitt's questions and requests to see documents. He would not share the reports of Say and de Grunne. Griffin dismissed Moffitt saying, "Like you, I am persuaded that the seeming contradictions are not terribly important."[201] Griffin told Moffitt that the cause of Merton's death was "accidental electrocution" and that the supposed contradictions and unanswered questions would be ignored. Not surprisingly, Moffitt was not persuaded.

Griffin told Moffitt that he had changed his opinion about the time of death at 3:00 p.m. and offered new incorrect times moving the time of death to slightly before 3:00 p.m. Griffin still argued that de Grunne "heard Tom's cry."[202] Moffitt knew that the new times from Griffin were incorrect and that if Say did not hear any sound from Merton it was highly unlikely that de Grunne did, either.

Griffin's times were much later than Moffitt knew that they should be. Moffitt wrote to Griffin on November 22 and asked to see a copy of Say's June 25 letter that Griffin called a "detailed account," which Griffin then sent him. Moffitt saw there that Say's letter did not support the later times that Griffin had been telling Moffitt.

In November the Associated Press (AP) writer Bill Mann visited the Abbey of Gethsemani with an AP photographer. He interviewed John Howard Griffin and Griffin was photographed at Merton's hermitage. Mann's AP story about Griffin was published in Kentucky on November 23. The story reported that Merton's "life ended last December when he touched the exposed portion of an electric fan cord in Bangkok, Thailand."[203]

A few days later, Moffitt wrote to Griffin to tell him that he had seen the Associated Press article about Thomas Merton and John Howard

---

[200] Griffin letter to Moffitt, August 11, 1969, Moffitt papers.

[201] Griffin letter to Moffitt, November 5, 1969, Moffitt papers.

[202] Griffin letter to Moffitt, November 5, 1969, Moffitt papers.

[203] Bill Mann, Associated Press writer, *Messenger- Inquirer*, Owensboro, KY, November 23, 1969.

Griffin published in a Kentucky newspaper. Moffitt asked Griffin if the report that Merton died when he touched "an exposed portion of an electric fan cord" was a new development in Griffin's thinking or an invention of the reporter.[204] Moffitt stressed that he did not want to write that Merton died of electrocution if it could not be substantiated. Moffitt still had doubts that Merton had been killed by the fan.

Griffin denied that he was the source in the AP article that Merton died when he touched an exposed cord.[205] If Griffin was not the source, who was? Fox had written that he knew as early as December 10, 1968, that Merton "grabed [sic] a badly insulated hot wire."[206] The story that Merton touched an exposed cord had first been told by the AP's John Wheeler in his December 11, 1968, report, which he had attributed to an "anonymous Catholic source."[207] What possible legitimate reason could there have been for him not to have named that source if he really had one?

Griffin closed his letter by telling Moffitt that he had "no gross disagreement" with him. Then he added that there is no evidence of sudden heart failure and that there is "pretty overwhelming evidence that electric shock was the prime cause." Griffin was uncompromising in his insistence that Merton was accidentally electrocuted, although he did not provide any evidence that would dispel Moffitt's doubts.

December 1969

Unconvinced by Griffin, Moffitt continued to look for evidence. At the end of November, Moffitt wrote to Archabbot Egbert Donovan at the Saint Vincent Archabbey in Latrobe, Pennsylvania. Donovan had arrived at the scene of Thomas Merton's body with Say and Haas. Moffitt wanted

---

[204] Moffitt letter to Griffin, November 25, 1969, Moffitt papers.

[205] Griffin letter to Moffitt, November 28, 1969, Moffitt papers.

[206] James Fox, Letter to Gethsemani diaspora, February 1, 1969.

[207] John T. Wheeler, "Thomas Merton Dies in Electrocution Accident," Associated Press, December 11, 1968.

to know what Donovan remembered about the times of the events, if he saw burns on Merton's hands, and any other details.

Donovan's reply, dated December 5, 1969, is the only known account of what Donovan witnessed. He told Moffitt about the strange way that de Grunne approached them, half walking and half running and swinging his camera. At first, they thought that he was going to ask to take their picture. Donovan said that he vividly remembered the conversation because it was very odd under the circumstances. De Grunne opened the conversation with these words, "Pardon me, did you have a nice swim?" Haas and Donovan affirmed that their swim had been enjoyable. De Grunne then said, "Well pardon me, I must speak to you of a matter of a serious nature. He then told them that "he had heard this thump," tried to enter Merton's room and found it locked. He peeked inside and was worried that something had happened to Merton.[208]

At that point, about 4 pm, Donovan and Haas ran to Merton's cottage where they joined Say and entered Merton's room. Donovan told Moffitt that he could not confirm or deny that there were any burns on Merton's hands. He did write, "I can assure you that his arms were straight and lying at his side—a fact that somewhat puzzled me. I have been personally puzzled by the fact that his arms were in the position in which they were. It seems to me that if he was in any way touching the fan or had pulled it over on himself in falling, his hands hardly would have been in the position in which they were found."

In early December, Griffin wrote a short note telling Moffitt that when Penn Jones took photographs at the Red Cross Center in the spring, the "old enormous Hitachi fan" was still there.[209] Griffin was still trying to convince Moffitt that Merton died by accidental electrocution. It isn't clear why Griffin waited until December to tell Moffitt about photographs of the fan taken by Jones in the spring and then not share the pictures. This note confirmed that Penn Jones was the name of

---

[208] Egbert Donovan letter to john Moffitt, December 5, 1969, Moffitt papers.
[209] Griffin note to Moffitt, December 5, 1969, Moffitt papers.

Griffin's "investigator" who visited the Philippines and Thailand in the spring of 1969.

Griffin had hoped to bring Moffitt around to the conclusion of "accidental electrocution," but Moffitt continued to raise more questions and point out more contradictions. Moffitt wrote to Griffin again on December 7 to return Say's June 25 letter to Griffin, as Griffin had requested. Moffitt retained a copy for his files.

Moffitt told Griffin that there was no need for him to respond, and he then quoted the times in Say's letter as evidence that Merton and de Grunne left the lunchroom at 1:40 pm and not at 2:10 pm, as Griffin had been saying. Moffitt himself remembered that lunch was at 1:00 pm and he did not think that Merton would have lingered for more than an hour. He suggested that Griffin recheck his reports that contradict Say, because he had the utmost confidence in Say. Moffitt told Griffin that he would like to know the source of the incorrect departure time of 2:10 for Merton and de Grunne.

Moffitt enclosed the letter that he had received from Egbert Donovan to share with Griffin. Moffitt added this tease, "I am on the track of some other interesting clues, which I somehow failed to note and bring up when I saw you."[210] In September Griffin had confidently told Brother Patrick that Moffitt's speculations had easily been taken care of, but Moffit had not given up.

Moffitt wrote to Fr. Say at the end of November to ask him the same questions that he had asked Donovan. Moffitt wanted to know if Say had seen burns on Merton's hands and if he would go over the times of the events and details again.

Say replied on December 11, and told Moffitt, "Definitely, I do not remember seeing any burns in his palms." Say went over the times of events again, confirming that Merton may have died a few minutes before or after 2 pm. Moffitt probably asked Say if Haas had been stuck to the fan, because Say repeated that Haas had recoiled from the fan and that Haas told him that the shock "was not very strong."

---

[210] Moffitt letter to Griffin, December 7, 1969, Moffitt papers.

Moffitt may have also asked Say if the body was wet because Say told him, "I remember that his body was dry." Griffin's agent Penn Jones must have made an impression upon Say because he told Moffitt again about the American journalist [Penn Jones] who told him that Merton may have been a victim of those who opposed his views and that his death may have been tied to the assassinations of Kennedy and Martin Luther King.[211]

When Griffin unwisely revealed that Penn Jones was the name of his investigator, Moffitt had enough information to make the connection that Griffin's own agent had told Say that Merton may have been assassinated. Moffitt must have wondered what Griffin and his man Jones were up to.

In 1970, the Notre Dame University Press was set to publish Moffitt's account of the proceedings at the monastic conference where Merton had died. Moffitt felt obligated to include with it an account of Merton's death. As the publication deadline drew near, Moffitt was still seeking a way to make sense of what had happened.

Moffitt Writes Abbot Flavian

On December 11, Moffitt decided to approach Abbot Flavian at Gethsemani. He knew that Griffin was working with Flavian, but Moffitt wanted to know Flavian's thoughts on Merton's death. The letter began with an amiable mention of a poem honoring Thomas Merton that was published in *America* magazine on the anniversary of Merton's death. Moffitt then changed the subject, saying that the purpose of his letter was not about the poem but concerned the manner of Thomas Merton's death.

Moffitt told Flavian that what he would share should remain completely confidential between them. He wrote that he knew that the abbot was aware of his constant communication with John Howard

---

[211] Say letter to Moffitt, December 11, 1969, Moffitt papers.

Griffin. Moffitt reminded the abbot that he had lodged in the cottage above the room where Merton died.

Moffitt revealed that from the moment he learned of Merton's death in Thailand "he had received the strong intuition that more than an electrocution occurred." However, in talking to John Howard Griffin, he had the impression that Griffin was convinced that there was no other cause than electrocution (emphasis by Moffitt). Moffitt told the abbot that his difficulty was that he had an obligation to present "a factual account" of what happened on December 10.

Moffitt told Flavian that he was at his disposal and that he would not want to write anything that would go against the abbot's wishes. Then Moffitt added that, "I do not wish to state something that I do not feel to be true: namely, that Fr. Louis died simply of an electrocution, because I do not feel that such a statement can be honestly made."[212]

Moffitt told Flavian that he needed his help and that anything the abbot might tell him would not be used without permission. Moffitt then added that what he was about to say should be in absolute confidence, "as if [he] were making a confession" to Abbot Flavian. Then Moffitt told Flavian that one of the organizers of the conference also believed that the electrocution was the immediate but not the only cause of Merton's death. This person thought that "a cardiac crisis is a cause just as plausible as electrocution."

Moffitt wanted the approval of Abbot Flavian to state in his published account that there is a strong possibility that Merton suffered a heart attack accompanied by an electric shock. Then Moffitt could rationalize how the fan came to be on top of Merton because he could have grabbed it during his heart attack and pulled it on top of himself, and at the same time cause a frayed wire to electrify the fan. In summary, Moffitt tells Flavian that he had already worded his account to state that "it is impossible to say if it was a heart attack or electrocution." Moffitt wanted Flavian's approval to state this.

---

[212] Moffitt letter to Abbot Flavian Burns, December 11, 1969.

152

CHAPTER 14

The Abbey's United Front

December 15, 1969

O n December 15, Abbot Flavian promptly responded to Moffitt's letter and told him that at Gethsemani they were quite certain that Fr. Louis' heart was in good condition. Flavian told Moffitt that he agreed with Griffin. Flavian said that all they could do was guess, and his guess was that Merton undressed, bathed, and tried to move the fan. Flavian added that there were "no fuses." He told Moffitt that his guesses came from poring over the handwritten reports of the primary witnesses.[213]

---

[213] Flavian Burns letter to John Moffitt, December 15, 1969, Moffitt papers. We may contrast this response to Moffitt with what we find in Chapter 4. Recall that Abbot Flavian later wrote that he had called the U.S. Embassy in Thailand and had been told that Merton had died from an accident; and James Fox, in his February 1 letter to the diaspora, was very explicit in what he said the embassy had told Flavian about how Merton had been electrocuted by the faulty fan when he tried to move it. Why, we must wonder, would Flavian have relied on

Flavian was united with both Fox and Griffin. Flavian cited the secret documents held by the abbey as evidence. Brother Patrick also used this same strategy. Flavian used his authority as the abbot to dismiss Moffitt by saying that his guesses were based on the reports. But, in fact, the official reports contain no evidence that Merton "bathed and tried to move the fan." There are no witness statements to support these claims by Flavian. There is no evidence that there were "no fuses." Abbot Flavian's strategy was either to persuade Moffitt to believe that he had such evidence or simply to convince him that the death story was immutable, for whatever reason, and that it was, at best, futile to challenge it.

If there had been any evidence to support what Flavian wrote to Moffitt, the abbey certainly would have made it available as proof that Merton died by accidental electrocution. Say's letters and photographs reveal the deceit of Fox, Griffin, Flavian, and Brother Patrick. That is obviously why Griffin told his companions "...these photos and negatives should be kept from publication – at least for many years and probably never."[214] Later Griffin stressed to Brother Patrick, "They should be kept by you, deeply hidden...this kind of thing should not, I feel, be made available to anyone."[215]

The only handwritten report that the abbey released was by Edeltrud Weist. Her report does not say that Merton was undressed, bathed, moved the fan or that there were no fuses.

There were six letters by Say that we know of, but only four are available; one that was sent to Flavian and another that was sent to Griffin remain secret. Say's letters are very specific, and he made it clear that Merton took no shower. His photographs prove that Merton was not undressed for bathing because he was wearing shorts, and there was nothing about fuses in any of his letters or in any of the known official reports.

---

guesswork to explain Merton's accidental death in his response to Moffitt, not mentioning these "facts" if they were true?

[214] Griffin letter to Flavian and Brother Patrick, June 30, 1969, Griffin papers.
[215] Griffin letter to Brother Patrick, July 24, 1969, Griffin papers.

Flavian did not approve of Moffitt's wish to say that it was impossible to know if the cause of death "was a heart attack or electrocution." Flavian, Griffin, and Fox were committed to the accidental electrocution story, consistent with what John Wheeler had written in that initial Associated Press report based upon anonymous sources, containing provably false information, and taking no note of the official statement that Merton had died of sudden heart failure.[216] Fox had taken the lead at the abbey in announcing the "accidental electrocution" in his letter on February 1, 1969. Just as Flavian would later tell Moffitt, Fox had written that this was based on "reports received." The official reports that did not conclude that the cause of death was "accidental electrocution" were kept secret.

Fox, Griffin, Flavian, and Brother Patrick would all continue to state publicly that the reports supported "accidental electrocution" as the cause of Merton's death. They were confident that those reports and Say's photographs would remain unpublished. Later, they would invent additional stories that Merton was wet from a shower and that he was a klutz, as further "evidence" that Merton died by "accidental electrocution."

Flavian's letter to Moffitt affirmed that Fox, Griffin, and Flavian rejected the official cause of death as stated on the Thai death certificate and on the Foreign Service Report from the U.S. Embassy in Thailand. They would all ignore the Thai police report that stated Merton had died before he encountered the fan.

Abbot Flavian's dishonesty about what was stated in the reports and witness statements casts serious doubt on Flavian's story that the U.S. Embassy told him that Merton's death was "accidental." We have seen nothing to support it. He never provided the name of the person that he spoke to. The U.S. Embassy was specific in its Foreign Service Report, that Merton's death was caused by "Sudden heart failure (according to the official death certificate)." The embassy was also specific that the

---

[216] John T. Wheeler, "Thomas Merton Dies in Electrocution Accident," Associated Press, December 11, 1968.

source for the cause of death in its report was the death certificate. There is no reason to believe that the embassy would have told Flavian anything different.

Flavian Failed to Order an Autopsy

Flavian had the authority to request an autopsy to determine the exact cause of death, but he didn't. So, as matters stood, he came closest to the truth when he wrote to Moffitt, "As for the accident itself, the best we can do is guess."

What kind of family member would be satisfied to simply guess how their loved one had died, especially under mysterious circumstances that demand answers? It was not necessary to guess. It should not have been the best that they could do. Putting yourself in their position, in effect, as a bereaved family member, you can easily see it was the worst thing you could have done. The situation virtually screamed for an autopsy, something that the puzzled witnesses fully expected to take place. Was Merton's cause of death related to that odd bleeding wound in the back of his head? An autopsy would almost certainly have given a definitive answer to that question.

Flavian knew that he had the responsibility to order an autopsy to determine the cause of Merton's death. The Thai officials also had a duty to order an autopsy. The Thai officials falsified their reports to state that an autopsy had been performed at a hospital. Similarly, as we have noted, the story that was almost certainly written at the abbey and supplied to *The Kentucky Standard* in Bardstown reported, "An autopsy was performed in Oakland, Calif. before the body was flown to Louisville..." There is no evidence that there was any autopsy in Oakland. Abbot Flavian's statement in 1984 that he had requested an autopsy, leaving the impression that there had been one, had a similar deceptive purpose.

Moffitt Caves In

Moffitt finally capitulated, apparently bowing to the will of Abbot Flavian. At the end of December, Moffitt wrote to Griffin and conceded that he had been incorrect to think that a heart attack may have caused Merton's death. His letter included a long quote from Flavian in which the abbot stated that he agreed with Griffin. Flavian had insisted that Merton had no heart trouble. Moffitt wrote that he would not do anything to "undermine what Fr. Flavian told [him]." Moffitt wrote that he was finished investigating if Merton had any heart problems.[217]

Moffitt enclosed the letters that he had received from Donovan and Say. He mentioned that Say "definitely" did not see burns on Merton's hands. Following up on what Griffin had said previously, Moffitt asked Griffin if his investigator (Penn Jones) learned anything and if he took any pictures. Moffitt added a "p.s." to say, that there was "no need to burn this" letter.

In early January, Griffin replied, stressing Flavian's point again that Merton had no heart trouble because it was not mentioned in his journals.[218] He did not comment on the letters Moffitt had sent to him from Say and Donovan. Moffitt had asked Griffin if there was a report or any photographs from his investigator Penn Jones. Griffin ignored Moffitt's question.

---

[217] Moffitt letter to Griffin, December 28, 1969, Moffitt papers.
[218] John Howard Griffin letter to John Moffitt, January 5, 1970, Moffitt papers.

CHAPTER 15

The Books by Moffitt and Griffin

In 1970 John Moffitt and John Howard Griffin would each release books that would comment on the death of Thomas Merton. Moffitt's was one he edited, *A New Charter for Monasticism*, which was on the proceedings of the monastic conference in Thailand on December 9-15, 1968. Moffitt furnished the introduction and three pages at the end of the book titled, "The Death of Father Louis."

This time, Moffitt's account of Merton's death did include the names of the witnesses who were at the scene, except for that of Sr. Edeltrud Weist, whom he just calls a sister from South Korea who was a doctor, and he accurately gave the times of events that Merton left the dining hall at 1:40 pm, arriving at the cottage with de Grunne at about 2:00 pm. Say arrived at the cottage a few minutes later.

However, Moffitt stopped very short of revealing everything that he knew. He did not mention that Say took photographs of the scene before anything was disturbed. He didn't reveal that he had one of those photographs, so he did not describe the picture. Moffitt also did not say anything about the wound on the back of Merton's head that he had to know about from Weist's report. He also left out the very crucial information that there was no autopsy.

Moffitt not only withheld information, but he also added false information. Moffitt had received two letters from Say, and he had read Say's letter to Griffin, so he knew that Odo Haas recoiled when he touched the fan. Say wrote, "Later I asked him if the shock was strong, he said that it was not very strong."[219] Weist in her statement had also called it a "slight electric shock." Moffitt knew, then, that the shock was not very strong. In his final analysis Moffitt wrote the opposite of what he knew to be true. Moffitt wrote that Odo Haas, "received a strong shock and his hands became paralyzed by the current. As quickly as he could the Philippine prior unplugged the fan from the wall."

Moffitt had to have taken that false information from the fake Haas document. As we have seen, Moffitt put question marks and underlinings on things that Griffin sent him that he thought were not true. For public consumption, though, he ended up going even further than Brother Patrick was willing to go in his postscript to *The Asian Journal of Thomas Merton*, who would write only that Haas received a "strong shock." Moffitt knew just as Brother Patrick knew that the story of Odo Haas being stuck to the fan was not true, but he wrote it anyway.

Moffitt accurately stated that the Thai doctor's report said that Merton's death was the result of "acute cardiac failure and electric shock." He was right about that, but he also had a copy of the police report that stated that the same Thai physician said that Merton was already dead of heart failure before he encountered the fan.

Moffitt concluded his report by quoting Sister Pia Valeri, a nun who had been at the conference but was not a witness at the scene of Merton's death. Sister Pia learned that some pills were found in Merton's luggage, and she assumed that it may have been heart medication. Merton had not been taking heart medication. He had been

---

[219] Fr. Celestine Say letter to John Moffitt, December 11, 1969, Moffitt papers.

160

taking pills for stomach and intestinal conditions.[220] Moffitt had accepted Sister Pia's guess to build his own theory that a heart attack caused Merton to fall, grab and damage the fan.

Abbot Flavian had told Moffitt that he disagreed with his heart attack theory. Flavian assured Moffitt that Merton had no heart trouble, and he took no heart medication.[221] By quoting Mother Pia Valeri, Moffitt let her make the argument for him. Moffitt called her statement a "balanced comment." Pia said that no one could say with certainty if Merton died by heart failure or electrocution and that it may have been both.

This was Moffitt's final public word on Merton's death. Moffitt knew that documents were being kept secret and he knew about the secret photographs. Moffitt was careful not to mention secret documents like the police report that the abbey had shared with him. Moffitt never revealed anything that he knew was being kept secret. No one mentioned the police report publicly until 1973 when Brother Patrick, to build his reputation as an authority on Merton's death, stated in his postscript to *The Asian Journal of Thomas Merton* that he had read it.

Griffin had remained at the Abbey of Gethsemani for a few days following Merton's funeral. At that time, he met with Abbot Flavian and Brother Patrick discussing photographs that Merton had taken and others that he had taken of Merton. Griffin said that from these discussions he got the idea for a picture book.[222]

When Griffin was chosen in April 1969 by the Merton Legacy Trust to be the official Merton biographer, he had asked trustees James Laughlin and Naomi Stone to act as his agent with Houghton Mifflin for his book of pictures.[223] In anticipation of the unauthorized biography of Merton by Edward Rice there was an urgency to publish Griffin's book. Brother Patrick wrote to Griffin to tell him that Naomi "was giving Houghton

---

[220] Thomas Merton letter to Elsie Hauck Holahan Jenkins, June 16, 1965, *Road to Joy: Letters to New and Old Friends*, Farrar, Straus & Giroux, 1989.

[221] Flavian Burns letter to Moffitt, December 15, 1969, Moffitt papers.

[222] *A Hidden Wholeness: The Visual World of Thomas Merton*, Houghton Mifflin, 1970, p. 5.

[223] Griffin letter to Naomi Burton Stone, April 23, 1969, Griffin papers.

Mifflin a push on that so it gets out at least simultaneously with Ed Rice's thing."[224]

The resulting book, *A Hidden Wholeness: The Visual World of Thomas Merton*, is an oversized and expensive coffee-table style book, mainly of photographs taken by Griffin and Merton. It has only a few pages of text about Thomas Merton. Most of the book consists of photographs of Merton that were taken by Griffin and some photographs of Merton with friends. There are also photographs taken by Merton of nature, his hermitage, and peeling paint. In the book's epilogue, Griffin mentions Merton's death on December 10, 1968. In his one brief passage on the death, he manages to write a falsehood, saying only that Merton "was found dead on the floor of his room with a large stand-up electric fan lying across his chest."[225] This story originated in the fake six Trappist letter. Fox, recall, had written similarly in his February 1, 1969, letter to the Gethsemani diaspora that Merton's chest had been burned deeply, and on the tenth anniversary of Merton's death Fox would repeat his story about the fan lying "across his exposed breast, burning a deep red line into his flesh."[226]

Griffin, as we know, had examined the official Thai reports and witness accounts. He had seen the photographs of Merton's body that were taken by Say before anything was moved. Griffin had to know that the fan was not found lying across Merton's chest, yet he put this false information in his book. The purpose of this invention that the fan was across Merton's chest was undoubtedly to neutralize the Thai authorities' conclusion that Merton had died of heart failure. That supposedly strong electric charge in proximity to Merton's heart was more likely to have caused it to fail than if it were lower down on his body. Never mind that Haas had told Say that the shock was not strong when he recoiled from the fan and the Thai police report stated explicitly that Merton was already dead from heart failure before he encountered the fan. The public had not yet been told either of those facts.

---

[224] Br. Patrick Hart letter to Griffin, October 4, 1969, Griffin papers.
[225] *A Hidden Wholeness*, p. 143.
[226] Lucas, p. 334.

162

During 1969 both Moffitt and Griffin had spent months studying and discussing the evidence from witnesses and the official records. They both had seen Say's photograph. In 1970, though, they both published books that concealed this evidence, while writing things about Merton's death that they knew were not true.

In reflecting upon Moffitt's radical about face, from seeming to be a sincere seeker of the truth about Merton's death to being just one more participant in the cover-up, we might try to put ourselves in his shoes when he was in his earlier mode, exchanging letters with Griffin. He would have still been in Thailand when John T. Wheeler's AP report on Merton's death had saturated the American public with the initial story that Merton had been accidentally electrocuted. He might have even read the English-language Thai newspaper, *The Bangkok Post*, which doubtless would have been the primary source of news available at the conference he was attending with Merton and the others. It reported in a short notice on page 5 of its December 12 edition that Merton had died of a heart attack, with no mention of any fan or accident.[227] He also would not likely have seen Abbot Fox's February 1 letter pushing the accidental electrocution story nor the six Trappists letter that reinforced it to a degree.[228]

---

[227] John Howard Griffin, *The Hermitage Journals: A Diary Kept While Working on the Biography of Thomas Merton* (Edited by Conger Beasley, Jr.), Image Books, 1983, p. 4. Griffin's source for that information is an article entitled *"Dernier Souvenirs,"* in French by the conference attendee, Jean Leclercq. He does not say where the article appeared.

[228] Heretofore we have suggested that the Trappists' letter, in the absence of an original document and for several other reasons, was wholly spurious. That is not necessarily so, any more than the typewritten Haas statement was a complete invention. In the original letter sent around privately by the abbey, the British spelling "centre" is used. In the version that was published in *The Asian Journal of Thomas Merton* the spelling has been Americanized to "center." None of the remaining Trappists at the conference was an American. There likely was a letter of some sort, but who knows what it said and how many of the Trappists signed on to it? Just as the editors of the *Asian Journal* removed "in his pajamas" from what the abbey had sent around, the abbey could have doctored such an original letter any way they wanted to before first sharing it privately for the purpose of reinforcing the accidental electrocution story.

In short, Moffitt might not have grasped the futility of any honest inquiry into Merton's death. He might not have known how thoroughly the fix was in, how powerful were the forces working against the truth. Just from examining the record of his letters, it appears that his epiphany came when he wrote Abbot Flavian and got Flavian's response, which backed John Howard Griffin's interpretation of things to the hilt, however unsupported Griffin's conclusions might have been.

We can only speculate about what other reasons there might have been for Moffitt's transformation. He was a journalist, after all, based in New York City and writing for the Jesuit-run *America* magazine. Perhaps Griffin put in a word with the folks who were pulling his own strings, and they then leaned on Moffitt's employer. Maybe someone like Merton Legacy Trustee James Laughlin, at the suggestion of someone in Griffin's orbit, invited Moffitt to lunch and explained the lay of the land to him. Nothing needed to be in writing. There didn't even need to be an explicit threat. In the end, it probably wouldn't have taken very much to get Moffitt to write what he knew was not true. All his truth-seeking had been private, after all, and even in the letters—at least in the ones that didn't get burned—he steered carefully away from the subject of the wound in the back of Merton's head and what might have caused it. As far as he ever seemed willing to go, even privately, was that the cause of death might well have been heart failure or a heart attack instead of accidental electrocution.

In August of 1970 Moffitt traveled to Rome and met with Rembert Weakland. After his journey, Moffitt wrote a two-page paper titled, "Reflections on the death of Thomas Merton." In parentheses Moffitt typed, "Not to be shared with others" and he sent his reflections to Griffin and Brother Patrick.

Moffitt's first paragraph concluded with this statement, "I believe that no one can state with assurance what caused the fall." Sr. Weist, who had arrived at Merton's body with Weakland, concluded that Merton must have fallen "for some reason" and that reason was not known.

Moffitt also reflected on the falling of the fan. He wrote, "how could the fan have fallen?" Moffitt wondered how a falling fan becomes

164

electrified. If Merton had not grabbed the fan, thought Moffitt, "there is no logical reason for the fan to have fallen."

Moffitt never considered the possibility, if not the likelihood, at least not in any written record that we could find, that someone had placed the fan on top of Merton to make his death appear to have been an accident.

Moffitt thought of as many possible explanations as he could, excluding foul play. In the end, Moffitt concluded with what Weakland had said to him at the time of Merton's death, "Perhaps we should just accept it as a spiritual mystery."

Though he would never concede privately that accidental electrocution was the cause of death, nor that Merton had taken a shower and was wet when he encountered the fan, in the end, he kept his misgivings to himself. As a writer for *America* magazine, Moffitt might be considered a part of the mainstream media, and to this day not one person in the mainstream media has broken ranks with John T. Wheeler's original incorrect, unsourced story about Thomas Merton's death, and it would be unrealistic to have expected John Moffitt to be the first.

Griffin never wrote a biography of Thomas Merton. Only in 1983, three years after Griffin's death, was the product of his years of labor published under the title, *Follow the Ecstasy: Thomas Merton, The Hermitage Years, 1965-1968.* Michael W. Higgins in his review concluded that what had been produced under Griffin's name could hardly be described as biography but rather was little more than a well-written paraphrase of Merton's journals from the period.[229] Since it was

---

[229] *The Merton Seasonal,* Volume 9, Winter-Spring 1984, "Testament of Griffin's Friendship," http://merton.org/ITMS/Seasonal/09/9-1Higgins.pdf. The origin of Griffin's book title is of some interest. The notable Chilean poet Nicanor Parra and Merton's publisher James Laughlin had driven Merton to a furtive meeting in Louisville with the young, attractive nurse, Margie Smith, with whom Merton had fallen in love. Laughlin didn't think well of what they had done, but Parra was delighted and said something along the lines of "one must follow the ecstasy," doubtless translated from the Spanish as Merton recalled it. This vignette is from page 65 of the updated version, *Follow the Ecstasy: The Hermitage Years of Thomas Merton,* edited and with a foreword by Robert

virtually just a paraphrase of Merton's journals, one might even wonder how much of it might actually have been written by its editor, Robert Bonazzi. Bonazzi and Griffin had had a long association, all the way back to 1966.[230]

Poor health or not or whether he was the primary writer of *Follow the Ecstasy* or not, Griffin was no biographer, but his early selection as Merton's "official biographer" positioned him perfectly for orchestrating the cover-up of Merton's murder, as we have seen. He was also well situated to see to it that whatever there was in Merton's writings that the abbey or Griffin's handlers didn't want to get out suffered the fate of all those letters that Griffin suggested should be burned.

Eight years after he had been named the authorized biographer people grew tired of waiting, or, at least, that was the story. In 1977, an attorney representing the Merton Legacy Trust notified Griffin that he had been removed as the official biographer. He was ordered to return all materials or reproductions of materials belonging to the Merton Legacy Trust.[231] The negatives that Fr. Celestine Say sent to Abbot Flavian were the property of the Abbey of Gethsemani. In 2017, we discovered the negatives that Griffin had told Brother Patrick should be "deeply hidden" among the papers of John Howard Griffin at Columbia University.

Bonazzi, Orbis Books, 1993. Since Griffin had been dead for three years when the book was published, he can hardly be blamed for the unfortunate choice of a title.

[230] Richard Marc Rains, "Publisher Gives Authors Latitude," *Fort Worth Star-Telegram*, August 3, 1990.

[231] John J. Ford, counsel for the Merton Legacy Trust letter to John Howard Griffin, February 11, 1977.

CHAPTER 16

Brother Patrick Hart

Brother Patrick took the Cistercian habit in 1951 and his solemn vows in 1957. That same year he became the secretary to Abbot James Fox. For ten years Brother Patrick served as Fox's secretary where he witnessed firsthand the turbulent relationship between Merton and "his nemesis." Merton would request a transfer to the Carthusians or another more contemplative order, Fox would refuse the request and tell Merton that he was not following the will of God, and this would be repeated. Brother Patrick was assigned to handle Merton's manuscripts for censorship, he delivered Merton's mail, and relayed calls and messages from Fox. Brother Patrick may have delivered the message to Merton that his book *Peace in the Post Christian Era* could not be published because "it falsifies the monastic message," according to the order of Dom Gabriel Sortais, Abbot General of the Cistercian Order.

When invitations were sent to Merton they were blocked by Fox. Fox convinced others, and perhaps himself, that he was acting to save Merton's eternal soul. Fox would undermine Merton's reputation by telling people that Merton was mentally unstable and that he needed Fox's protection. Brother Patrick witnessed these events firsthand.

In 1966, Merton described how Brother Patrick's eyes looked away in discomfort when they met.[232] Fox's secretary, as Merton put it, would give him a smile of embarrassment over all that he knew but pretended not to know.[233] Later that year Brother Patrick went to work and study at the headquarters of the Cistercian Order in Rome.

With Brother Patrick at the Generalate in Rome were other monks from Gethsemani. One day they were at lunch with Timothy Kelly, also from Gethsemani. After complaining about the food and the Master of the Students, the topic turned to their common source of angst back at Gethsemani, Abbot James Fox. As the monks exchanged incidents, it turned into a game of "Can you top this?" Brother Patrick hurriedly left the table. Later when Kelly asked Brother Patrick why he had left. Brother Patrick said that he only had gratitude for Abbot Fox.[234]

Clearly, Brother Patrick's warm feelings toward Fox were not shared by Merton and other monks in the community. Merton wrote that Fox was detested by many of the monks who were embarrassed by his vanity and his boasting about his importance.[235] When the time for Merton's big trip drew near, Brother Patrick was recalled from Rome to serve as Merton's secretary while he was away.

Merton's Secretary?

Following Merton's death, Brother Patrick, the loyal secretary to James Fox, was refashioned into the secretary of Thomas Merton. Brother Patrick had served Fox for many years and was assigned to be Merton's secretary a few months before Merton left Gethsemani in September of 1968. Following Merton's death, Abbot Flavian entrusted Brother

---

[232] Thomas Merton, *The Journals of Thomas Merton Book 6, Learning to Love,* HarperOne Kindle edition, 2010, p. 84.

[233] *Learning to Love,* p. 304.

[234] Timothy Kelly, O.C.S.O., "Homily for the Funeral Mass of Br. Patrick Hart," February 28, 2019.

[235] *Learning to Love,* p. 164.

Patrick with the responsibility of the Merton legacy and to work with the Merton Legacy Trust.[236] Brother Patrick would locate in Merton's vast trove new literary material for publication. Through Brother Patrick's efforts over a period of many years, royalties from Merton's literary work continued to flow into Gethsemani.

There is a popular photograph of Brother Patrick and Merton together. *The Merton Seasonal* dedicated the Summer 2019 issue to Brother Patrick and published the photograph of Brother Patrick and Merton. It cements in the public mind the false impression that they were friends. Among the books we find that photograph featured are the authorized biography of Merton by Michael Mott and the biography of James Fox by F. Dean Lucas.

Brother Patrick Hart, Fr. Thomas Merton, Brother Maurice Flood

The photograph was taken on the day of Merton's departure from Gethsemani. In the original picture, Br. Maurice Flood was standing on the other side of Merton. Flood was also a secretary to Thomas Merton. [237] Flood is often cropped out of the picture. Br. Philip Stark, another

---

[236] Timothy Kelly, O.C.S.O., "Homily."
[237] Cistercian Father Maurice Flood Dies at 85, *Arlington Catholic Herald*, September 7, 2021.

secretary to Merton, took the photograph with Merton's camera. Their goal was to use up the film that was remaining in Merton's camera before he left on his journey. Merton invited his three secretaries, Flood, Brother Patrick, and Stark to his hermitage to celebrate his final Mass before his departure. Following Merton's death, only Brother Patrick retained the title of "Merton's secretary," and the cropped photograph rounds out the picture.

In the *Merton Seasonal* issue devoted to Brother Patrick, Mary Somerville, a member of the Merton Legacy Trust, recalled this supposed Merton friend with his "candor and sly sense of humor" telling a group of people that Merton's death resulted from the fact that he was an accident-prone klutz.[238] Brother Patrick was echoing his mentor. We learn from Fox's biographer, Lucas, that there were some of the monks at Gethsemani who speculated that there might have been a conspiracy behind Merton's death, but that this was not the consensus, because those who knew Merton best were familiar with his "accidental ways." To drive the point home, he tells of a visit to Dom James sometime after Merton's death by Ann Skakel McCooey, who asked him if he was surprised at what had happened. Fox responded that he was not, telling her that the man was not "mechanically inclined."[239]

Abbot Flavian Burns pushed the same line in an article published later in a book. He used the fact that Merton never learned to drive to show that he was impractical with mechanical things, overlooking the fact that his life had been such that he was never in a position where he needed to know how to drive. Then he went completely off the deep end by volunteering that many at the monastery were surprised that Merton had not suffered his fatal accident sooner at his hermitage, as clumsy and inept as he was.[240]

From 1969 to 2013 Brother Patrick served as secretary for successive Gethsemani abbots: Flavian Burns, Timothy Kelly, Damien

---

[238] From the compilation edited by Patrick O'Connell, "Heart to Hart: Memories and Reflections," *The Merton Seasonal*, Summer 2019, p. 52.

[239] Lucas, p. 162.

[240] Wilkes, pp. 105-06.

Thompson, and Elias Dietz. In 1974 he joined the board of directors of Cistercian Publications. Brother Patrick edited numerous books by and about Merton. He was a founding member of the International Thomas Merton Society and founding co-editor of *The Merton Annual*.

He often acted as spokesman for the abbey on Merton's death. Brother Patrick consistently maintained that the reports said the cause of death was "accidental electrocution." Donna Kristoff, O.S.U., coordinator of the Cleveland Chapter of the ITMS, wrote that Brother Patrick was a man to be trusted.[241] We might observe that it depends on what is meant by the term, "trusted." Brother Patrick was certainly trusted to perpetuate the "accidental electrocution" story by concealing Say's photographs, witness accounts, and official documents, and, above all, by inventing the shower story.

No one believed that Brother Patrick would lie. Jim Forest, Merton's friend, wrote in a letter published in the *Catholic Worker*, "Anyone who knew Brother Pat knows he was as honest a man as you and I are ever likely to meet."[242] Michael Plekon, a professor emeritus of Sociology and Religion and an Orthodox priest wrote that one of Brother Patrick's greatest gifts was his honesty.[243]

February 5, 1970

On February 5, almost one year after Fox had sent his letter first announcing that Merton had died by "accidental electrocution," Brother Patrick sent Moffitt a draft copy of his foreword and postscript to be published in *The Asian Journal of Thomas Merton*. Brother Patrick asked for Moffitt's thoughts and comments. There were three statements in the postscript that Moffitt challenged, the cause of Merton's death, that Merton had taken a shower, and the time of Merton's death.[244]

---

[241] Donna Kristoff, O.S.U., from "Heart to Hart," p. 45.

[242] Jim Forest, letter to editor, *Catholic Worker*, Spring 2020.

[243] Michael Plekon, from "Heart to Hart," p. 51. At this point an old Groucho Marx line comes to mind, "Integrity is everything. If you can fake integrity, you've really got it made."

[244] Moffitt letter to Brother Patrick, February 8, 1970, Moffitt papers.

Brother Patrick was not a superior at the abbey and he could not have shared any documents concerning Merton's death with people outside the abbey, including Moffitt, without permission. Brother Patrick did not have the independent authority to make decisions on the question of when and how Merton died, and that applies to the question of whether he had taken a shower. Brother Patrick very likely had a guiding hand behind what he wrote—or signed off on—in the postscript.

There is evidence that John Howard Griffin may have been, at the very least, assisting Brother Patrick with both his foreword and postscript to *The Asian Journal of Thomas Merton*. In December of 1969, Brother Patrick sent a note to Griffin telling him that John Laughlin "liked the foreword and postscript." Brother Patrick told Griffin that he had been worried about what the reaction of Laughlin might be.[245]

Whoever doctored the six Trappists letter very likely assisted in getting it into *The Asian Journal of Thomas Merton*. The letter complemented Patrick's postscript shower story and Fox's revised letter that said that Merton's feet were "wet." The six Trappist letter said that the fan was on Merton's chest, and this agreed with Fox's false statement that Merton's chest was burned. The person or persons who doctored that letter revised it further for publication in *The Asian Journal* by removing "in his pajamas" from the description of Merton's body as it was found. Brother Patrick was hardly authorized and would not appear to have had the talent for that kind of work.

Fox seems likely to have been assisting his longtime right-hand man, Brother Patrick, and Griffin. Fox reviewed writings from Griffin and thanked him for his delicate and charitable handling of his own nineteen years as Merton's superior.[246]

In his postscript, Brother Patrick wrote that a phone call from the U.S. Embassy in Bangkok came through to the abbey at noon on December 10. Brother Patrick wrote, "We learned that death was caused by accidental electrocution at 3 o'clock (Bangkok time) on December 10th."

---

[245] Brother Patrick letter to Griffin, December 15, 1969, Griffin papers.
[246] Fox letter to Griffin, February 8, 1970, Griffin papers.

According to Brother Patrick, the U.S. Embassy in Bangkok contacted the abbey twice, by cable at 10:00 am and again by telephone at noon. This presents a contradiction. *The New York Times* reported that according to the abbey spokesman, the cable said that "heart failure" was the official cause of death and Brother Patrick said that the phone call said that "accidental electrocution" was the cause of death. As we noted earlier, the official report that the embassy mailed to the abbey confirmed that "heart failure" was the cause of death. Not mentioned in Brother Patrick's postscript was a second cable from Hobart Luppi at the State Department in Washington, D.C., that only said that Thomas Merton had died.

Brother Patrick's postscript did not say who called from the embassy and said that the cause of death was "accidental electrocution." James Fox is the only person to support Brother Patrick's statement. Fox wrote that he learned about the "accidental electrocution" when Brother Patrick told him that the abbot received a call from the embassy in Bangkok. Brother Patrick's draft postscript agreed with the account that Fox had written one year earlier and sent to the Gethsemani diaspora. Fox was not mentioned, though, in Patrick's draft or in the final postscript.

As we have seen, there are numerous indications that the story by Fox and Brother Patrick about a call on December 10 around noon from the embassy to the abbey is a fabrication. If it had been known on December 10, 1968, that Merton died by "accidental electrocution," it appears that Brother Patrick and his friends did not tell anyone. Brother Patrick had been in close contact with Naomi Burton Stone, a Merton Trustee and co-editor of *The Asian Journal of Thomas Merton*. Stone wrote to Moffitt on May 7, 1969, "I do realize that no one can know if Tom was electrocuted, or had a heart attack, or what." In August, John Howard Griffin wrote a letter to John Moffitt on Abbey of Gethsemani stationery telling Moffit that he was working closely with Brother Patrick. Griffin then wrote about Merton's death, "I am certainly not yet satisfied that things actually happened the way they are alleged to have happened." Brother Patrick himself suggested to Moffitt that Merton's

173

death be accepted as a "mystery" and "leave it at that."[247] In 1969, Stone, Griffin, and Brother Patrick all on occasion gave the impression that they did not know for sure that Merton had died by accidental electrocution.

Moffitt challenged Brother Patrick's definitive statement in the draft postscript that Merton had died that way.   He had spent considerable time studying Merton's death and contacting witnesses and Moffitt knew that there was no proof that accidental electrocution was the cause of death. He suggested that Brother Patrick's statement "was caused by accidental electrocution" should be qualified to state, "appeared to have been caused." Moffitt conceded that the fan may have caused Merton's death, but he felt that there was no way of knowing that this was a fact.

Moffitt also questioned Brother Patrick's statement that Merton had taken a shower asking, "What is the proof of this?" Moffitt reminded Brother Patrick that according to eyewitnesses Merton was dry and appeared to be getting ready to shower.

Most convincingly, Moffitt disputed Brother Patrick's statement that Merton died at "3 o'clock." Moffitt sent Brother Patrick a detailed chart that he had made with the times of events according to witnesses. Moffitt proved that Merton must have died around 2 o'clock.

Brother Patrick had stated that these "facts" were told to the abbey by the embassy in Bangkok. One would think that what the embassy had said could not be changed. Nevertheless, in the published version of the postscript, Brother Patrick changed the time of death "that the embassy had told the abbey" from 3 o'clock to 2 o'clock. Brother Patrick's shower story and the cause of death by "accidental electrocution" remained in the published postscript.

Even though Moffitt disagreed with what Brother Patrick had written, he remained committed to keeping some things about Merton's death secret. Moffitt quoted Weist's written statement that she was uncertain how the fan came to lie on Merton. Moffitt then told Brother Patrick, "Though this is confidential material, I am sure that you have seen it. Naturally I cannot use any of those words in my account." In the end,

---

[247] Brother Patrick letter to Moffitt, August 22, 1969, Moffitt papers.

Moffitt was signaling to Brother Patrick that he would not reveal secret evidence that did not support the abbey's narrative of Merton's death.

CHAPTER 17

Abbot James Fox's "Stay Awake" Homily

A decade after Merton's death, the "accidental electrocution" story had become widely accepted as established fact. In 1978, Fox used the tenth anniversary to preach on Thomas Merton's "accidental electrocution." Using Merton as his example Fox's sermon warned that death could come unexpectedly.

Fox's demonstrated ignorance of small things and large about Merton's death revealed his lack of concern for the truth. He began, for instance, by saying that Merton was in Bangkok. This popular error, which began with the AP reporter John Wheeler's error-filled initial dateline-Bangkok article on Merton's death, persists in many accounts today, even at the Abbey of Gethsemani website.

Fox incorrectly stated that Merton was staying in a cottage with three other monks. Only two of the three other men were monks. Fox did not name any of them, but he correctly stated that Merton was in one of the two rooms on the ground floor. John Moffitt, not a monk, was in the room on the second floor above Merton's room. Moffitt was away sightseeing with a group from the conference in Bangkok at the time of Merton's death.

Fox incorrectly said that the monk in the room above Merton's heard a shout. François de Grunne was on the second floor, but he was not above Merton's room, rather, he was above Fr. Celestine Say's room. De Grunne first made conflicting statements that he had heard a shout and eventually he denied hearing a shout. Celestine Say, the other monk in the cottage sharing the first floor with Merton did not hear any such shout.

Fox drifted far from the truth by saying that the monk on the second floor who had heard the shout was later joined by another monk and that these two monks entered Merton's room after removing a "partition wall." The truth is that about two hours after the alleged shout, de Grunne told Say that Merton was in trouble. De Grunne then left the cottage and told two abbots, Odo Haas and Egbert Donovan, that Merton had had an accident. These two abbots rushed to the cottage and with Say the three of them entered Merton's room after unlatching the door. No partition wall was removed, de Grunne did not return to the cottage, and he did not enter Merton's room.

At this point in his homily, as we have previously noted, Fox added more false information, saying that the fan was on Merton's "exposed breast, burning a deep red line into his flesh" and that Merton grabbed the fan and that Merton "could not let go of it." Fox's error that de Grunne entered Merton's room is found in the fake Haas document that falsely stated that Haas had been stuck to the fan. It's completely original with Fox, though, that Merton had grabbed the fan and couldn't release it. Here he also went beyond his wholly original assertion in his February 1, 1969, letter that he had only grabbed the fan, not that he was stuck to it in the manner of Odo Haas in the fake document. The photograph of the body shows both of his hands far from the fan, and there was no physical indication that he had ever grasped the fan.

Fox originated the false story that the fan was across Merton's "exposed breast, burning a deep red line into his flesh" when he wrote that he knew this "fact" on the day that Merton died.

178

Fox concluded his sermon by comparing Merton's "accidental electrocution" with the Gospel. Fox said, "We know that lightning is electricity" so Merton's death was like lightning. "Like lightning which appears in the west and disappears in the east so shall the coming of the Son of Man be. (Luke 17:25)"[sic, that's Luke 17:24]. The reality is that Merton was not accidentally electrocuted and therefore Fox's "Stay Awake" homily was essentially rubbish.

People might wonder how Abbot Flavian and Brother Patrick could listen to Fox preaching and saying things that they surely knew were not true. They had to know that there were not three monks in Merton's cottage, de Grunne did not enter Merton's room with Say, there is no evidence that Merton grabbed a fan, and the fan was not found on Merton's chest. One can't help feeling that the only thing that really mattered to them was that everything the former abbot had to say was consistent with the prevailing accidental electrocution story. He did that with flying colors, with a clever little Biblical reference at the end to further nail it down in the minds of his audience.

CHAPTER 18

Lesser Betrayers

Jim Forest

Jim Forest was a writer, antiwar activist, and longtime correspondent with Merton from the early 1960s. Merton dedicated his 1968 book *Faith and Violence* to Father Phil Berrigan and to Forest, and Forest was the author of the 1980 book *Thomas Merton: A Pictorial Biography*[248] and the 2008 book, *Living with Wisdom: A Life of Thomas Merton.*[249] He was also among the many people who repeated the popular accidental-electrocution story, like so many others providing spurious details that give the impression that he knew a lot more than he did.[250]

Early in our researching of Merton's death, because we knew that Forest was purported to have been a friend of Merton and because he shared the antiwar position that we felt might been a motivating factor

---

[248] Paulist Press.

[249] Orbis Books.

[250] He has had lots of company through the years in that regard. See http://www.themartyrdomofthomasmerton.com/articles.html.

in Merton's likely assassination, we had corresponded with Forest for any assistance that he might be able to give us. We were surprised and disappointed when what little interest he showed in our inquiries might well be characterized as hostility. Because of that experience, we were hardly surprised at a letter to the editor that he sent to the *Catholic Worker* in 2020. Forest wrote that he was disappointed that they had published the generally favorable review by Anthony Donovan of *The Martyrdom of Thomas Merton: An Investigation* in their August-September 2019 issue.[251] He said that our discovery that the monks at Merton's abbey were, and remain, involved in a cover-up was to "enter into the weirder zones of Conspiracy Land."

Forest conceded that there was no evidence that Merton had taken a shower. He suggested that Brother Patrick Hart had only guessed what had happened "based on what he had been told by people who were present at the conference." Forest's defense of Brother Patrick was that he was an honest man trying to make sense of what had happened. Forest concluded by stating that a Benedictine, Abbot P.C. "Cees" Tholens, had been at the conference in Thailand and he thought that "Merton had died of accidental electrocution after taking a shower."

Forest was unable to refute any of the evidence in our book. His only course of action was resorting to pejorative, saying our book came from "Conspiracy Land." If Forest wanted to defend Brother Patrick by saying that he only guessed, "based on what he had been told by people who were present at the conference," he should have provided supporting evidence. Who are those people, and what did they tell Brother Patrick? Furthermore, unlike biographer Michael Mott, who was explicit that he was guessing about the shower and notably avoided citing Brother Patrick's assertions written many years previously as the source of his information, Brother Patrick wrote explicitly that Merton "proceeded to take a shower."

251

http://www.themartyrdomofthomasmerton.com/ewExternalFiles/Catholic%20
Worker.pdf.

We know that the three people who shared the cottage with Thomas Merton did not say that he took a shower. Two of these witnesses were in the cottage, in a position to see or hear if Merton took a shower, and they didn't think he took a shower. Father Celestine Say, whose room was right next to the shower room, was quite definite, in fact, that Merton did *not* take a shower. The third man, John Moffitt, was also convinced from his later serious inquiries that Merton did not take a shower. Moffitt challenged Brother Patrick when he read Brother Patrick's draft postscript with his statement that Merton took a shower. Moffitt told Brother Patrick not to write anything that was not true. In addition, the photographs of Merton's body as it was found show Merton wearing shorts with the fan lying across him, which would have been odd, indeed, if he was wet from a shower when he encountered the fan. Brother Patrick knew how destructive that evidence would have been of the shower story, which is certainly why he and the other editors removed "in his pajamas" from the description of the body as it was found from the version of the six Trappists letter that they published, accompanying Brother Patrick's postscript, in *The Asian Journal of Thomas Merton.*

We also know that none of the official reports, the death certificate, doctor's report, police report or U.S. Embassy report, made any mention of Merton having taken a shower. Brother Patrick had access to all these reports, reports of eyewitnesses, and the photograph of Merton's body wearing his pajamas. In short, Brother Patrick had all the evidence that made it quite clear that Merton did not take a shower.

Jim Forest offered no evidence of anything that Brother Patrick was told that would provide a basis to guess that Merton took a shower. Forest and a few others have claimed to have a hard time believing that Brother Patrick would make up a story that Merton took a shower. There might be a grain of truth in what they say. Brother Patrick, the long-time secretary to Abbot James Fox, might not have been the man to invent the shower story, just as Brother Patrick also would not have been the person to add the word "wet" to Merton's feet in the published version of Fox's February 1, 1969, letter to the Gethsemani diaspora, but both are obvious inventions.

In our opinion, Brother Patrick was likely directed to put his name on the shower story in his postscript to *The Asian Journal of Thomas Merton*. Brother Patrick told us later, in so many words, that there was no evidence that Merton took a shower, saying only that it was hot and Merton "must have taken a shower." But he had taken credit for the shower story, indicating deceptively as he did so in his postscript that it was based on the reports that the abbey had received.

Forest mentioned Cees Tholens as someone who was present at the conference who thought that "Merton had died of accidental electrocution after taking a shower." Forest ignored the best evidence in favor of basically useless evidence. The best evidence is from the eyewitnesses at the scene with Merton's body, the official reports, and the photographic evidence, all of which indicate that Merton did not take a shower. Tholens may have been present at the conference, like many other people, but he was not a witness at the scene. Tholens didn't see or hear anything inside the cottage where Merton died. His view is mere hearsay and would not be permitted in a court of law.

We might also mention, for what it is worth, that Fr. Vincent Shigeto Oshida, OP, of Japan was also at the conference in Thailand where Merton died, and it has been reported that he believed that Merton had been assassinated by the Korean CIA.[252] Although we don't know the basis for his opinion, we can say with some confidence that its foundation is no weaker than that of Forest's "authority," Cees Tholens.

In his letter to the *Catholic Worker*, Forest lamented that on account of his death Brother Patrick "cannot defend himself." Our book was published almost a full year before Brother Patrick's death. Brother Patrick had ample time to defend himself. It is Thomas Merton who cannot defend himself. It is indeed unfortunate that Forest can no longer defend himself, either. He died on January 13, 2022. We welcome all

---

[252] Paul M. Pearson, "'A Dedication to Prayer and a Dedication to Humanity': An Interview about Thomas Merton with James Conner, OCSO," *The Merton Annual*, 2010, http://www.merton.org/Itms/Annual/23/Pearson212-239.pdf.

challenges to our discoveries. When the best that they can do is revealed to be no better than what Forest had in his *Catholic Worker* letter, it only strengthens our case.

James Laughlin

Laughlin's friendship with Merton goes back to the early 1940s when, upon the recommendation of the man who had been Merton's professor of English literature at Columbia University, Mark Van Doren, Laughlin's publishing company, New Directions, published a volume of Merton's poems. Laughlin would later visit Merton at the Gethsemani Abbey and would become one of the three founding members of the Merton Legacy Trust.

Laughlin makes the "betrayer" list because he was also one of the three editors of *The Asian Journal of Thomas Merton.* That means that he put his seal of approval upon the spurious assertion in the postscript signed by Brother Patrick Hart that Merton had taken a shower before encountering the faulty fan and upon the inclusion of the questionable six Trappists letter from which the "in his pajamas" had been removed. Putting one's imprimatur on such legerdemain is virtually unforgivable.

Naomi Burton Stone

A native of England, Stone's friendship and professional association with Merton went back even further than Laughlin's. She was working in New York City for the literary agency Curtis Brown Ltd., with offices in both London and New York, when Merton brought his first novels and a long poem to Curtis Brown for possible publication in the spring of 1940 when he was a graduate student at Columbia University. Her efforts on his behalf would bear no fruit at the time, but she would continue as his literary agent until his death.

Naomi Stone destroyed letters from John Howard Griffin and concealed Say's negatives. She agreed with John Laughlin to keep information from Tommie O'Callaghan. Stone was the third editor along with Brother Patrick Hart and James Laughlin of *The Asian Journal of*

Thomas Merton and must share the blame for its crucial falsehoods that directed the blame for Merton's death to Merton himself.

We should note that as members of the New York City book-publishing industry, Laughlin and Stone were every bit as much a part of the corrupt national opinion molding apparatus (NOMA) as were journalists John T. Wheeler and John Howard Griffin.

John Moffitt

In *The Martyrdom of Thomas Merton*, we characterized Moffitt as the Hamlet of the affair. In this volume we have fleshed out that description. Ultimately, though, unlike Hamlet, his hands might have been tied by those to whom he owed a higher loyalty, his employer. *America* magazine, like Patricia Lefevere's employer, *The National Catholic Reporter*, unfortunately, may be counted as part of the NOMA.

Reverend Doctor Bonnie B. Thurston

Rev. Dr. Bonnie B. Thurston was one of the founders and was the third president of the International Thomas Merton Society, and she is the author of over fifty articles and prefaces about Thomas Merton.[253] The Rev. Dr. Thurston, a Disciples of Christ minister from Wheeling, West Virginia, was a professor of Christian Spirituality at Emmanuel School of Religion in Johnson City, Tennessee, and is a former professor of New Testament at Pittsburgh Theological Seminary.

In 2020, which was a full two years after *The Martyrdom of Thomas Merton: An Investigation* was published, Thurston wrote, "In Bangkok, on December 10, 1968, after giving a talk to superiors of Asian religious communities, Merton died of accidental electrocution."[254] This came hard on the heels of her writing the preface for Jaechan Anselmo Park's previously mentioned 2019 book in which he wrote that Merton was accidentally electrocuted by an electric fan. Thurston added a footnote

---

[253] The Merton Seasonal, Winter 2019, edited by Patrick O'Connell, p. 34.

[254] Bonnie B. Thurston, *Shaped by the End You Live For: Thomas Merton's Monastic Spirituality*, Liturgical Press, 2020, p. 11.

at the end of her sentence indicating that she had a reference with evidence for her statement.

Thurston's footnote stated that there were "rumors that Merton's death was not accidental," and that the CIA or some other group was involved. Thurston declared confidently that there was absolutely no evidence for these rumors. She said that she had read the accounts of witnesses who examined Merton's body and that she had seen pictures of the corpse. Her footnote stated that one of the witnesses was an abbess at the meeting who was also a medical doctor. Thurston wrote that an ungrounded fan was found across Merton's body. She wrote, incredibly, that Merton had had a heart attack and had fallen against the fan or had touched it and was electrocuted. Thurston added that electricity in less developed countries is undependable. The long footnote concluded by stating that a Merton scholar, Robert Grip, concluded the death was accidental and he had done a lot of research on Merton's death.

There is no evidence in Thurston's footnote that Thomas Merton was accidentally electrocuted or that he died in Bangkok. Merton died in Samutprakarn, Thailand.[255] This basic information is publicly available, and copies of the official death documents were published in our book. To say that Merton died in Bangkok would be equivalent to saying that someone who died in Bethesda, Maryland, or Arlington, Virginia, had died in Washington, D.C. Thurston would be accurate to say that Merton died near Bangkok, about 15 miles away, but Thurston was incorrect to state that Merton died "in Bangkok."

For over fifty years, the scholarship on Merton's death has been inadequate and Thurston's determined ignorance is predictable. She is not alone. To name a few, the following people have said that Merton died in Bangkok: Bishop Fintan Monahan; Christopher Pramuk, Regis University; Steven P. Millies, Catholic Theological Union; Alan Jacobs, Baylor University; Cristóbal Serrán-Pagán y Fuentes, Valdosta State University; Sarah Coakley, University of Cambridge; Jon M. Sweeney,

---

[255] Thomas Merton Death Certificate, American Foreign Service Report on the Death of an American Citizen, National Archives, Silver Spring, Maryland.

Paraclete Press; Father Richard Rohr, OFM; Mary Ann Poust, National Catholic Reporter; Rev. Timothy Radcliffe, OP; David Griffith, University of Notre Dame; Fr. James J. Martin, *America* magazine; and Sophfronia Scott, Alma College. They may all have taken their cue from John Wheeler of the Associated Press, who, as we have previously noted, said it first with his initial report.

Exactly where Merton died may appear to be a technical matter, but getting it wrong is representative of poor scholarship generally. Had Thurston taken the time to examine the rudimentary official documents concerning Merton's death that are published with our book and on its accompanying web site, she would know more than where Merton died. She would know that the official cause of Merton's death was not "accidental electrocution." She would know that the death certificate and doctor's report falsely stated that Merton's body had been taken to a hospital for an autopsy as required by law. Thurston was close to the stated findings of the police report when she suggested that Merton was stricken naturally before encountering the fan, but they said he was already dead, while she has the fan, which the police report says had somehow come to be mis-wired, administering the *coup de grace* by electrocution.

Thurston wrote that she had read the accounts (plural) of those who first examined the body without identifying whose accounts she had read. Thurston tentatively identified one witness as, "one of the abbesses at the meeting who was also a medical doctor." She was doubtless speaking of Doctor Edeltrud Weist.

Weist was a prioress and not an abbess. Weist identified herself in her handwritten statement as "Prioress of the Missionary Benedictine Sisters in Taegu/South Korea." Had Thurston read the account of Sr./Dr. Weist carefully, she could have noticed her proper title. Weist's title was also stated in the conference program.

Here is probably the key portion of the Weist statement that Thurston is relying upon:

> I only could give the declaration of death. I was convinced it was due to
> an electric shock by the fan.

188

However, I could not decide if this was the first reason, or if F. Merton first fell down (by fainting, dizziness, or heart attack?), pulling the fan over himself, or if he first got a shock from the electric fan, and then falling down, had dragged it along. That he had fallen down was obvious by a bleeding wound on the back of the head.

What Weist was describing was a scene that clearly puzzled her as much as it puzzled everyone. She believed that the death must have been caused by the fan because it had produced burns on his body and had shocked one of the discoverers of the body when he touched it. But she states very clearly that based upon her cursory examination she could really do no more than declare that Merton was dead and that anything else was just guesswork.

Her guesswork was not very good, though. She was convinced, for instance, that the bleeding wound in the back of Merton's head must have been caused by a heavy fall backward. It didn't occur to her that a fall against a level floor, no matter how heavy it might have been, is unlikely to have produced such a wound and that it is much more likely to have been produced by a sharp object or a bullet. She was also unable to reconcile her opinion that the shock from the fan killed Merton by her observation later in her statement that the witness who attempted to move the fan had received only "a slight electric shock."

The fact that Weist was a medical doctor was virtually irrelevant to the situation in which she found herself, and she said as much with that first sentence, "I could only give the declaration of death." The scene was extraordinarily peculiar, of a sort that no one had encountered before. Not only was an autopsy called for, but so was an honest police investigation. How did a Hitachi fan that had been working quite well suddenly become mis-wired so that it shocked people? How could it shock one person only slightly and kill another person on the spot? Wouldn't Merton have recoiled from the fan just like Abbot Haas did, none the worse for wear? If the fan had shorted out, why didn't the short circuit cause a fuse to blow, thereby cutting off all electricity to the fan as would commonly be the case? How did Merton come to be lying flat on his back with his arms by his side with the fan lying across his body? If he had grabbed the fan, as Abbot Fox said in his February 1, 1969, letter and is repeated often elsewhere, why were his hands so far from the fan in the end?

Thurston added that she had seen photographs of Merton's body, but what she failed to say was how they contradicted the electrocution story as it has come to be told, that Merton was wet from a shower when he touched the fan. The photographs were suppressed by the abbey precisely because they undermine that scenario. The photographs show Merton wearing shorts and Weist in her statement speaks of Merton's shorts. She also drew a little sketch accompanying her statement that shows just what the photographs do. He has shorts on, and the fan is diagonally across his body at the pelvis and lower abdomen. He had obviously not just come out of the shower.

Thurston wrote further that "an ungrounded fan was found across his body." For what it is worth, she provided no evidence that the fan was ungrounded., but it hardly makes a difference. Grounded electrical outlets are safer than ungrounded, but an ungrounded lamp, toaster, or fan is not *per se* lethal. Prior to 1962 most electrical appliances were ungrounded. Many American homes still have old ungrounded fans that are not a mortal danger to anyone.

At that point in her long footnote, Thurston hedged her position by saying that Merton either had a heart attack or was electrocuted, seeming to realize that she wasn't making a particularly strong case for electrocution.

Yet another argument offered by Thurston was that "in the less developed world" electricity is undependable or an adventure. This argument plays to the popular imagination, but the Red Cross center where Merton died was a modern facility and the fan was a very high-quality Hitachi product. Very much like the "Merton was a klutz" argument, Thurston's "less developed world" argument is irrelevant.

Finally, Thurston concluded by stating that Robert Grip has done research and concluded that the death was accidental. In other words, Thurston's proof is, "because Robert Grip said so." If Grip has published any evidence, Thurston did not say where it might be found, and we have not discovered it. For the record, the journalist Grip, like Thurston, is a former president of the International Thomas Merton Society.

The Thai death certificate, police report, and the report by the U.S. Embassy were all available to Thurston. She ignored all the official reports that did not support her statement that "Merton died of accidental electrocution."

Reading Thurston's very disingenuous observations about Thomas Merton's death, brought forward so late in the game, we are almost forced to conclude that she must be the "prominent Merton scholar" who put her seal of approval on the similarly slipshod work of Judith Valente in Valente's book review that we mentioned in the foreword. Maybe, though, it was Deborah Kehoe, as we shall see in the next section.

The Merton Annual

The stated mission of *The Merton Annual* is to provide a regular outlet for substantial Merton-related scholarship. The co-editors of *The Merton Annual* in 2018 were Joseph Quinn Raab and Deborah Kehoe. In July of 2018 we submitted an article entitled, "New Directions' Misdirection in Thomas Merton's Death," but it was rejected on the grounds that it did not measure up to that publication's scholarly standards. Our article is available on David Martin's web site at https://dcdave.com/article5/180 911.htm, and one may read it and decide for himself about the level of scholarship demonstrated.

Our book, *The Martyrdom of Thomas Merton: An Investigation*, announced that the official Thai documents concerning the death of Thomas Merton had been found. Professor Michael W. Higgins in his review of our book commended our research in "acquiring official documents," but then he never stated what official documents our research found.

We expected that there would be some interest in the historic documents that we discovered. Almost two years after the publication of our book nothing was published in the Catholic or secular press concerning these official reports. The *Merton Seasonal*, a quarterly publication that contains articles, book reviews and other information of interest to members of the International Thomas Merton Society said nothing about the discovery of the documents that had been missing for 50 years. The International Thomas Merton Society *Newsletter,* published twice a year, did not report that the historic records had been found.

After no scholarly articles appeared concerning the documents that were discovered, we submitted an article to The *Merton Annual* titled, "Official Thai Reports on Thomas Merton's Death." The concluding paragraph stated:

> The most surprising discovery in the official Thai records of Merton's death is that the stated cause of death is "sudden heart failure" and not "accidental electrocution" as the monks at Gethsemani have said for over 50 years. The story that Merton took a shower before his "accidental electrocution" originated with Brother Patrick Hart in 1973, so it is no surprise that there is no mention of any bath or shower by Merton in the official Thai reports. The New York City chapter of the International Thomas Merton Society website states, [Merton] slipped in the shower, grabbed a rotary fan, and was electrocuted." There is no known original source to support this popular story.

We thought that our article met the stated purpose of *The Merton Annual,* "to provide a regular outlet for substantial Merton-related scholarship." We included copies of the official reports to document what was discussed in our article.

Deborah Kehoe, co-editor of *The Merton Annual* acknowledged she had read our submission, but she rejected the article stating that, "we do not run material that has substantially appeared in print elsewhere." Technically, she is correct because we did write about the official documents in our book, but the mention in our book was not comparable to a competing academic journal, magazine, or news outlet. If the documents are to be ignored by those who should have the most interest in them, they might as well have not ever been found.

With the truth suppressed by *The Merton Annual,* Kehoe can get away with saying things about Thomas Merton that are false. On June 28, 2020, in a lecture on Thomas Merton at St. Paul's Episcopal Church in

Corinth, Mississippi, she said, "The official cause of death remains accidental electrocution from stepping out of a bath and grabbing a badly wired electric fan."[256] Kehoe had read our article and she had the official Thai documents, so she surely knew that what she was saying was completely false. That was never the official cause of death, and the evidence is overwhelming that Merton was never in a bath of any sort before encountering the fan.

It is interesting that Kehoe's co-editor at the time, Joseph Quinn Raab, at *The Merton Annual* does not share her opinion. In 2021, as we noted in the introduction, Professor Raab wrote, "It is no longer plausible to conclude that Merton's death was the result of accidental electrocution."

The Standard (Account) Bearers

As we allude to in the foreword, in his review of *The Martyrdom of Thomas Merton*, Professor Paul Dekar uses, alternatively, the terms "standard account" and "generally accepted account" as shorthand for the conclusion that Thomas Merton died because of an accident. He is forced to use those terms because he can't call it the official account, as with, say, the John F. Kennedy assassination and the lone-gunman explanation, because, by the only official account, Merton died of heart failure. As it happens, though, when we look into the details of the various accounts by scholars, we find that the account is not all that standard.

Bishop Fintan Monahan of Ireland, for instance, said that Merton was electrocuted by an air-conditioner.[257] Former UN Ambassador Andrew Young said that the bald Merton was found electrocuted in his bathtub with an electric hair dryer.[258] Father John McCloskey wrote that a fan fell

---

[256] Deborah Kehoe address at St. Paul's Episcopal Church, Corinth, MS, June 28, 2020, 16 min. 40 sec. mark at https://www.youtube.com/watch?v=vqXf0ICmTDQ.

[257] Bishop Fintan Monahan, Diocese of Kilalloe, speaking at his book launch in Dublin, Ireland, November 2020.

[258] James W. Douglass, Keynote address to the International Thomas Merton Society, June 13, 1997, Spring Hill College, Mobile, AL.

into Merton's bathtub.[259] Father Timothy Radcliff, O.P., former Master of the Order of Preachers, said that Merton was electrocuted in the shower.[260] Another Dominican friar disagrees. Fr. Jacob Restrick, O.P., wrote that Merton touched a live wire in a floor lamp after taking a shower.[261] Fr. Restrick also wrote that Merton died on December 5 and not December 10. When we asked Fr. Restrick to correct his errors he told us that he did not think his Dominican community would give him permission, even though the motto of the Dominican Order is *Veritas*.

Quentin Hardy, in an article titled, "The Dangers of Everyday Activities," wrote that Merton died when a radio fell into his bathtub.[262] Father John Dear wrote that after taking a shower Merton bumped into an old, upright electric fan.[263] Anthony Podavano said, "Certainly, the story of Merton's death is very straightforward...He touched a fan after a bath in the afternoon...I did ask the monks at Gethsemani, Patrick Hart his secretary most prominently, about what they thought of his death...Hart said, 'Most of us are amazed that he didn't kill himself in the hermitage. He was unbelievably klutzy. He never learned to drive a car. We kept expecting he was going to be found dead electrocuting himself in the hermitage.'"[264] Virginia Spencer Carr said that Merton "emerged dripping from his shower and stumbled over an electric fan with faulty wiring; electrocuted at 53."[265]

According to Morgan Atkinson, "Thomas Merton always could make an exit. He returned to his room and took a nap, then a shower, there's a wet floor, a fan with bad wiring, 220 volts. The official explanation is

---

[259] Rev. John McCloskey, review of *The Seven Storey Mountain*, "The Christian Review," March 2015.

[260] Rev. Timothy Radcliffe, OP, *Alive in God: A Christian Imagination*, Bloomsbury Continuum, February 4, 2020.

[261] Rev. Jacob Restrick, OP, *Sister Mary Baruch: The Early Years*, Tan, 2019.

[262] Quenton Hardy, "The Dangers of Everyday Activities," *Forbes*, May 13, 2010.

[263] Rev. John Dear, *Thomas Merton Peacemaker*, Orbis, 2015.

[264] Anthony Podavano, *Soul Searching: the journey of Thomas Merton*, Liturgical Press, 2008, p. 177 .

[265] Virginia Spencer Carr, review of Michael Mott's *Seven Mountains of Thomas Merton*, *The Merton Seasonal*, Autumn 1985.

death by accidental electrocution."[266] Jon Sweeney said that Merton "was a klutz and accidentally electrocuted himself in the bathroom; not a heroic death, to be sure."[267] A member of the Merton Legacy Trust, Mary R. Sommerville, quoting Brother Patrick Hart, "Merton was always a klutz, never to be trusted with machinery. He was accident prone. His death was just that, an accident."[268] As noted, Abbot James Fox wrote that Merton either had a heart attack and grabbed a fan, or just grabbed a fan, or he had been fixing a fan when he touched a badly insulated wire.[269]

There is an endless variety of descriptions of Merton's "accidental electrocution." Some people even have their own competing versions of Merton's death. Notre Dame Professor Emeritus Lawrence Cunningham maintains that "the facts seem more straightforward: he died either from electrocution directly or from a heart attack precipitated by the shock he received, or he had a heart attack and fell over the fan."[270] Even the official Merton biographer Michael Mott has more than one description, "What seems the most likely reconstruction is that Merton came out of the shower either wearing a pair of drawers or naked...Merton may have slipped and drawn the fan sharply toward him for support, or he may have simply tried to change its position."[271] Father James J. Martin, S.J., has several descriptions of Thomas Merton's death: First, Merton was found "lying on the floor grasping a fan...Merton had come out of the bathtub, slipped on the tiled floor, and grabbed a fan to break his fall. The fan electrocuted him and he died instantly."[272] Second, "...in Bangkok, on a warm day while taking a bath, he slipped in the bathtub,

---

[266] Morgan Atkinson documentary, *The Many Storeys and Last Days of Thomas Merton*, 2015, aired on PBS.

[267] Jon M. Sweeney, *Born Again and Again*, Paraclete Press, 2005, p. 125.

[268] Mary R. Sommerville quoting Brother Patrick Hart, *The Merton Seasonal*, Summer 2019, p. 52.

[269] James Fox, letter to the Gethsemani Diaspora, February1, 1969.

[270] Lawrence Cunningham, *Thomas Merton & the Monastic Vision*, Eerdmans Pub., 1999, p. 179.

[271] Michael Mott, *The Seven Mountains of Thomas Merton*, Houghton Mifflin Harcourt, 1984.

[272] Rev. James J. Martin, *Becoming Who You Are*, Paulist Press, 2006.

grabbed an electric fan and was electrocuted."[273] And third, "...stepped out of a bathroom shower during a visit to Bangkok. Slipping on the wet floor, he grabbed a poorly wired fan for support and was electrocuted."[274]

In 2021, The International Thomas Merton Society awarded Sophronia Scott the prestigious Thomas Merton Award. In her book, *The Seeker and the Monk: Everyday Conversations with Thomas Merton*, Scott wrote, "...he died in Bangkok, Thailand, while attending a monastic conference. His cause of death is listed as accidental electrocution, the result of him touching a faulty fan after getting out of a shower."[275] Even Jim Forest in his letter attacking our book had conceded a year before, "Turley and Martin are right that there is no certain evidence that Merton had taken a shower."[276]

---

[273] Rev. James J. Martin, Thomas Merton, A Man of Contradictions, Loyola Press, https://www.loyolapress.com/catholic-resources/saints/saints-reflections/thomas-merton-a-man-of-contradictions/.

[274] Rev. James J. Martin, "Thomas Merton: Still Controversial," *America Magazine*, December 10, 2008.

[275] Sophronia Scott, *The Seeker and the Monk*, Broadleaf Books, 2021, p. 14.

[276] Jim Forest, letter to the editor, *The Catholic Worker*, March 2020.

CHAPTER 19

Conclusion

The Merton Murder Mystery

You say he died of an accident,
Then would you explain to me
Why the story has come to us
Wrapped in lies and secrecy?

U ndoubtedly, the reason why so many explanations for Thomas Merton's death by electrocution persist right up to the present day is that there was never any clear-cut explanation for it. As we have seen, the only official investigation that was ever conducted, the one by the local Thai police, stated, in fact, that the cause of death was "heart failure" and that Merton's contact with the faulty fan after he was already dead was, in effect, coincidental.

If you were living in the United States, your only chance of reading about that "heart failure" would have been if you were a reader of *The New York Times.* Even then, you would likely have concluded that the heart failure conclusion was a mere technicality, because the reporter,

Israel Shenker, first said that Merton's body was badly burned by the fan that had toppled over on him and that "the cause of death was *officially listed* as heart failure." The mind naturally leaps to the conclusion that the shock from the bad fan caused the heart failure. As we have seen, though, *The Times*—or perhaps the leadership at the Gethsemani Abbey—felt that it had given out too much information and the "heart failure" mention was cut out of the wire service version of its report that went to newspapers around the country.

The Associated Press and John T. Wheeler

Everything goes back to that initial, dateline Bangkok, AP story by John T. Wheeler. To be sure, Abbot Flavian Burns said that he received a phone call from the U.S. Embassy in Thailand in which he was told that Merton was electrocuted by a faulty fan, repeated by James Fox in his February 1969 letter, but there is no evidence for such a phone call. As we have seen, the early news reports from the abbey said that they didn't know the cause of death. At best, there is no known source at the embassy for that information, nor did Wheeler name any source for his own information.

It is evident that neither Wheeler nor anyone working for the AP or for any other news organization actually went to the site of the death and did any investigation of their own. Neither Wheeler nor the people at the *Bangkok Post* even knew where Merton had died, after all. They said it was in Bangkok. John Moffitt was a journalist after a fashion because he worked for a magazine, but he was the poetry editor for *America*, and he didn't put on his journalist's cap at the time and ask any probing questions of witnesses that we know of. We also know that Dutch and Italian film crews were there, but they had either left for the day or saw no reason to do any news gathering, either.

Is it any wonder that there should be such a proliferation of widely varying stories? We are reminded of Jesus' story in Matthew's Gospel of the foolish man who built his house upon the sand. The accidental electrocution story is built upon such a foundation. We can see why Bonnie Thurston would seize upon that one sentence in Dr. Weist's statement, "I was convinced [the death] was due to an electric shock by the fan." But, as we have also seen, that was based upon her superficial impression of the moment, which, in our studied opinion, was the impression intended by the people who rigged the fan and placed it across Merton's supine body. Dr. Weist, like the other witnesses, was also greatly puzzled as to how the scene they witnessed, with the fan lying across Merton's body with his arms down by his side could possibly have originated. That's why they memorialized the scene with Fr. Celestine Say's photographs. Thurston also avoids mention of the fact that Dr. Weist said later in her statement that the witness Fr. Odo Haas received only "a slight shock" when he attempted to move the fan.

Even though the undated, unsigned Thai police report concluded that Merton died of heart failure before encountering the fan, it did provide some grist for the accidental electrocution mill by saying that there was a faulty cord installed in the fan that caused an "electrical leakage" that was "strong enough to cause the death of a person if he touched the metal part." But it also reported that when Fr. Haas touched it, he merely jerked away, which is consistent with the "slight shock" that Weist reported and with what Fr. Say says Haas told him about the shock when he inquired about its severity.

So, the definitive conclusion that Merton was electrocuted by a faulty fan traces back to the AP's John T. Wheeler, who was fed the story by an anonymous source. It's hardly a leap of logic to conclude that the story was already written in advance of the dirty deed, perhaps even weeks in advance.[277]

---

[277] The corruption of the Associated Press goes way back. Upton Sinclair's 1919 *The Brass Check* has a good analysis of the organization that remains timely. Surprisingly, Wikipedia has a good treatment of the subject on its *Brass Check* page: "Press watchdogs at the time of publication and recently find The Brass Check's analysis of the media accurate and valuable. It is 'muckraking at its

The Gethsemani Abbey and James Fox

We believe that we have shown to the satisfaction of almost any objective person that Merton was assassinated. The assassination would have involved a great deal of planning. An important part of the planning would have been the planning of the cover-up. In planning for the cover-up, the killers had to think of what the greatest threat to the cover-up might be and how it could be neutralized. Anyone who knows the first thing about the news media knows that it would not come from there. Rather, they knew they could count on the news media's active cooperation in the cover-up. The biggest threat would surely come from those who cared most about Father Louis, the great poet and philosopher, the earnest prophet for peace, known to the world as Thomas Merton. Would that not have been Merton's surrogate family, his home abbey?

The killers had to know in advance that they would have no more of a problem with the Abbey of Gethsemani than they would have with the Associated Press, *The New York Times*, and all the others. And that proved to be the case in spades. Had the abbey really cared about knowing the truth, Abbot Flavian Burns would have insisted that an autopsy be performed. He did not, even though much later he would leave the impression that he did. (See chapter 4.) He recognized the

---

best' and 'astonishingly prescient in its critique of the coziness of big media and other corporate interests.'

"However, on its publication 'most newspapers refused to review the book, and those very few that did were almost always unsympathetic. Many newspapers, like the *New York Times*, even refused to run paid advertisements for the book.' And 'those historians who bother to mention *The Brass Check* dismiss it as ephemeral, explaining that the problems it depicts have been solved.'"

For evidence that those problems have not been solved, with heavy reference to *The Brass Check*, see David Martin, "Upton Sinclair and Timothy McVeigh," June 2, 2001, https://www.dcdave.com/article4/010602.htm.

importance of an autopsy early on when the abbey was the obvious source of the story that appeared in *The Kentucky Standard* eight days after the death that stated falsely that an autopsy had been performed in Oakland, California, when the body was on its way home.

We have seen how energetically the abbey has sold the accidental electrocution story, and it stands to reason that the killers would have been assured in advance that that is just what they could expect from them. With that realization in mind, we are forced to take another look at the setting of the stage for Merton's murder. It was convenient, indeed, for the killers that it would take place so far removed from scrutiny in the United States, that the one news choke point would be John T. Wheeler of the Associated Press, a man whose usual beat was playing the propagandist role of covering the Vietnam War. The other information choke point would have been the abbey, itself.

As we alluded to previously, for Abbot Fox to have allowed Merton to leave the abbey for virtually any reason other than medical treatment would have been an enormous break in precedent for him. For Merton then to end up dying suspiciously would have cast a huge cloud of suspicion on Fox. Fox seemed to be quite similar in personality to the man who was the President of the United States at the time, Lyndon Johnson, and his situation might well have been analogous:

> Once he had attained his lifelong goal, no one ever reveled in—indeed wallowed in—the power of the office more than did Johnson. He was also an extraordinarily stubborn man, as best evidenced by his Vietnam War policy. That's why it came as such a shock to almost everyone when he announced at the end of a speech on March 31, 1968, that he would not seek reelection that fall. That is also why, right up to the present day, there are almost as many explanations for it as there are people offering them.[278]

Abbot Fox also seemed to enjoy the power of his position very much, and it looks as though even after he had formally retired, he continued to exercise some of that power. But he had freed himself of the suspicion

---

[278] David Martin, "Did Lyndon Step Down So Bobby Could Be Killed?", September 22, 2014, https://dcdave.com/article5/140923.htm.

that he might have intentionally sent Merton off to his demise. He would later write privately, as we have seen, that if he had continued to be the abbot that Merton would still be alive because he would never have allowed him to go to Thailand.

As retired abbot, Fox was also at the head of the parade at the abbey in selling the accidental electrocution story, beginning with his February letter. Fox wrote that he knew at exactly 12:45 P.M. on December 10, 1968, that Merton was "electrocuted by a faulty wire in a large electric fan." And Fox wrote, that according to the early reports Merton had been "in his wet bare feet" and a "large segment of his bare chest had been burned deeply, where the fan had fallen on him, pinning him down."

All the other false information about a shower, Haas being stuck to the fan, no fuses, Merton being a klutz, the embassy calling Flavian, the time of death, and the fake documents came after Fox claimed to know what had happened. Everything that was suppressed by the abbey, Say's photographs, the death certificate, doctor's report, embassy report, and witness accounts, was suppressed because it contradicted what Fox said had happened.

Brother Patrick, Abbot Flavian, and Griffin never claimed to know as much about Merton's cause of death on December 10, 1968, as did James Fox. Fox, in his own words, was the first to know that the cause of death was "accidental electrocution," and it was to be blamed on Merton for his "wet bare feet" around electricity.

The Deep State and John Howard Griffin

In the public mind, John Howard Griffin is almost as much a cardboard character as are the people in his famous work, *Black Like Me.* He is the courageous man who taught white Americans what it is like for Black Americans to live under the oppressive conditions then current in the Deep South.

We have seen, though, that Griffin is very much a man of mystery. Perhaps the best way of approaching him is to recognize that, like John T.

Wheeler, Griffin was a professional journalist, though not so clearly deeply embedded in the heart of the U.S. journalistic establishment. Rather, he was working on the less reputable fringes until his big chance came. Upon closer examination we have found that if Griffin was embedded anywhere, it was in the bowels of what had not yet come to be called the Deep State. Much of what his authorized biographer, Robert Bonazzi, has written about him stands up poorly to scrutiny. That also applies to what Griffin's widow, who married Bonazzi, has written.

Griffin's official military record is largely inconsistent with what Bonazzi tells us about it. That record, and much of what Griffin did after leaving the service, has the strong earmarks of intelligence work. One of his obituaries tells us that it was explicitly intelligence work during the time he lived in Mexico. His known assignment living with a primitive tribe in the Solomon Islands would generally have been under the purview of military intelligence, and we can only guess about what he might have been doing in all those other places his military record tells us about, but Bonazzi doesn't.

The books that Griffin wrote seemed to get publicity that was well beyond what they merited. That applies to his lesser-known novels as well as to *Black Like Me*.

He showed up at the Gethsemani Abbey shortly after Merton's writings took a political, anti-war, and anti-establishment turn. His reason for going there, just for a religious retreat, having nothing to do with the fact that Merton happened to be there, hardly passes the smell test. In fact, in the words of Shakespeare, "He protesteth too much, methinks"

The evidence strongly suggests to us that Griffin arrived at the abbey on assignment. With his apparent intelligence background, he would appear to be the key nexus between the leadership of the abbey and those who assassinated Merton. As we have seen, very soon after Merton's death, Griffin virtually took charge of the public handling of the event. His handling of it consistently reflected a couple of key features of intelligence tradecraft, secrecy and mendacity.

Hardly anything nails down Griffin's Deep State bona fides more than his use of Penn Jones, Jr., to go to the Philippines to determine if the honest and sincere Benedictine monk, Fr. Celestine Say, posed a serious threat to the cover-up. Jones pretended to believe that there was a good chance that Merton was murdered in an obvious attempt to draw Fr. Say out.

An early critic of the official version of the John F. Kennedy assassination, Jones's subsequent positions and associations mark him as almost certainly fake opposition, put in place to overshadow real opposition and to keep skeptical inquiry within acceptable bounds. Jones's job might have been to deceive people, but as his close confederate, Griffin would not have been among those that he deceived. Rather, the evidence is very strong that Griffin and Jones were partners in deception.

The Culprits Revisited

In the foreword to our previous book we wrote, "In *The Martyrdom of Thomas Merton* we identify four men who have been most instrumental in imprinting upon the public mind the wholly unsupported notion that Merton died from accidental electrocution—a conclusion that had not been reached by the investigating police in Thailand." Those men were Abbot Flavian Burns, Brother Patrick Hart, John Howard Griffin, and Michael Mott. Clearly, upon reflection, we missed the most important one of all, the AP's John T. Wheeler. We do make mention of his short initial report on the death, but we were laboring under what we now believe was a misconception that the abbey had a source at the U.S. Embassy in Thailand for the accidental electrocution story. But then, Wheeler himself had no ultimate source for it. Someone fed him the story, and we can see that whoever that was was not at the conference, because he also said falsely that Merton was missed when he didn't show up for lunch. The only conclusion that one can come to is that Wheeler had been fed the story by the same people who rigged the fan to give the appearance that Merton had been electrocuted. The story, like the fan, was very likely to have been prepared in advance.

Abbot Flavian certainly deserves his share of the blame for the false story. Although the abbey for the first few days said it had not been told how Merton had died, Abbot Flavian did write later that he had called the U.S. Embassy and had been told that Merton had died from an accident, and had he really wanted to know the truth about Merton's death, he was in a position to insist upon an autopsy. We have seen that Abbot Flavian backed John Howard Griffin to the hilt in rebuffing the challenges by John Moffitt to the accidental electrocution story. But as long as James Fox was at the abbey, it is evident that he was the man calling the shots, particularly in relation to dealings with Thomas Merton's death. He made that apparent with his February 1, 1969, letter to the Gethsemani diaspora. We can see that no one was looking over his shoulder or it wouldn't have gone out with the flagrant misspellings. Abbot Flavian was little more than Fox's agent in this matter.

What we have said about Flavian Burns in that regard goes double for Brother Patrick Hart. He was Fox's longtime secretary, and he was Fox's man. Brother Patrick stands above Abbot Flavian in one good thing that he did. As we noted earlier, Volume 7 of *The Journals of Thomas Merton*, published in 1998, has an introduction by Brother Patrick that is virtually identical to that postscript of his in the 1973 *Asian Journal of Thomas Merton* in which he broke the phony Merton-shower story, but with one big exception. In his earlier account, when the witness Odo Haas touched the fan lying across Merton's body, he received a "severe" shock. In his later account, Brother Patrick tells us that Haas received only a "slight" shock. He changed an obviously false statement to a truthful one. In doing so, whether he realized it or not, he was strongly suggesting that the electrified fan lying across Merton's body was no more than a stage prop, incapable of killing anyone at the touch, in contrast with what we have been given to believe about it and it is also in contradiction to how the Thai police characterized the strangely mis-wired fan in their report.

As we suggested earlier, there could have been more than conscience at work here, because James Fox died in 1987 and Brother Patrick had become free of his censure.

We see at least a couple of things in Michael Mott's account of Merton's death that suggest that he might have wanted the truth to get out, but he was laboring under serious constraints. He—and Brother Patrick as well—might be compared to a hostage who has been forced to make a public statement that is pleasing to his captors, but for one who can read between the lines, he is saying that the thrust of his message should not be believed.

From all our research, Mott is the only source we have encountered for the very important information that the wound in the back of Merton's head had "bled considerably." He couldn't have made that up. Doubtless, it was in one of those witness statements that Griffin promised to Moffitt but never delivered and the abbey now seems to have "lost." One can only wonder what else might be in those statements that undermine the accidental electrocution narrative. Mott quickly neutralizes this major revelation with his very next sentence, saying that the "obvious solution" was that it resulted from Merton's head striking the floor. The fact of the matter is that it is not the least bit obvious. If Merton fell, it is more likely that he would have fallen forward rather than backward, and no matter how heavily he might have fallen backward, it would have been onto a level floor. There was nothing in the area that would have produced such a laceration. The Thai police, in their acknowledged cover-up, apparently recognized the importance of that wound by the fact that they made no mention of it. That it was more than just a wound, but one that had bled quite a bit, tells you unmistakably that it was a deep wound. Do we really need any more evidence than that that it must have been the cause of Merton's death? What possible cause is more likely?

Mott was also under no obligation to give us a long direct quote of the conclusions of the Thai police report, the passage in which they say that the "dead priest," having died naturally from heart failure, fell into the fan which just happened to have been somehow mis-wired and ended up

206

causing those burns on his body—and also on his shorts, as the quoted police report says. It makes the whole Thai police "investigation" look ridiculous. Why bother to cite those parts of it that seem to lend support to the prevailing narrative such as that the fan, in its mis-wired state, was capable of killing someone when they could come to such an absurd conclusion?

We shouldn't let Mott completely off the hook, though. As we stressed in our first book, Mott consciously lied when he said that Fr. Say took his photographs of the body after the scene had been disturbed and he strongly intimated that the body might have been dressed for modesty's sake. That left open the possibility that Merton had just emerged from a shower when he encountered the fan. But Mott certainly knew that that was not true, because he had Say's letter in which Say explained that they took the picture of the body as they found it precisely because the death scene that they witnessed seemed so peculiar.

Mott also said that the witness Odo Haas was held to the fan by the electrical charge when he tried to move it and that Françoise de Grunne was among the four initial witnesses to enter Merton's room. In that case, though, he would have the rather poor excuse that he was using the phony Haas document for his source, although he never references it.

Merton's "Friends"

Michael Mott doesn't belong on any list of friends who betrayed Thomas Merton, because he was a Johnny-come-lately to the Merton story. They never knew one another. It's really not clear why he was chosen to take over for Griffin when Griffin was apparently unable to continue on account of his health. Mott's professional history was similar to Griffin's in that both had a journalism background and that, apart from that, their writing was in fiction rather than non-fiction. Mott had also had several books of poetry published. Neither had previously written a biography. Other than what he had to say about Merton's death, Mott seemed to do a commendable job. His book was popular and very well received critically.

For a man who spent the last few years of his life as a hermit, Merton was very gregarious. In fact, he was outgoing and friendly by almost any standard. He had a very wide circle of friends and correspondents. Brother Patrick Hart should hardly be counted among such friends, though. The notion that they were friends has been perpetuated to a great degree by the wide circulation of the photograph or the two men together, with Brother Maurice Flood cropped out. The idea has also been enhanced by the fact that he is always described as Merton's secretary, when he had been Fox's secretary for a decade and had only become one of Merton's three secretaries just before Merton's Asia trip. As a man whose first loyalty was to Fox, he could be counted on to go along with the accidental electrocution story that Fox pushed from the very beginning.

James Fox's relationship could hardly be characterized as one of friendship, either. As we have seen, as personalities go, as well as in their backgrounds and interests, they were pretty much oil and water. The notion of their friendship was something that Fox went to great lengths to cultivate in that long February 1, 1969, letter to the Gethsemani diaspora, though.

Of all the people involved in the cover-up of Merton's almost certain murder, John Howard Griffin would seem to have the strongest claim to friendship. From the discoveries we have made about Griffin, though, we believe that that assessment needs to be reconsidered. Despite the many things that they might seem to have in common, at least on the surface, the only thing that they ever seemed to interact over was photography. One might well conclude that his photographic skill was merely a good way for Griffin to worm himself into Merton's confidence.

In the final analysis, Merton's true friends were the new acquaintances that he had made in Thailand, because they were the only ones concerned enough about him to want to know, and to want everyone else to know, the true cause of Merton's death. They were the four members of the Order of Saint Benedict to whom we dedicated *The*

Martyrdom of Thomas Merton, Father Celestine Say, Sister Edeltrud Weist, Father Egbert Donovan, and Father Odo Haas.

Why it matters

A very common reaction that we have encountered among professed Merton admirers to our revelations about Merton's death has been that they are far more interested in Merton's life and work than in how his life ended, because it is so much more important. A main reason why Merton's works are important, though, is that they so much embody a Christ-like pursuit of the truth. It greatly dishonors his memory for the widely believed story of how he died, perpetuated by his own home abbey, to be the precise opposite, the purest embodiment of falsehood.

And we chose the title for our earlier book, "The Martyrdom of Thomas Merton," for a reason. The biographer Michael Mott sold Merton greatly short when he wrote that "no convincing motive has come to light" for his murder and that "Merton's death would have furthered the political ends of no group."[279] Merton was a very influential, incorruptible opponent of the American warfare state.

We are reminded of the observations of Professor Cristóbal Serrán-Pagán y Fuentes, the native Spaniard who teaches philosophy and religious studies at Valdosta State University in Georgia, made in the wake of David Martin's presentation in Rome of "What We Know about Thomas Merton's Death." He told the group that he once responded to a person who made light of skepticism over Merton's death by saying that it didn't really make much difference, "Does it matter how Christ died?"

Martin was inspired to compose "Thomas Merton's Martyrdom" that very evening. Claudia Burger, the Austrian administrative coordinator of that Merton Symposium, typed up the handwritten poem, made copies, and placed them at the desks of each of the attendees the next day.

---

[279] Mott, p. 586.

Thomas Merton's Martyrdom

They say his death was meaningless.
That's what they want us to swallow.
But in light of all the evidence,
Their argument rings hollow.

His life was full of purpose,
But we must to the world confide:
His words had no more meaning
Than the things for which he died.

Appendices

1. What We Know About Thomas Merton's Death

Paper by David Martin and Hugh Turley presented to
Thomas Merton Symposium, Pontifical Atheneum, Rome, Italy, June 13, 2018

The state of knowledge of Thomas Merton's death can best be described as highly unsatisfactory. Michael Mott's 1984 authorized biography, *The Seven Mountains of Thomas Merton*, has been taken as the last word on the subject. Everyone who has written about Merton's death since then—and there are many—has apparently accepted his explanation of how Merton was electrocuted by a defective fan, departing from his description on occasion only with their own embellishments, based solely upon imagination rather than new research.

This is unfortunate because Mott leaves a lot of loose ends. First, he quotes directly from the just-then-revealed conclusion of the Thai police report, a document that only a few people had previously seen and of whose full contents few are even now aware:

> However, the Investigating Officer questioned Dr. Luksana Narkvachara, whose views were that Reverend Thomas Merton died because of:
>
> 1. Heart failure.
>
> 2. And that the cause mentioned in 1. caused the dead priest to faint and collide with the stand fan located in the room. The fan had fallen onto the body of Reverend Thomas Merton. The head of the dead priest had hit the floor. There was a burn on the body's skin and on the

underwear on the right side which was assumed to have been caused by electrical shock from the fan.

Therefore the cause of the death of Reverend Thomas Merton was as mentioned. There were no witnesses who might be suspected of causing the death. There is no reason to suspect criminal causes.

Mott softened the blow of that revelation by preceding it with a quote from the report that said that a "defective electric cord" had been installed inside the fan's stand that caused an "electrical leakage" sufficient to kill a person who touched the metal part, but that's not what the attending doctor said killed Merton, hence the "however."

"The police investigation had not inspired much confidence," writes Mott, and who could be surprised that it hadn't? "Many felt electrocution was deliberately played down to protect the reputation of the conference center. It may have been so."

What Mott has just told us, using nice language for it, is that the official investigation of Merton's death amounted to a cover-up. This is a very poor beginning for learning what the actual cause of death was. Then Mott provides us with only one possible motive for the cover-up, to protect the reputation of the local conference center. But that center was run by a large, powerful international organization, the Red Cross. It would sound like a big scandal if one were to say that there was a cover-up to protect the Red Cross, so Mott says essentially the same thing, but in different words.

But there is another big, powerful organization involved here. If a family has a member killed by a defective fan in a public facility, a product liability lawyer would advise the family to sue whoever might be responsible, and the deeper the pockets of the responsible party the better. That would not just be the Red Cross, but it would be the maker of the fan. Mott doesn't say who that was, but according to several witnesses, the fan was made by Hitachi.

Now we're looking at a major scandal involving a big multinational corporation. Might the Thai authorities have performed their cover-up on behalf either the Red Cross or the Hitachi Corporation? Merton's home abbey of Gethsemani in Kentucky was, in effect, his surviving family. One might well ask why the abbey did not bring suit for damages against either the Red Cross or Hitachi, or both. Does that mean that the abbey privately accepted the verdict that Merton actually died of natural causes and that they were willing to do so in the absence of an autopsy?

That's right. There was no autopsy, even though the official doctor's certificate stated, "a post-mortem examination has been done in accordance with the law." Mott offers a variety of weak excuses for the absence of an autopsy but says nothing about the statements by the Thai authorities that give the unmistakable impression that there was one. He also fails to tell us that the police report made no mention of the curious bleeding wound in the back of Merton's head. Mott, himself, does mention that injury, employing the passive voice: "Little attention seems to have been given to a wound on the back of Merton's head that had bled considerably. The obvious solution appears to be that it was caused when his head struck the floor."

The big story here, though, is that an investigating police force that Mott has virtually acknowledged engaged in a cover-up should pay absolutely no attention to the bleeding wound in the back of Merton's head. Merton fell upon a level floor. Mott notwithstanding, it's not the least bit obvious that the floor caused such a wound. How deep did the wound go? Did it reach the brain? If the wound were probed might one find a projectile of some sort? An examination on the spot—even without a full autopsy—might have provided an answer to some of these questions, but the Thai police failed even to acknowledge the wound's existence. At this point one must begin to ask if they conducted their cover-up on behalf of someone even bigger and more powerful than the International Red Cross or the Hitachi Corporation.

The police report also said nothing about Merton having been wet from a shower when he came into contact with the fan. Mott, on the other hand has this passage: "What seems the most likely reconstruction is that Merton came out of the shower either wearing a pair of drawers or naked. His feet may have been wet still from the shower."

Does that not also suggest that the police are covering up for those responsible for the faulty fan that killed Merton? At this point, readers may be surprised to learn that it is the police and not Mott who are on the firmer ground. In fact, speaking of the loose ends in Mott's explanation of the event, it's really very hard to say what ground Mott is on. Notice that he doesn't even say for certain that Merton was wet from a shower, though he even leaves open the possibility that Merton donned his shorts while still wet from the shower, something that is even less likely than a Hitachi fan shocking someone to death.

The police, in this instance, had good reason to make no mention of Merton having taken a shower. That is because he didn't. He left lunch at the main building of the conference center at around 1:40 p.m. in the company of Father François de Grunne, O.S.B., of Belgium to take a break from the conference, which was to resume at 4:30. The cottage where they were staying was a 10 to 15 minute walk away. Father Celestine Say, O.S.B., from the Philippines, followed about five minutes behind them, and he could see them far ahead of him in conversation. By the time Say arrived at the cottage, de Grunne had gone upstairs to his room and Merton to his room on the first floor. Say's room was also on the first floor. John Moffitt, the poetry editor of the Jesuit *America* magazine was the fourth person in the cottage, with a room upstairs, but he had joined a group for a short sightseeing trip into Bangkok for the afternoon.

The doors with their frames for the private rooms seem to have been more or less permanent structures, but the walls were not. They were nothing but a wire mesh, with bed sheets hung next to them for privacy. Air could pass through, an important feature in the tropical climate with no air conditioning, and so, too, could sound. A shower room was accessible from the parlor between the two private rooms. The fan that was found lying on Merton was in his room, which was some distance from the shower.

Say said that he could even hear Merton when he was walking barefooted in his room, but from the time that he arrived at the cottage, he never heard a sound from Merton. He could even see that Merton was not lying in his bed but thought that he might be reclining on the floor, either because it was cooler or for penance. Say was awake the whole

216

time from when he arrived at the cottage shortly before 2:00 p.m. until de Grunne came downstairs and told him to come have a look into Merton's room at around 4 :00 p.m. Say even took a shower himself when he was unable to take an intended nap because of the noise de Grunne was making pacing up and down upstairs directly above him. At no time after his arrival at the cottage did Say hear or see Merton take a shower.

The testimony that de Grunne gave to the police was included with the police report when it was sent to the Gethsemani Abbey in 1969, but it seems to have disappeared. De Grunne wrote several letters to Moffitt in that year, and he makes no mention of Merton having showered, either. The shower was absent from contemporary news reports, as well.

A few weeks after the conference, Sister Marie de la Croix, O.C.S.O., who was at the conference, prepared a 5-page report in French whose English title is "The Last Days of Thomas Merton." In that report she wrote that the first thing Merton did upon returning to the cottage was to take a shower, but then, she says, he took a nap before his encounter with the fan, so the shower would have been immaterial to the supposed electrocution. At any rate, she was not a witness, having been on that same excursion into Bangkok with Moffitt and was probably just repeating erroneous scuttlebutt.

One other early document makes mention of a shower. That is a letter sent on December 11, 1968, the day after the death, purportedly from "the six Trappist delegates at the Conference" to Abbot Flavian Burns at the Gethsemani Abbey. There were actually seven remaining Trappists in attendance at the conference after Merton's death. If there was ever such an actual signed letter, it has also disappeared. Whoever wrote the letter merely speculates, saying only that Merton might have taken a shower, but none of the Trappists would have been in any better position than Sister Marie de la Croix to testify to the fact since none of them were witnesses, either.

Mott is bad enough with his hedging and equivocating, but he is most unreliable when he is most definite. Right at the beginning of his narrative of what happened at the cottage he says, "At some time before three o'clock Father de Grunne heard what he thought was a cry and the sound of something falling. There were noises at all hours in the area around the cottage, but this sound seemed to come from below."

With this passage, he has planted in the mind of the reader that that was the moment of Merton's fatal encounter with the fan. On this point Mott seems to be close to agreement with the police report. "At 3:00 P.M., on the same day, Reverend De Grunne who stayed in an upper room over the scene, while walking into the bathroom, heard a loud noise coming from the lower story which sounded like a heavy object falling onto the floor," they say.

Notice that the cry is missing from the police report. Perhaps Mott got that from Father Say, who he implies failed to hear the noise because he was brushing his teeth at the time and the water was running.

Say did, indeed, report that de Grunne came down and asked him if he had heard a "shout," and Say was brushing his teeth at the time, but the time of his experience is quite different. According to Say, the first thing he did upon returning to the cottage was to take off his habit and to go brush his teeth. It was at that moment, which would have been around 2:00 p.m., that de Grunne came down, knocked on the bathroom door, and asked Say if he had heard a shout, which Say said he had not. Say later reported in a letter that it would have been an easy matter for de Grunne to look into Merton's room and see his condition, but he did not. He simply went back upstairs and paced the floor.

What one would never gather from Mott, or from the police report, for that matter, is that de Grunne behaved a great deal more like a suspect than a reliable witness. It looks like he was inviting Say to make the discovery of Merton's body, but Say only noticed upon returning to his room that Merton was not lying in his bed, looking no further, out of respect for Merton's privacy.

De Grunne interrupted his almost two hours of pacing around, according to Say, to leave the cottage for a short time and then to come back. After coming down that third time at around 4:00 p.m., either to ask Merton to go for a swim or to ask him for the key to the cottage,

218

depending upon which of the two mutually exclusive reasons de Grunne has given, he made his "discovery" and then invited Say to come look into Merton's room. Neither of de Grunne's reasons for going to Merton's room at that time is plausible. He had already gone out and come back into the cottage, either using the key to regain reentry or without needing a key for an unlocked outer door, and it was too late to go for a swim. The conference was set to resume at 4:30.

Say then saw Merton lying in his shorts on the floor of his room with the fan lying across him. The door was latched from inside (though later gaining entry without breaking the door proved relatively simple). De Grunne left toward the main building, ostensibly to go for help. Upon encountering two abbots, Fr. Odo Haas, O.S.B. and Fr. Egbert Donovan, O.S.B., his first words were to ask them if they had had a good swim. Even Mott thought this pleasantry odd, but he dismissed it on account of de Grunne's "nervousness." Say later wrote that de Grunne's manner generally had given him "the creeps." Donovan wrote that de Grunne told them that he had come down and discovered Merton because of the noise that he had heard. Now we have a third possible time for the crucial noises from down below that de Grunne claims to have heard.

In July of 1969, in a letter responding to John Moffitt, de Grunne took it all back. In that letter he said that whatever noises he might have heard must have been coming from the nearby neighborhood.

There is another source for the 3:00 p.m. time. An unsigned statement, purportedly to be from Fr. Haas, says, "We met Rev. Fr. Grunne [sic] and he told us that about 3 pm he heard a cry and the fall of a heavy object in or nearby the house. After some time he wanted to go look in the room where Fr. Merton was, off on the right."

There's the 3:00 p.m., but now we have a third reason for de Grunne to have come down and look into the room, and after a long, implausible delay, at that. Because it has a number of clear errors, however, we have concluded that this document cannot be authentic. Mott has seized upon the biggest error, though, apparently because it is essential for the lethal-fan argument. Haas, Donovan, and Say were the first people into Merton's room. The Haas statement says that when he tried to remove the fan from Merton's body, he got a strong electric shock and could not free himself from it until Say rushed to unplug it. Say reported, however, that Haas recoiled from the shock and when asked, said that the shock was not too strong. Even the police report said that Haas "jerked away from the fan." For Mott, that turned into Haas dramatically being "jerked sideways and held to the fan" until Say could unplug it.

Finally, the reader may have noticed that we say that the witnesses found Merton in his shorts. Say even photographed the scene. Mott, however, purposely neutralized the photographic evidence by writing that the photograph was taken after the scene had been disturbed and that the body by that time might have been dressed for modesty's sake. He had to have known that that was not true, because he had seen the same letters from Say that we have seen and he knew that Say's purpose in taking the photograph was precisely to preserve the death scene as the witnesses had seen it, because they thought it was so peculiar. Mott also fails to explain how there could have been a burn on the underwear—as he quotes from the police report—if the body had been found naked.

In summation, the widespread trust in Michael Mott's account of Thomas Merton's death has been very badly misplaced.

2. The Strange Case of the Monk in the Shower

THE STRANGE CASE OF THE MONK IN THE SHOWER -QUESTIONS SURROUNDING THE DEATH OF THOMAS MERTON

by

Patricia Lefevere, December 2018

(Published with permission of Patricia Lefevere)

Priests are an endangered species. Hardly a month passes without headlines of a priest murdered in Africa. Cameroon, Central African Republic, Nigeria and South Sudan have all lost Catholic clergy this year due to violence. Two years ago an ICIS jihadist stabbed and slit the throat of an elderly French priest on his parish altar in Normandy.

Catholics are now praying to St. Oscar Romero, canonized in October just 38 years after he was shot by an assassin as he lifted the host in the act of consecration. Scores of missionaries in Latin America, Asia and Africa have lost their lives to violence since Romero's killing in 1980.

But what about Trappist monk Thomas Merton, whose death 50 years ago this week (Dec. 10, 1968) in Bangkok, Thailand is being marked by thousands of his devoted readers? Was he murdered by CIA or other assassins for his outspokenness against the Vietnam War, his critical stance on nuclear weapons, on made-in-America racism, or his cry against capitalism's empire-building by way of global violence?

In *The Martyrdom of Thomas Merton, an Investigation*, Hugh Turley and David Martin conjecture that the monk was struck in the back of the head by either a pointed object or a bullet fired from a gun with a silencer while in his room at the Sawangke Vivas center, 15 miles south of Bangkok. Merton and other religious were staying at the center while attending an international meeting of Catholic abbots. The monk had returned to his room after giving a speech earlier that morning and after eating lunch.

The authors call "preposterous" the long-held explanation that Merton stepped out of the shower and then tried to move a large floor fan with an apparently faulty cord and was electrocuted. They describe Merton as lying on the floor, his legs and arms straight, his palms facing down as if placed in a coffin.

Turley and Martin base their description on a photo taken by Benedictine Fr. Celestine Say as Merton's body lay on the floor, the fan still atop his thigh and reaching to the opposite side of his lower waist.

Say of the Philippines and Benedictine Archabbot Egbert Donovan of St. Vincent Archabbey in Latrobe, Penn. both shared rooms close to Merton's and were among the first to come upon his body, the authors report. Both found the death scene with the still-running fan "suspicious," the authors write, and Donovan urged Say to take a photo before Merton's body was moved. "His body had several cuts and burns," according to an obituary in the Kentucky-Standard of Bardstown Dec. 19, 1968.

A copy of Say's photo is part of the archives of the Thomas Merton Center at Bellarmine University in Louisville, Ken. and of the Abbey of Our Lady of Gethsemani in Trappist, Ken., where Merton lived 27 years, Dr. Paul Pearson said. Pearson directs the Merton Center at Bellarmine.

The original film, which includes two photos of the death scene, is part of the John Howard Griffin archives in Columbia University's Butler Library. Griffin was the first official biographer of Merton, but was unable to finish the project due to ill health.

Neither photo appears in the book as the authors failed to gain the permission of Fr. Elias Dietz, the Abbot of Gethsemani, to reproduce them. However they are described in great detail.

Whether Merton's death was an accident or a crime might well have been determined 50 years ago with an autopsy. None was done. Instead the Abbey was told by the U.S. Embassy that according to Thai law if an autopsy was done, Merton would have to be buried in Thailand. The monks wanted him to be buried at Gethsemani. But the authors say there was no such law, only an invention of the embassy.

Though many people might have been glad to see Merton out of the way, or at least relieved that his prolific outpourings of essays and letters critical of the war – two written to President Lyndon Johnson --had been halted, the authors have no proof of his presumed murderer. But the curious reader may find intriguing their descriptions of a Belgian Benedictine, who has seemingly managed to fall off the face of the earth – and his abbey-- since the deed was allegedly done. The monk, Fr. François De Grunne, was the last person known to have been with Merton when he returned to his room after lunch.

A confession

A few years ago Matthew Fox spoke with two CIA agents who were in Southeast Asia at the time of Merton's death. Fox asked them if they killed Merton. The first replied: "I will neither affirm it nor deny it." The second talked about how inundated with money they were at that time in Southeast Asia and how there was no accountability whatsoever, said Fox, a spiritual theologian and Episcopal priest in the Diocese of Northern California.

"Any CIA agent who felt Merton was a threat to the country could have had him killed with no questions asked," Fox said via e-mail. He also reports this in his book, *A Way to God: Thomas Merton's Creation Spirituality Journey.*

More recently Fox met a third CIA agent and asked him pointblank: "Did you guys kill Merton?"

"Yes," the agent replied, adding: "The last 40 years of my life I have been cleansing my soul from the actions I was involved in in the name of the CIA in Southeast Asia as a young man."

For Fox that admission is proof the CIA killed the monk. "Merton died a martyr for peace – as did his friend, Dr. Martin Luther King, Jr., at the hands of the U.S. Government," said the former Dominican priest and author of 36 books.

Conjectures about Merton's death may still be rife when the centenary of his passing arrives in 2068. A heart attack as suggested in the Thai police report. Electrocution from a faulty fan as in the most-quoted death scenario. Head wounds as a result of a fall. These are all possibilities, Pearson noted. "The cause of (his) death is uncertain."

Commemorations of the 50th anniversary of whatever death Merton experienced have been going on for months across the nation and the world. From Argentina to Britain, Canada to Poland and across 12 American states exhibitions, Masses and services of remembrances have been held or are planned.

Louisville artist Joe McGee wondered what is it about Merton that "draws so many of us together like a magnet 50 years after he left this Earth." The answer may be found not only in McGee and artist Penny Sisto's art works on display at Bellarmine, but also in many of the 70 books the monk authored.

Merton once said he would rather hoe beans or pitch hay than write books. He often disowned the main character in The Seven Story Mountain, his sensational autobiography written at the Abbey and published in 1948. But Fr. Daniel Walsh, his teacher and friend since their days at Columbia in the late 1930s, said Merton loved when readers told him the book "brought them closer to God."

In his homily preached at Merton's funeral and available on the Merton Center website, Walsh speaks of the monk's lifelong search for God, which was at times "thorny," but one in which he "never wavered in his steadfast devotion to the God of his deeply religious faith." In return Merton "was given great gifts of mind and heart," Walsh said. "His humility, patience and perseverance were the added reward of his abiding faith."

Walsh likened Merton's spiritual and intellectual gifts to those of John XXIII with whom he exchanged letters and gifts. The Trappist and the

Pontiff shared the charism of recognizing "the unity of spirit and person in all of us." Both men understood that "the spiritual is primarily the work of God… not man," Walsh said, calling this truth "humbly satisfying to the people of God."

Merton's superior and friend, Abbot Flavian Burns told monks at a Mass the day following Merton's death that the monk was ready for death. The two spoke of death before Merton set off on his Asia trip. "The possibility of death was not absent from his mind," Burns said. "He even saw a certain fittingness in dying over there amidst those Asian monks, who symbolized for him man's ancient and perennial desire for the deep things of God," the abbot said.

Merton's death at 53 while sad and shocking was celebrated – and continues to be recalled – with the alleluias of Easter. Would that have been possible 50 years ago in the midst of a terrible war had anyone suspected he had been murdered? The question – like the search for God – continues.

3. Thomas Merton's "Death Shout"

By

David Martin

November 14, 2019

Before there was the "shower," there was the "shout." The great anti-war Trappist monk and writer, Thomas Merton, died suddenly and mysteriously on the afternoon of December 10, 1968, in his room in a two-story, four-bedroom cottage at a Red Cross retreat center outside Bangkok, Thailand. The standard, widely believed, story of how he died is that he was wet from a shower or a bath when he touched a defective fan that killed him by electrocution. Hugh Turley and I reveal in our book, *The Martyrdom of Thomas Merton: An Investigation*, that the story that Merton had taken a shower originated with Merton's secretary at his home abbey of Gethsemani in Kentucky, Brother Patrick Hart, in 1973, almost five years after the death. Hart wrote in an authoritative voice that after giving a talk and having lunch at the main conference building where an international monastic conference was taking place, Merton returned to his cottage (a 10-15-minute walk) and "proceeded to take a shower." That was in the postscript that he wrote for *The Asian Journal of Thomas Merton*, a volume that he co-edited. As we explain in the book and in "New Directions Misdirections in Thomas Merton's Death" Brother Patrick made up the shower story out of whole cloth.

Well before that, only a few weeks after Merton's death, a Japan-based Trappist nun by the name of Marie de la Croix, who was also an attendee at the event, had written in a 5-page paper that Merton had taken a shower, but then she said that he took a nap before he

227

encountered the fan, so the shower would have had no connection to his supposed electrocution. Her observations are faulty in other ways, as well. She was not an immediate witness at the scene, and what she wrote has deservedly been generally ignored.

The only other early mention of a shower was in a letter, supposedly composed the day after the death by the remaining six Trappist monks at the event and sent to the Gethsemani Abbey. The letter was sent around to various interested parties by the abbey to provide some information about Merton's death, but it seems not to have made it into the press or any publications at that time. Like Sister de la Croix, who was actually the seventh surviving Trappist at the conference, none of the Trappists was a witness to the death scene. Their letter actually has virtually no useful information, providing only speculation and conference scuttlebutt instead. They speculate that Merton might have been electrocuted by the fan and he might have died of a heart attack. They also say that Merton might have taken a shower. The letter also states, "Not long after [Merton] retired a shout was heard by others in his cottage but after a preliminary check they thought they must have imagined the cry." The letter plants in the mind of the reader that that must have been the moment that Merton encountered the lethal fan. In fact, the only "others" in the cottage were Father Celestine Say, a Philippine Benedictine monk on the first floor with Merton and Father François de Grunne, a Belgian Benedictine, in a room directly above Fr. Say. Only Fr. de Grunne ever reported hearing any such shout.

Mott and the Death Cry

That letter first gained wide exposure when it was included as an appendix to the previously mentioned *Asian Journal* volume. The purpose for including it, we may speculate, is that with its conjecture about a possible shower it complements in some small degree Br. Hart's flat assertion that Merton did take a shower. Hart has nothing to say about the supposed death shout. It remained for Merton biographer Michael Mott to bring the shout into relative prominence. At the beginning of his narrative about the events at the cottage in his 1984 biography, *The Seven Mountains of Thomas Merton*, he writes, "At some time before three o'clock Father de Grunne heard what he thought was a cry and the sound of something falling. There were noises at all hours in the area around the cottage, but this sound seemed to come from below."

Positioning his declarative sentence about the shout right at the beginning of his narrative, like the letter by the six Trappists, he suggests to the reader that that was the instant of Merton's fatal encounter with the fan. He also does not say that Fr. de Grunne *said* that he heard such a noise. Rather, he states it as a fact that Fr. de Grunne *heard* that noise that comports so conveniently with the thesis that that was the moment of Merton's fatal fan encounter. One has to be particularly observant to notice that he hedges his statement a bit by saying that de Grunne *thought* it was a cry and the sound of something falling and that the sound *seemed* to come from below. He also carefully hedges on the time, getting three o'clock on the record, but by saying "some time before three o'clock" it might not have been as near to three o'clock as the reader might naturally infer.

There is one thing that you can hang your hat on in Mott's statement, though. Fr. de Grunne is the source, and he is the only source that there ever was, for any such sound supposedly emanating from in or near Merton's room. For its part, the Thai police report says that at 3:00 p.m. de Grunne "heard a loud noise coming from the lower story which sounded like a heavy object falling on the floor." The sound of the falling object accords with Mott's account as does the 3:00 p.m. time, except that the police report is more precise about it. The shout, quite noticeably, is missing, however. Whatever de Grunne might have told them, they couldn't very well report that there was a death shout, because their official conclusion was that Merton died of heart failure and was already dead when he encountered the fan.

The U.S. State Department's Report on the Death of an American Citizen, dated December 13, 1968, took the time of that reported noise, 3 p.m., as the time of Merton's death and gave the cause as "Sudden Heart Failure (according to official Death Certificate)".

A statement purported to be from the witness, Father Odo Haas, apparently ties it all up into a nice, neat bow. Haas's document states that around 4 p.m. he and Father Egbert Donovan "met Rev. Fr. Grunne [sic] and he told us that about 3 p.m. he had heard a cry and the fall of a heavy object in or nearby the house." It was curiosity about that sound, de Grunne said, that drew him downstairs to look into the room, whose wall was only temporary netting that one could see through where a privacy sheet was not hung, and he had seen Merton lying on the floor. The door was locked, so he was on his way to the main building to get a key.

The very influential account of Merton's death by the biographer Mott relies heavily, without attribution, upon this Haas statement. Unfortunately for all those people who have repeated Mott's account in one variation or another, the statement is as full of holes as a Swiss cheese. First, the door was secured by an inner latch, not by a key. And what, one well might wonder, took de Grunne so long to satisfy his curiosity? De Grunne, in fact, said to other people that his reason for coming downstairs at that time was, alternatively, to ask Merton if he would like to go for a swim in the retreat's pool or to ask him for the key for the outer door. As it happens, neither of those explanations is any better than curiosity over the noise he had heard an hour before. Fr. Say had heard de Grunne go out of the cottage and come back in earlier, so he either already had the key to the outer door, or the outer door was not locked. It was too late to go for a swim, because the conference was scheduled to resume at 4:30. It looks like de Grunne gave up on Say discovering that Merton was dead, and he finally had to go and do it.

Fr. Say Has Last Say

The biggest problem of all, though, is with that sound that de Grunne supposedly heard, and, again, it is the testimony of the best witness, Fr. Say, that reveals it. Fr. Say was about five minutes behind Merton and Fr. de Grunne as they entered the cottage after walking together from the main conference building, approaching 2 p.m. The first thing he did, he

230

said, was to remove his habit and then go to the bathroom off the parlor that separated his room from Merton's to brush his teeth. At that point, he heard a knock on the bathroom door, opened it, and there was Fr. de Grunne. The first thing de Grunne said to him was, "Oh, I thought you were Merton." Then he said, "Did you hear a shout?" Say responded in the negative. In fact, he never heard the slightest sound from Merton's room from his moment of his arrival at the cottage.

So, according to Say's report—and he is a rock-solid witness, in stark contrast to de Grunne and the dodgy Haas and six-Trappists documents—if there was ever any "death shout" heard by de Grunne, it would have been at around 2 p.m. and not 3 p.m. Oddly, instead of at least looking into Merton's room or knocking on Merton's door to satisfy his supposed curiosity about the "shout," de Grunne simply went back upstairs. Say, out of respect for Merton's privacy, did not look in on Merton and simply returned to his room after brushing his teeth.

Had there ever actually have been any such shout or cry from Merton's room, Fr. Say almost certainly would have heard it. As it turns out, perhaps the best evidence that there was no such noise, either from Merton's mouth or from a falling fan (which would have hardly made any noise at all falling squarely onto Merton's supine body where it was found) comes from de Grunne, himself. On July 6, 1969, in a letter in response to a query by John Moffitt, the poetry editor of the Jesuit *America* magazine who was the fourth occupant of the cottage but had gone into Bangkok sightseeing that fateful afternoon, de Grunne minimized the importance of the sound that he had supposedly heard, saying that there were lots of sounds from a nearby house and, whatever it was he heard and whenever it might have occurred, it must have come from that other house.

As a final note, Say's observations also destroy another myth originating with the Haas document and perpetuated by Mott. When the three crime-scene witnesses—not four as reported in the Haas document and repeated by Mott (de Grunne had continued on to the main building)—the document says that Haas attempted to remove the fan from Merton's body but received a strong electric shock from which he could not pull free until Say unplugged the fan. Say, however, said, much more plausibly, that Haas recoiled from the shock and that, when he asked him about it, Haas had said that it was not too strong. Interestingly, Br. Patrick, in that postscript in 1973 in which he introduced the shower to the Merton tragedy, like Mott mentioned the "severe" shock that Haas had received when he attempted to remove the fan, but when Br. Patrick repeated that postscript almost verbatim in the introduction to Volume 7 of *The Journals of Thomas Merton* entitled *The Other Side of the Mountain, The End of the Journey*, published in 1998, the "severe" shock had turned into a "slight" electric shock. Some lethal fan, indeed!

4. Key False Document in Thomas Merton Death Case

by
Hugh Turley and David Martin
January 3, 2019

In the paper that we presented to the Thomas Merton Symposiom in Rome, "What We Know about Thomas Merton's Death," we noted that on the subject of Merton's death, Michael Mott's authorized biography, *The Seven Mountains of Thomas Merton* has been treated as the ultimate authority, that is, up until we published *The Martyrdom of Thomas Merton: An Investigation* in March of 2018. Unfortunately, the International Thomas Merton Society (ITMS), which has 45 U.S. chapters, conducts four-day conferences biennially, and publishes the quarterly *Merton Seasonal* and the *Merton Annual* jointly with the Thomas Merton Center of Bellarmine University, in a most benighted fashion, still seems to be treating Mott's flawed and dishonest work as definitive. In one vital part of his narrative, Mott relies upon information contained in a document that we have determined must surely be fraudulent. Worse than that, he fails to reference the document, as though he is aware of its fraudulence. We know that is where he must have gotten his information because it is found nowhere else in the record, and it is directly at odds with much more reliable information that is on the

233

record. We hardly have to guess about this, because the document is among his archived papers at the library of Northwestern University.

We are speaking of Mott's assertion that Father Odo Haas, one of the three witnesses who found Merton's body in his room with a defective fan lying across his pelvic area, attempted to remove it and suffered a strong shock, finding himself stuck to the fan until another witness, Father Celestine Say, was able to unplug it. That is not at all what happened, according to Fr. Say. Mott also writes that there were four initial witnesses, including Father François de Grunne, a "fact" which only could have come from the suspect document. We know that according to the testimony of several others that Fr. de Grunne was not there.

Phony Documents and Cover-Ups

In the case of government cover-ups, made up or misrepresented documents are almost standard fare. A notable example is Vincent Foster's somewhat gloomy memorandum to himself, belatedly found in his briefcase days after it had apparently been emptied out in the presence of several people, torn into 28 pieces with no fingerprints on it, and with one piece missing where a signature might have been. That document served for the press as Foster's suicide note, though it isn't addressed to surviving loved ones and gives no indication that anything in it is serious enough that the writer might be even considering taking his own life. Furthermore, three notable handwriting examiners have declared it to be a forgery.[280]

A similar document played a central role, from the very first day, in the press and government declarations that recently resigned Secretary of Defense James Forrestal had taken his own life on May 22, 1949, when he fell from a 16th floor window of the main tower of the Bethesda Naval Hospital where he had been confined. In this case the surrogate suicide

---

[280] "Foster Suicide Note Was a Forgery, Say Independent Experts," October 26, 1995, https://www.independent.co.uk/news/world/foster-suicide-note-was-a-forgery-say-experts-1579504.html.

234

note was the supposed transcription by Forrestal of a morbid poem by Sophocles, "Chorus from Ajax," in which the main character in despondence apparently contemplates suicide. That transcription turned out not to be even an attempt at a forgery.[281] Perhaps the writer was confident that it would never see the light of day, because the handwriting doesn't begin to resemble Forrestal's.[282]

A more common type of phony document is a falsified witness statement. Sylvia Meagher's seminal 1967 examination of the Warren Commission Report on the John F. Kennedy assassination, *Accessories after the Fact,* is replete with examples (pp. 323-326) of misrepresentation of witness statements by the FBI interviewers. A clear example of an FBI-falsified statement in the Foster case is that of the witness, Patrick Knowlton. Knowlton described to the FBI a car parked at Fort Marcy Park, where Foster's body was found, that was older and of a distinctly different color from Foster's car,[283] but the FBI interview report stated blandly that Knowlton saw Foster's car.

We have encountered a document in the Merton case that appears to be a combination of the two types of falsifications that we have described. It is apparently not a misrepresentation of what a witness told interviewers; rather, it looks very much like a witness statement that has been entirely manufactured. It has not been as central to the Merton case as the two notes were to the Forrestal and Foster cases, but it is important. It provides the only "evidence" that the bad wiring of the fan might have been such that a person touching it might possibly have been killed on the spot.

It is represented as the written statement of Fr. Odo Haas. It would appear to be what he submitted to the Thai police on the day of the death, and that was how it has been characterized in correspondence between those responsible for constructing the narrative approved for

---

[281] https://www.dcdave.com/article4/041103a.htm.

[282] David Martin, *The Assassination of James Forrestal,* 2nd edition, McCabe Publishing, 2021, pp. x-xiii.

[283] *The Vince Foster Cover-up: The FBI and the Press,* www.youtube.com/watch?c=eii7LBSziSM&t=399s.

public consumption. However, initial authorized Merton biographer, John Howard Griffin, in a letter to *America* magazine editor John Moffitt, described the witness statement that he had seen, and that the Gethsemani Abbey had in their possession as "handwritten."[284] He promised that he would send it to Moffitt, but what he eventually sent Moffitt was this typed statement.

The document's legibility is poor, so we transcribe it here so that readers might join us in evaluating its authenticity:

Report on the Discovery of the Corpse of R.Fr. Thomas-Louis Merton

10 Dec.1968

About 4 p.m. In Bangkok- Swanganivas on Sukhumvit Rd. –Thai Red Cross Haus No. ii

Reporter: Odo Haas, osb, Abbot of Waegevan [sic]

*****

About 4 pm I went by Haus no. 2 together with Rt. Rev. Archabbot E. Donovan/Vincent-Latrobe (USA-Penn.) where Rev. Louis-Thomas Merton was living. There were living with him in the same house: Rev. Celestine Say, om[sic]/Prior of Manila

Rev. Francois de Grunne/St. Andrè-Belgium

MR.Moffitt/Editor of America Magazine

We met Rev. Fr. Grunne [sic] and he told us that about 3 pm he had heard a cry and the fall of a heavy object in or nearby the house. After some time he wanted to go look in the room where Fr. Merton was, off on the right. He saw Fr. Merton lying on the floor as he looked through the screen. The door was locked. He took off immediately to get a key.

The three of us immediately hastened to the door of the room. There we met Fr. Say.

I was going to break the door-window open and it gave way right off so that we could easily open the door.

---

[284] Moffitt Papers, October 6, 1969.

Fr. Merton lay on the floor before us. He was dressed only in his shorts. He lay between the bed and a stand where his habit was hanging to dry. The feet lay about 40 inches from the feet-end of the bed with the head in the corner of the room in front of the clothes-stand. On his body lay a fan (made in Japan), about 45 inches high. The feet of the fan lay between the legs of Fr. Merton, with the switch on the top seam of the shorts and the fan itself on the face or the head of Fr. Merton.

The toes of both feet seemed to be cramped.

At the point where the switch touched the shorts and the body a wound, a hands-breadth in width, gaped open. The raw flesh was visible and the base of the wound was blood-shot.

The face was deep blue. The eyes were half open. So was the mouth. On the left side between the body and the arm I observed a pool of fluid. It was not water. I thought it was fluid from the wound or from the body. (Fr. Say advised me to take a picture of the scene. It is doubtful whether it took since it was too dark.) An odor filled the room which, from earlier experience, I had learned to recognize as burnt human flesh.

The fan was still going. And so I wanted to take it off the body right away. In doing so I got a strong electric shock. It kept me from getting free of the fan. Fr. Say pulled the plug of the fan out of the socket as quickly as he could (it was behind the bed in the other corner of the room).

We four together verified the death of Fr. Merton. And so Rt. Rev. Donovan gave him the blessing (presumably general absolution). I did the same.

Immediately I hastened to Rt. Rev. Abbot Primat [sic] R. Weakland who appeared at the scene about 3 minutes later. About 4:10 p.m. the Abbot Primate gave Fr. Merton extreme unction.

(signed) Eyewitness; Odo Haas, osb

Abbot of Waegwan/S. Korea.

(The typewritten document was *not* signed. ed.)

Considering the fact that this statement was supposedly given within a few hours after the actual event, its clear errors can hardly be explained away on account of the witness's faulty memory. The most obvious error is that de Grunne joined Haas and Donovan after he had informed them of Merton's plight: "The three of us hastened to the door of Merton's room."

We know for certain that that is not true. Everyone else said that the three people who first entered Merton's room were Haas, Donovan, and Say and that de Grunne had gone on to the main building. De Grunne, himself, in a letter to John Moffitt said that he went quickly to the main building after informing Haas and Donovan of the Merton emergency. Say also wrote to Moffitt that he had noticed that de Grunne did not return after going for help, and he reflected that de Grunne must have been hit hard emotionally by what had happened to Merton.

We can also see that this misstatement is not just a slip-up, because near the end of the document the writer says quite definitely, "We four together verified the death of Fr. Merton." The four that he is clearly referring to at that point are Say, Donovan, de Grunne, and himself. One of them could not be Dr. Edeltrud Weist, whom he does not mention in his statement, and it could not be Weakland, who didn't get there until a few minutes later, almost simultaneously with Dr. Weist.

The error looks very much like the sort of inadvertent one that a person would make who was not actually there at the scene. It is very difficult to believe that Haas would have made such a major mistake. Another error of that type concerns the matter of the key that de Grunne supposedly left the death scene to pursue. The door to Merton's room was not secured by a lock that required a key, but by an internal latch. And if getting the key were so important in de Grunne's mind, why would he not have continued on to the main building to try to get it?

The Document's Poison Pill

Such inadvertent mistakes may be contrasted with the statement's central inaccuracy, which appears to be the main reason that the statement was concocted. We are talking about the "strong electric shock" that the writer says he got that "kept [him] from getting free of the fan" when he attempted to lift it off Merton's body.

238

That is not what Say reported that he witnessed at the time, saying only that Haas "recoiled" from the shock and that Haas told him that the shock was "not too strong." There is an absolutely fundamental difference between these two descriptions, representing the difference between a would-be killer fan and a fan that one would jerk back from in the manner in which one jerks back from an electric fence. It is extremely hard to believe that a witness like Say, who has proved to be so consistent and reliable in every other way, could possibly have been so wrong about what he saw when Haas touched the defective fan and in what Haas told him about the nature of the shock. Surely Say would not have found such an episode so forgettable that he would never tell anyone else about it, that is, that he had to rush to unplug the fan so that Haas could free himself from it. It is also quite difficult to believe that Haas would describe such an extremely painful and, indeed, life-threatening experience in such a matter-of-fact way.

Whoever wrote this statement—which tellingly lacks Haas's signature and dating at the bottom where a signature is supposed to be—must have realized that reinforcement was needed for the notion that Merton had been killed by a defective fan. The idea had to be planted that the fan might have killed Haas, too, but for the quick thinking of Say to rush to unplug it.

The short statement has other anomalies, likely errors of both the intentional and inadvertent type. In that latter category, the writer has the fan lying on Merton's body with its base between his legs and the blades of the fan on Merton's head. Since the diagonal placement of the fan across Merton's body was so radically different from this, one can hardly believe that this could be the writing of an actual witness.

The document also describes a wide, open wound on Merton's body mentioned by no other witnesses or the police report and not apparent in the two photographs of the scene that we have.

The writer also says that Say suggested that he take a picture of the scene, but we know that it was Say who actually took photographs, and, according to Say, it was Haas who suggested that he do so. Say, we know, after observing the conduct of the Thai police, became wary of them and decided not to reveal to the police that he had taken photographs of the body for fear that they would confiscate his film. Haas is likely to have shared Say's wariness of the police and would not have divulged that he had taken any photograph for the same reason.

Another likely inadvertent mistake in the statement is that the fan was still running, suggesting that the blades of the fan were still turning. Donovan, however, wrote in a letter to Moffitt, that the blades of the fan were still when they entered Merton's room. It is a good deal more likely that a short-circuited fan would not be running, so Donovan's observation seems more believable.

It is highly unlikely that Haas would have begun his statement by misspelling the hometown of his abbey in Korea. It is equally unlikely that he would have written the initials for the Order of St. Benedict that follows his name in lower case letters. This is never done.

In the intentional misinformation category, the writer reports that de Grunne, as soon as he encountered Haas and Donovan, told them that he had heard "a cry and the fall of a heavy object" at about 3:00 p.m., but, curiously, he hadn't gone to check on it until about an hour later. This fits very well with the "loud noise" that the police report says that de Grunne heard at about that time, but it's very strange that Haas would report such a thing so routinely. Wouldn't he have found it odd that de Grunne would have waited so long to check on such alarming sounds?

It also fits with Dr. Weist writing that she had been told that de Grunne heard a shout at about 3:00 p.m., causing her to speculate that this could have been the time of Merton's death. (M. Edeltrud Weist, Report on the first impressions after Rev. F. Thomas Merton's tragic death given by an eyewitness, handwritten note, Bangkok, December 11, 1968, the Merton Center.) De Grunne very likely did tell others what the police say in their report that he told them. For the record, John Moffitt, after studying the evidence, had concluded by 1970 that de Grunne could not have heard any shout or sound of an object falling–never mind the time–because de Grunne was upstairs on the opposite side of the cottage with a door closed between the two floors. Merton's body falling onto

240

the terrazzo floor would hardly have made any noise. Neither would the fan falling on top of Merton's body have made much noise.[285]

In fact, in a letter to Moffitt, that's not at all how Donovan remembered the encounter. The thing that stood out in his mind was how de Grunne first oddly asked them if they had had a good swim, and only then told them that he had heard a thump, and when he promptly checked he saw Merton on the floor of his locked room. Donovan said that on hearing this from de Grunne, he and Haas quickly went to Merton's cottage. Not only does that account have a greater ring of truth, but it also correctly reports, in agreement with de Grunne and Say, that only Haas and Donovan rushed to look about Merton.

Say reported that Haas had told him he thought it most unusual that de Grunne should greet them with a casual query about their swim, but it seems not to have been remarkable enough for mention in this statement that is purportedly by Haas, which is just another reason to doubt its authenticity.

The Shower Story Came Later

Readers may note that the statement says that Merton was found wearing shorts and that whatever liquid was present was not water. This gives the lie to any notion that Merton was wet from showering when he touched the fan. One might wonder why the perpetrators of a cover-up would manufacture a document that is so incriminating on this point. But we must remember that the wet-from-showering scenario was not yet part of the story that the public had been told. It was not in the police report, and it was not in any news reports and would not be for a few years. That would not come until 1973 when, as we reported in "New Directions' Misdirection on Thomas Merton's Death,"[286] Merton's secretary at the Gethsemani Abbey in Kentucky, wrote it in the postscript to *The Asian Journal of Thomas Merton.*

---

[285] John Moffitt, letter to Brother Patrick, February 8, 1970, Moffitt Papers.
[286] https://dcdave.com/article5/180911.htm.

241

Even though it did not support the shower story, this "Haas statement" was still used to support the approved account, even after the wet-from-showering story had become a part of it, though carefully, as we have pointed out, without direct acknowledgment. A major reason why Michael Mott, who was one of the few people even to be aware of this document, could make no direct reference to it was precisely because of what the statement accurately said about Merton's body with shorts on it and the absence of water at the scene. By the time Mott published his biography in 1984, the shower story had become thoroughly incorporated into the myth of Merton's death.

If this is indeed a statement that Haas made for the Thai police, and it was in possession of the U.S. Embassy at the time that they ostensibly translated the police report, there is no conceivable innocent excuse for either of them to have mangled the spelling of the names of Haas and Say, as they did in the copy of the police report that was supposedly furnished to the abbey. Those names are right there in this statement for them to see.

The statement, in fact, in great contrast to the police report, is downright meticulous about people's names as well as their proper titles and occupations. In that regard, it seems to reflect more the concerns of a fussy bureaucrat than those of a witness at the scene, which is just one more reason to doubt its authenticity. Since neither the Haas statement nor the police report was signed and neither had the embassy's official stamp, as other documents related to Merton's death did, it further raises the question of whether either of the documents even came through the embassy.

As we discuss in more detail in Chapter 8 of *The Martyrdom of Thomas Merton*, the typewritten witness statement by Dr. Weist has a big problem of its own, that is, that it omits the concluding two paragraphs of Dr. Weist's signed, handwritten version of the statement. The important information thereby left out is that, according to Dr. Weist, Haas told Say that the shock that he had received upon touching the fan was not very strong. It is hard to escape the conclusion that someone

242

realized how damaging to the electrocution story it was that the fan had only mildly shocked Haas, so that part was deleted.

This explanation would be all nice and neat, except for the fact that it was the original handwritten version of Weist's statement that was sent to the abbey with the police report. We obtained our typed copy of it from Father Rembert Weakland, Abbot Primate of the Benedictine Order who presided over the conference. Weakland was not even aware of the police report. Perhaps someone just messed up when he or she provided Weist's handwritten statement and not the typed one to the abbey. Why would they have even bothered to type it up if it were not designed to be the official one for public consumption?

Finally, Dr. Weist's handwritten statement and Fr. Say's letter giving his eyewitness account are not the only sources that contradict this Haas account of the "strong electric shock" that kept him stuck to the fan until Say could unplug it. The police report itself, which Michael Mott had in his possession, along with the statement of Dr. Weist and the letters of Fr. Celestine Say, when he wrote Merton's biography, says that Haas "jerked back" from the fan, and Brother Patrick Hart in the introduction to *The Other Side of the Mountain*, Volume 7 of *The Journals of Thomas Merton*, published in 1998, described the shock to Haas as "slight." He had previously described the shock as "strong," however, in that postscript in which he introduced the shower story back in 1973. Hardly surprisingly, Brother Patrick has no source for either of these assertions that contradict one another.

Sir Walter Scott's famous line, "Oh what a tangled tale we weave, when first we practice to deceive," seems particularly appropriate for what we have described in all of the foregoing.

John Moffitt copy of Haas document with his notations

Report on the Discovery of the Corpse of Fr.Thomas-Louis Merton
10 Dec.1968
About 4 p.m. in Bangkok- Samganivas on Sukhumvit 54.-Thai Red Cross
Haus No. 11

Reporter: (de Haas,osb,Abbot of Waegevan
※※※※※※

About 4 pm I went by Haus no. 2 together with Rt.Rev.Archabbot R.Donovan/St.
Vincent-Latrobe ("PA-Penn.) where Rev. Louis-Thomas Merton was living. There
were living with him in the same house: Rev. Celestine Say,osb/Prior of Manila
Rev. Francois de Grunne/St.André-Belgium
Mr.Moffitt/ Editor of "America"-magazine.

We met Rev.Fr.Grunne and he told us that about 3 pm he had heard a cry and the
fall of a heavy object in or nearby the house. After some time he wanted to go
look in the room where Fr. Merton was,off on the right. He saw Fr. Merton lying
on the floor as he looked through the screen. The door was locked. He took off
immediately to get a key.
The three of us immediately hastened to the door of the room. There we met Fr.
Say.
I was going to break the door-window open and it gave way right off so that we
could easily open the door.
Fr. Merton lay on the floor before us.He was dressed only in his shorts. He lay
between the bed and a stand where his habit was hanging to dry. The feet lay
about 40 inches from the foot-end of the bed with the head in the corner of the
room in front of the clothes-stand. On his body lay a fan(made in Japan),about
45 inches high. The foot of the fan lay between the legs of Fr.Merton, with
the switch on the top seam of the shorts and the fan itself on the face or
the head of Fr. Merton.
The feet toes of both feet seemed to be cramped.
At the point where the switch touched the shorts and the body a wound,a hand-
breadth in width, gaped open. The raw flesh was visible and the base of the wound
was blood-shot.
The face was deep blue. The eyes were half open.So was the mouth.
On the left side between the body and the arm I observed a pool of fluid. It

244

was not water. I thought it was fluid from the wound or from the body.(Fr.Day
advised me to take a picture of the scene. It is doubtful whether it took since
it was too dark.) An odor filled the room which,from earlier experience,I had
learned to recognize as burnt human flesh.

The fan was still going. And so I wanted to take it off the body right away. In
doing so I got a strong electric shock. It kept me from getting free of the fan.
Fr.Day pulled the plug of the fan out of the socket as quickly as he could(
it was behind the bed in the other corner of the room).

We fourxxxxxxxxxxxxxxxxxxxxxx together verified the death of Fr. Merton. And so
Rt.Rev. Donovan gave him the blessing(presumably general absolution). I did the
same.

Immediately I hastened to Rt.Rev.Abbot Primat R.Weakland who appeared at the scene
about 3 minutes later. About 4:10 p.m. the Abbot Primate gave Fr.Merton xxx extreme
unction.

(Signed) Eyewitness:Odo Haas,osb
                    Abbot of Waegwan/S.Korea.

245

5. John H. Griffin Military Discharge

ENLISTED RECORD AND REPORT OF SEPARATION

HONORABLE DISCHARGE   #4-85/482

1. LAST NAME - FIRST NAME - MIDDLE INITIAL	2. ARMY SERIAL NO.	3. GRADE	4. ARM OR SERVICE	5. COMPONENT
GRIFFIN JOHN H	38 098 381	S/SGT	AAF	AUS

6. ORGANIZATION	7. DATE OF SEPARATION	8. PLACE OF SEPARATION
424th Bombardment Squadron	27 Oct 45	Separation Center Fort Sam Houston Texas

9. PERMANENT ADDRESS FOR MAILING PURPOSES	10. DATE OF BIRTH	11. PLACE OF BIRTH
2223 Rand Rd Fort Worth Tarrant Co Texas	16 Jun 20	Fort Worth Texas

12. ADDRESS FROM WHICH EMPLOYMENT WILL BE SOUGHT	13. COLOR EYES	14. COLOR HAIR	15. HEIGHT	16. WEIGHT	17. NO. DEPEND.
Same 9	Grey	Brown	5'11"	219	0

18. RACE	19. MARITAL STATUS	20. U.S. CITIZEN	21. CIVILIAN OCCUPATION AND NO.
White X	Single Married Other X	YES X AC	Translator 0-58.320

MILITARY HISTORY

22. DATE OF INDUCTION	23. DATE OF ENLISTMENT	24. DATE OF ENTRY INTO ACTIVE SERVICE	25. PLACE OF ENTRY INTO SERVICE
9 Mar 42	-	9 Mar 42	Ind Sta Camp Wolters Texas

26.	27. LOCAL S.S. BOARD NO.	28. COUNTY AND STATE	29. HOME ADDRESS AT TIME OF ENTRY INTO SERVICE
X	# 6	Tarrant Co Texas	Same 9

30. MILITARY OCCUPATIONAL SPECIALTY AND NO.	31. MILITARY QUALIFICATION AND DATE
Radio Mechanic 853	AAF Technician Badge (Date Unknown)

32. BATTLES AND CAMPAIGNS
GO 33 WD 45   Bismarck-Archipelago Central Pacific Eastern Mandates New Guinea
Northern Solomons Luzon Western Pacific Air Combat Borneo

33. DECORATIONS AND CITATIONS
Asiatic-Pacific Campaign Medal with 8 Bronze Stars
Distinguished Unit Badge GO #63 WD 5 Aug 44 1 - Service Stripe
Good Conduct Medal   5 - Overseas Service Bars

34. WOUNDS RECEIVED IN ACTION
None

35. LATEST IMMUNIZATION DATES				36. SERVICE OUTSIDE CONTINENTAL U.S. AND RETURN		
SMALLPOX	TYPHOID	TETANUS	OTHER (specify)	DATE OF DEPARTURE	DESTINATION	DATE OF ARRIVAL
9 Jul 45	22 May 45	23 Dec 42	Typhus 6 Aug 45	10 Feb 43	AP	21 Feb 43

37. TOTAL LENGTH OF SERVICE		38. HIGHEST GRADE HELD			20 Sep 45	US	20 Oct 45
CONTINENTAL SERVICE	FOREIGN SERVICE						
YEARS	MONTHS	DAYS	YEARS	MONTHS	DAYS		
0	11	8	2	8	11	S/Sgt	

39. PRIOR SERVICE
None

40. REASON AND AUTHORITY FOR SEPARATION
Convenience of the Government (RR 1-1 Demobilization) AR 615-365 15 Dec 44

41. SERVICE SCHOOLS ATTENDED	42. EDUCATION (Years)
Radio Operator & Mechanic	Grammar High School College 8 4 3

PAY DATA

43. LONGEVITY FOR PAY PURPOSES	44. MUSTERING OUT PAY		45. SOLDIER DEPOSITS	46. TRAVEL PAY	47. TOTAL AMOUNT, NAME OF DISBURSING OFFICER
YEARS MONTHS DAYS	TOTAL	THIS PAYMENT			$450.00 Cash
7 19	300	100			Check CARLOS DE LIMA Capt

INSURANCE NOTICE

IMPORTANT IF PREMIUM IS NOT PAID WHEN DUE OR WITHIN THIRTY-ONE DAYS THEREAFTER, INSURANCE WILL LAPSE. MAKE CHECKS OR MONEY ORDERS PAYABLE TO THE TREASURER OF THE U.S. AND FORWARD TO COLLECTIONS SUBDIVISION, VETERANS ADMINISTRATION, WASHINGTON 25, D. C.

48. KIND OF INSURANCE	49. HOW PAID			51. Effective Date of Allot.	52. Date of Next Premium Due	53. PREMIUM DUE	54. INTENTION OF VETERAN TO
Nat. Serv. U.S. Govt.	Allotment Direct to V.A.					None	

55. REMARKS
Lapel Button Issued
ASR Score (2 Sep 1945) - 105

56. SIGNATURE OF PERSON BEING SEPARATED	57. PERSONNEL OFFICER (Signature)
John H. Griffin	H. L. CLIFTON CWO USA Ass't Mil Pers Officer

WD AGO FORM 53-55
1 November 1944

6. Turned Away by the Abbey of Gethsemani

I N March of 2019, Hugh Turley drove to Gethsemani from Maryland with his wife, Makiko. Makiko was paralyzed and suffering with severe dementia, so it was a challenging journey for them. He was a 24-hour caregiver to his wife and tended to all her needs. Their trip to Gethsemani would be their last road trip since travelling had become so difficult. They arrived at the Gethsemani on Saturday afternoon, March 23, and after their journey Turley sent the letter below to the abbey's Brother Paul Quenon, with whom he had corresponded previously:

April 8, 2019

Dear Brother Paul,

In February, I wrote to tell you that I wanted to come to Gethsemani to meet you. I asked you if I needed an appointment. You did not reply to me.

In March, I drove to Gethsemani from Maryland with my wife Makiko. My wife is paralyzed and has severe dementia, so it was a challenging journey for us. We arrived at the Abbey on Saturday afternoon, March 23.

I found Fr. Seamus Malvey at the reception desk, and he greeted us with a nice "hello," and an extra nice "hello" for my wife in her wheelchair. I told him that I would like to see you. He told us that you were not available because you were with a group of students from Bellarmine. I asked if I might see Abbot Elias Dietz. Fr. Seamus asked if the abbot was expecting me. I said, "No, but he will know who I am. My name is Hugh Turley."

Fr. Seamus picked up the phone and called the abbot. When he hung up, he told me that the abbot was busy and then angrily asked, "Why did you tell me you knew the abbot?" I said, "I never told you that I knew the abbot. I told you that he would know who I am." Ignoring my words, Fr. Seamus again falsely stated, "You told me that you knew the abbot."

Fr. Seamus looked uncomfortable, and his face became contorted. He said that I should have made an appointment. I asked him if he had read our book, *The Martyrdom of Thomas Merton*. Fr. Seamus said, "I've heard about it." I told him that I had written several letters to Abbot Dietz and that he does not answer my letters. Fr. Morey does not reply to my letters and when I asked you if I needed an appointment, you did not reply.

Fr. Seamus smugly said, "You have been rejected. You should not have come here." He called me "aggressive and rude" for coming to Gethsemani. I told him that my disabled wife and I had come a great distance and that we would like to meet with someone.

Fr. Seamus sarcastically clapped his hands slowly three times to belittle and make fun of us. "Why did you do that?" I asked. Gloating, Fr. Seamus said, "I wanted you to have some recognition." His hurtful words and actions were unbecoming a Trappist monk and Catholic priest. There was no point in talking to a fool so I told him that we would pray for him, and we left.

I stopped to visit Thomas Merton's grave and I saw the new grave of Brother Patrick. My wife and I made the two-day drive safely back home to Maryland.

Visiting your monastery has greatly helped my understanding.

Sincerely,

Hugh Turley

Perhaps we should not be surprised, but Father Mulvey and Abbot Deitz did not follow the Rule of St. Benedict, which is supposed to guide the actions of Catholic monasteries. In Chapter 53 of The Rule of St. Benedict it states, "1. All guests who present themselves are to be welcomed as Christ, for he himself will say: I was a stranger and you welcomed me (Matt 25:35). 2. Proper honor must be shown to all, especially to those who share our faith (Gal 6:10) and to pilgrims. 3.

Once a guest has been announced, the superior and the brothers are to meet him with all the courtesy of love. "

Makiko Turley died on June 16, 2022.

7. Letter to Abbot Dietz and Response

October 19, 2022

Abbot Elias Dietz, O.C.S.O.
Abbey of Gethsemani
3642 Monks Road
Trappist, KY 40051

Dear Fr. Dietz,

As you might recall, I got in touch with you in August of 2017 prior to the publication of our book *The Martyrdom of Thomas Merton: An Investigation*. Our book primarily concerned the events around Thomas Merton's death in Thailand in December of 1968. We made the official documents from Thailand available to the public for the first time and we shared important eyewitness accounts and revealed our discovery of two crucial death scene photographs that had been concealed for 50 years. Our purpose in writing you was to request permission to publish drawings of those photographs. You denied us that permission, so we were forced to describe them in detail.

Following the book's popular reception, but its cool reception from the mainstream and Catholic news media, many Merton scholars, and the Abbey of Gethsemani, we decided to investigate further. This time we directed our attention to the events in Kentucky before and after Merton's unexpected, mysterious death in Thailand. We were interested to know the origin of the clearly false "accidental electrocution" story and how it was successfully established and perpetuated.

In our latest book, Thomas Merton's Betrayers: The Case against Abbot James Fox and Author John Howard Griffin, we clear up some minor missteps in our earlier investigation and reveal more evidence that Merton was, indeed, the victim of foul play. The cover-up succeeded through lies, like the story that Merton was wet from a shower and that he was just a clumsy accident-waiting-to-happen, and secrecy, like the concealment of the official death documents, original witness testimony, and those negatives that we discovered in the papers of John Howard Griffin at Columbia University.

I think that you deserve another opportunity to grant us permission to publish the drawings of those photographs of Fr. Merton, and we are hereby requesting it for our upcoming book. We believe quite strongly that in the interest of truth and of justice to the memory of Thomas Merton they should be revealed to the public.

The light came into the world,

But men loved darkness rather than light because their deeds were wicked.

Everyone who practices evil hates the light;

He does not come near it for fear his deeds will be exposed.

But he who acts in truth comes into the light,

to make clear that his deeds are done in God.

    John 3:19-21

Sincerely,

Hugh Turley

On October 31, Turley received a terse response, dated October 28, 2022, from Father Dietz stating that nothing had changed regarding the granting of permission to display the drawings of the photographs of Thomas Merton's body and that he would appreciate it if he heard nothing further from us.

8. Thomas Merton's Stage Prop Fan

By
David Martin
December 30, 2021

To the tune of "Secret Agent Man"

There was a nice floor fan he used for cooling;
They rigged a substitute they used for fooling.
After he was whacked,
The ringer was unpacked.
Merton's work against the war found termination.

Merton's stage-prop fan.
Merton's stage-prop fan.
They killed a Christian warrior, and they used a fiendish plan.

Beware of pious folks who claim you're nuts.
Who say the monk they knew was just a klutz.
As though a lethal fan
Couldn't kill a handy man,
This sounds just like the voice of desperation.

Merton's stage-prop fan.
Merton's stage-prop fan.
They killed a peaceful warrior, and they sold a fiendish plan.

The living conscience of the nation one day,
Victim of a household appliance the next day,
I don't care where you go,
Searching high and low,
You'll find no better choice for canonization.

Merton's stage-prop fan.
Merton's stage-prop fan.
He should be a martyr, but we bought their fiendish plan:

Merton's stage-prop fan.

9. Seventeen Techniques For Truth Suppression

By

David Martin

December 28, 1999

Strong, credible allegations of high-level criminal activity can bring down a government. When the government lacks an effective, fact-based defense, other techniques must be employed. The success of these techniques depends heavily upon a cooperative, compliant press and a mere token opposition party.

1. Dummy up. If it's not reported, if it's not news, it didn't happen.
2. Wax indignant. This is also known as the "How dare you?" gambit.
3. Characterize the charges as "rumors" or, better yet, "wild rumors." If, in spite of the news blackout, the public is still able to learn about the suspicious facts, it can only be through "rumors." (If they tend to believe the "rumors" it must be because they are simply "paranoid" or "hysterical.")
4. Knock down straw men. Deal only with the weakest aspects of the weakest charges. Even better, create your own straw men. Make up wild rumors (or plant false stories) and give them lead play when you appear to debunk all the charges, real and fanciful alike.

5. Call the skeptics names like "conspiracy theorist," "nutcase," "ranter," "kook," "crackpot," and, of course, "rumor monger." Be sure, too, to use heavily loaded verbs and adjectives when characterizing their charges and defending the "more reasonable" government and its defenders. You must then carefully avoid fair and open debate with any of the people you have thus maligned. For insurance, set up your own "skeptics" to shoot down.

6. Impugn motives. Attempt to marginalize the critics by suggesting strongly that they are not really interested in the truth but are simply pursuing a partisan political agenda or are out to make money (compared to over-compensated adherents to the government line who, presumably, are not).

7. Invoke authority. Here the controlled press and the sham opposition can be very useful.

8. Dismiss the charges as "old news."

9. Come half-clean. This is also known as "confession and avoidance" or "taking the limited hangout route." This way, you create the impression of candor and honesty while you admit only to relatively harmless, less-than-criminal "mistakes." This stratagem often requires the embrace of a fall-back position quite different from the one originally taken. With effective damage control, the fall-back position need only be peddled by stooge skeptics to carefully limited markets.

10. Characterize the crimes as impossibly complex and the truth as ultimately unknowable.

11. Reason backward, using the deductive method with a vengeance. With thoroughly rigorous deduction, troublesome evidence is irrelevant. E.g., We have a completely free press. If evidence exists that the Vince Foster "suicide" note was forged, they would have reported it. They haven't reported it so there is no such

evidence. Another variation on this theme involves the likelihood of a conspiracy leaker and a press who would report the leak.

12. Require the skeptics to solve the crime completely. E.g. If Foster was murdered, who did it and why?

13. Change the subject. This technique includes creating and/or publicizing distractions.

14. Lightly report incriminating facts, and then make nothing of them. This is sometimes referred to as "bump and run" reporting.

15. Baldly and brazenly lie. A favorite way of doing this is to attribute the "facts" furnished the public to a plausible sounding, but anonymous, source.

16. Expanding further on numbers 4 and 5, have your own stooges "expose" scandals and champion popular causes. Their job is to pre-empt real opponents and to play 99-yard football. A variation is to pay rich people for the job who will pretend to spend their own money.

17. Flood the Internet with agents. This is the answer to the question, "What could possibly motivate a person to spend hour upon hour on Internet news groups defending the government and/or the press and harassing genuine critics?" Don't the authorities have defenders enough in all the newspapers, magazines, radio, and television? One would think refusing to print critical letters and screening out serious callers or dumping them from radio talk shows would be control enough, but, obviously, it is not.

Index

261

262

264

ABOUT THE AUTHORS

Hugh Turley is the author with David Martin of *The Martyrdom of Thomas Merton: An Investigation* and with John Clarke and Patrick Knowlton of *Failure of the Public Trust*, concerning the Vincent Foster death case. His work can be found at FBIcover-up.com and at DCDave.com.

David Martin is also the author of *The Assassination of James Forrestal* and *The Murder of Vince Foster: America's Would-Be Dreyfus Affair*. He was a founding member of North Carolina Veterans for Peace while in graduate school at the University of North Carolina during the Vietnam War. His writings are at DCDave.com, heresycentral.net, FBIcover-up.com, and Rense.com. He is the author of the poems in this volume.

www.ingramcontent.com/pod-product-compliance
Lightning Source LLC
Chambersburg PA
CBHW071317090426
42738CB00012B/2718